RAILWAY POLICY IN INDIA

RAILWAY POLICY

IN

INDIA

BY

HORACE BELL, M. INST. C.E.

GYAN

Published by

GYAN

Gyan Publishing House
5, Ansari Road
Daryaganj, New Delhi-110002
Phone: 011-47034999, 9811692060
E-mail: books@gyanbooks.com

Distribution Network
gyanbooks.com
India, USA, Canada, UK, Australia, France

ISBN: 978-81-212-7105-9 (PB)
First Published, 1894

2nd Impression 2024

Printed at: Gyan Press, Delhi.

RAILWAY POLICY IN INDIA
Author: HORACE BELL

RAILWAY POLICY IN INDIA

RAILWAY POLICY

IN

INDIA

BY

HORACE BELL, M.INST.C.E.

CONSULTING ENGINEER FOR STATE RAILWAYS
TO THE GOVERNMENT OF INDIA

RIVINGTON, PERCIVAL AND CO.

KING STREET, COVENT GARDEN

LONDON

1894

PREFACE

THIS work has, by permission, been based upon the records of the Government of India, but is no way whatever to be regarded as having any official authority. It professes to give no more than an outline of the policy pursued on Indian Railways, and the Author has designedly abstained from criticism, and from the assertion of his own views. It is hoped that it may be of interest, if not of some use, to those connected with Indian Railways, and perhaps to a wider circle of readers.

H. B.

CALCUTTA,
January 1894.

CONTENTS

CHAPTER VII

APPENDICES

MAPS AND PLANS

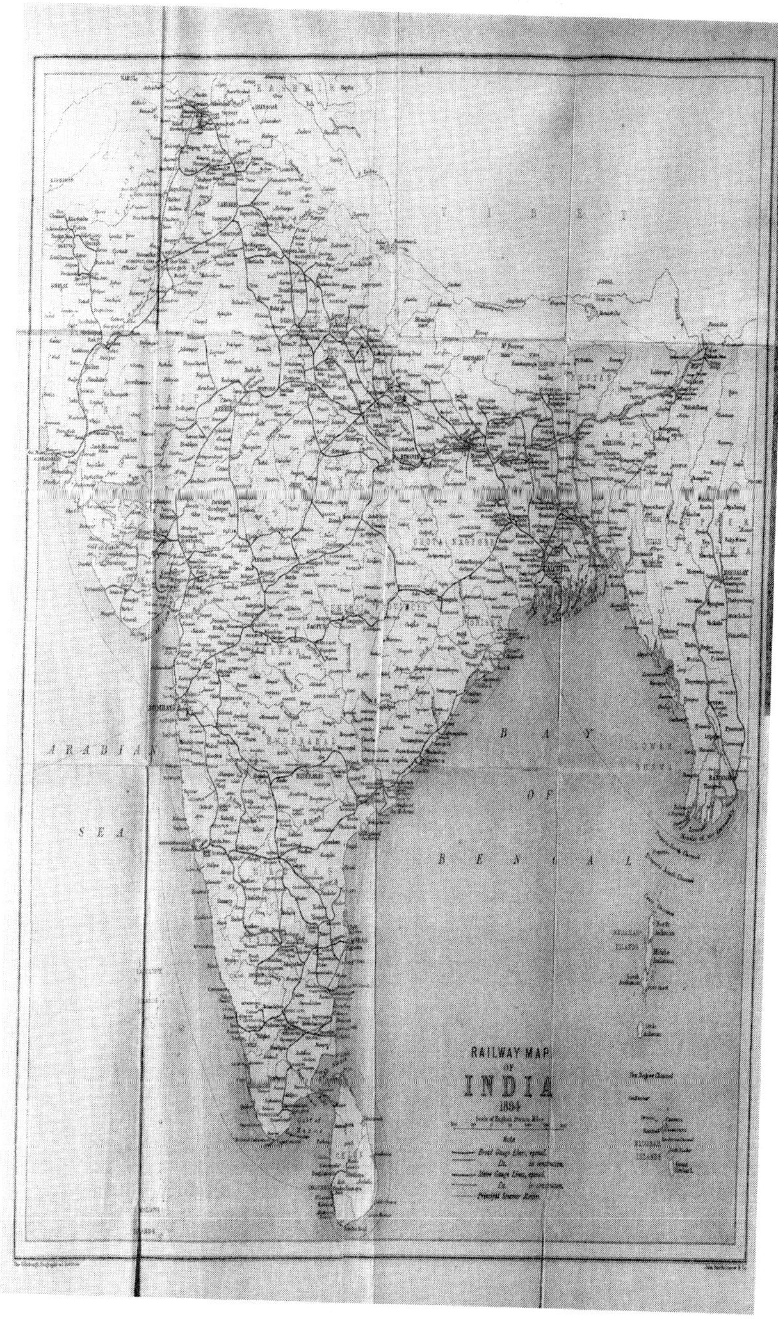

RAILWAY MAP
OF
INDIA
1894
T I B E T
ARABIAN
SEA
B A Y
OF
B E N G A L

CHAPTER I

HISTORICAL SKETCH

THE earliest proposals for constructing railways in India were put forward in 1843-44 by the promoters of a company, headed by Sir Macdonald Stephenson. We were then on the eve, in England, of the period known as that of the "railway mania"; the imagination of projectors drew railways penetrating into every known land; and while they expected that they should be mainly financed in Lombard Street, they were still more certain that they could only be carried out by English engineers. It is not to be wondered at that India should have received their early attention. Yet the condition of that country at the time could have given little hope of success. We had but recently conquered Sind, and with a new Governor-General, Lord Hardinge, were rapidly drifting into the struggle with Runjeet Singh, which was to end in an annexation of the Punjab. Thus, apart from the comparative novelty of railways, even in Europe, and in face of much more serious and urgent matters, it would not have been surprising if the "Honourable Board" in Leadenhall Street had regarded the proposals as untimely or premature. This, however, does not appear to have been the view taken at any time, either at home or in India, and notwithstanding that much more weighty business was in hand, the railway promoter found himself in favour, and a desire shown to help rather than retard the progress of his schemes.

Early in 1845, a formally drawn-up prospectus for a company was put before the Court of Directors of the East India Company, which proposed to raise a capital of one million sterling, for the construction of an "experimental" railway, starting from Calcutta, and extending for 140 miles towards Allahabad. The Company asked at the outset for a guarantee on its outlay of 3 per cent; but were willing, if this was considered objectionable, to be content with a bonus of £30,000 per annum, in order "to encourage the introduction of railways into India," but with the proviso that this bonus should be withdrawn when the net profits of the railway exceeded 3 per cent on the capital of one million. Subsequently, however, it was stipulated that a guarantee, or some equivalent pecuniary assistance, must be held to be an indispensable condition of the proposal. After many discussions, and much deliberation of this and other proposals, the Court of Directors addressed a despatch on the subject to the Governor-General, on the 7th May 1845; the beginning of a correspondence between the Home and the Indian Governments, which is now as bulky as it is interesting as a record of railway policy.

In England, or more properly in the United Kingdom, the progress of railway enterprise has received, and indeed needed but little more than guidance from the State and the Legislature. It sprang with marvellous rapidity into popularity and power. There were no doubts as to its adaptability to the habits and aims of the people, no serious difficulties at outset as to the raising of capital, nor was there any marked indication of an intention on the part of the Government to impose either legal or technical conditions in the shape of control. In India the position was widely different. The great Empire which we now either govern or control, from the Himalayas to Cape Comorin, was, in 1844, far from complete. We had yet to include in our territory the Punjab, Burma, Nagpore, and

Oudh. The people had scarcely yet realised that they were to become the subjects of one great and paramount Power, nor had they then more than a faint conception of its strength, as revealed in the Mutiny, or of the closeness of the bond now made possible by roads and railways between distant provinces. Moreover, the habits and condition of the people, except in the vicinity of Calcutta or Bombay, were scarcely altered from what we found them when we first came to the country. The palankin or the house-boat were the recognised vehicles for long journeys, whether for natives or Europeans; the one metalled and bridged road of any importance in the country was the Grand Trunk Road from Calcutta towards Peshawur; and the only means of getting from or to England was by sailing vessel round the Cape. But a still greater divergence between the past and the present was to be found in the system of triple Government, under which India then lay. At home it had the East India Company and a Board of Control, both directing and disputing over and with the Government in India.

It may be readily supposed that under such conditions opinions on proposals to initiate railways in India were curiously varied, and that men of even well-recognised abilities were led to base their views on what we now see were the crudest assumptions, and to anticipate failure in nearly every direction. It was thought then that railways in India might possibly get a fair share of the goods traffic, but next to nothing in the shape of passengers. It was imagined that the climate of the country would be a most serious obstacle. There was a fear of the disastrous effects of the periodical rains, of violent winds, and a vertical sun. The damage that would be caused by insects and by vermin to the banks and the timber sleepers was dwelt on, as well as the effects of tropical vegetation; while a more reasonable and valid objection was raised, in the difficulty which would be experienced in finding competent engineers and workmen for constructing and working railroads in India.

But the most singular feature in the despatch above referred to was the assumption that railways in India would have to deal mainly with goods traffic. The argument was put as follows: "According to the experience of this country (England), by far the largest returns are procured from passengers, the least from the traffic of goods. The condition of India is in this respect the reverse of that of England. Instead of a dense and wealthy population, the people of India are poor, and in many parts thinly scattered over extensive tracts of country; but on the other hand, India abounds in valuable products, of a nature which are in a great measure deprived of a profitable market by want of a cheap and expeditious means of transport. It may therefore be assumed that remuneration for railroads in India must, for the present, be drawn chiefly from the conveyance of merchandise, and not from passengers." The ignorance or inaccuracy displayed in this statement is very striking, more especially if it is borne in mind that this first railway proposal was to traverse one of the most densely populated territories in the world, which, at a moderate computation, must then have had a population on the average exceeding that of England to the square mile. That India was and is poor, as compared with England, was true enough, but it must even at that time, half a century ago, have been sufficiently evident that a large proportion of all classes were both able and willing to travel, whether on business, or pleasure, or from religious motives. The streams of pilgrims who then went across the country on foot may, however, have been thought likely to have scruples in visiting their shrines by railway; but if this idea existed, it has been very amply refuted since then, and, as a fact, in the first three years the receipts on Indian railways from passenger traffic largely exceeded the receipts from goods traffic; and to the present day have continued to show the most extraordinary development.

Shortly after sending this despatch to India, the Court of Directors came to the conclusion that it would be advisable to send out to India a railway engineer of experience, who should be associated with two officers of the Indian Engineer Corps "of tried and proved ability in that country," and who together, after due inquiry, would suggest some scheme of moderate length as a first experiment. Mr. Simms was the gentleman who was sent out from England, and he arrived in India in September 1845. The Directors of the East India Company were not averse to this construction and administration of railways in India by the agency of companies; but, recognising the haphazard way in which such schemes had been launched in England, they wisely determined that in India the trunk lines at least should be constructed on certain conditions which would give the Government powers of control, and, if necessary, powers of purchase. They therefore suggested for consideration that the detailed plans and estimates of any project, and the constitution and terms of agreement of any proposed company, should be submitted for examination and approval of the Government, and that the books and accounts should at all times be open to inspection by officers appointed for this purpose. In this we may see the first germ of a policy, and the commencement of a system of control, which has since then been gradually elaborated, and has become the distinguishing feature of our Indian railway system. Mr. Simms had not been many months in India before he drew up a memorandum, dated 6th February 1846, in which he made the following suggestions as to the terms which should be offered to English capitalists. As to the assistance to be given by Government, he proposed that a "lease" should be given to a company affording it power to construct, maintain, and "hold" certain lines for a term of years; that land should be given by Government free of cost for permanent works; that no tax should be imposed on the railway as it proceeds; and that a company should have complete control over its servants. On the other hand, the company should make the necessary surveys and plans and submit them for approval, should construct the lines in accordance with an approved specification, and maintain all works in perfect repair, until the expiration of the lease, when they should be handed over to Government *without payment.* No deviation from a sanctioned plan was to be made without the further sanction of Government, and the inspecting officer was to have power to condemn, stop, or order the reconstruction of any work. If any company failed in their engagements, the Government was to have power to take the whole property into its hands, and do with it as they thought fit. Further, he proposed that on the completion of any line, every working regulation, rule, or bye-law, the tariff of rates and fares for goods or passengers, the number of trains per diem, and times of starting of same, should be approved; in short, every detail was to be submitted for the acceptance of the Government, and no line was to be opened for traffic until all proposed rules had been sanctioned. Moreover, every railway was to carry mails, troops, and military stores at reduced rates. The failure to run one train a day from end to end of a line was to be held to be evidence that the railway had "ceased to be employed as such." All Indian railways were to be constructed on one specification, worked on one system, and supplied with stock of one uniform pattern; while every company was to keep its accounts in approved forms, and the Government to have power to call for any returns, financial or statistical, that might be thought necessary.

Many of these stipulations showed a wisdom and sound judgment which was probably the outcome of discussions with leading men in India, and most of them, with certain modifications, became the basis of the terms on which railways have since been made by companies. As if aware, however, that these proposals were somewhat one-sided, and unlikely to attract capital, Mr. Simms suggested that the Government might, in addition, "think it advisable" to guarantee a small percentage upon the actual cost of the works, which guarantee should not operate until the railway was opened for traffic, and should cease if a line was not worked regularly or satisfactorily. In the same month as saw the issue of this memorandum, the Report of a Committee of Engineers on the practicability of introducing railways into India was submitted to the Government, and both communications were dealt with together. The Report stated at the outset that "railroads are not inapplicable to the peculiarities and circumstances of India; but on the contrary, are not only a great desideratum, but with proper attention can be constructed and maintained as perfectly as in any part of Europe." The Report then went on to deal with the assumed difficulties mentioned above, and which had been referred to by the Directors of the East India Company in their despatch of May 1845. The Committee, while admitting that in some measure they were valid, did not consider them insuperable, or such as to prevent the immediate prosecution of railways in India. The Report then went on to recommend the construction in the first instance of a line from Calcutta towards Delhi.

In dealing with this Report, and with the suggestions made by Mr. Simms, the Government of India, then under Lord Hardinge, considered that the proposal to give land free of cost was right and proper, and this concession, which was subsequently adopted, has been a regular and leading feature in all railway concessions up to the present day. As regards the power of becoming eventually the proprietor of railways in India, the Government considered that the option of so doing should be reserved on certain conditions, at the expiration of a certain period, or of entering into new arrangements with a company. This also became a leading feature in all subsequent contracts. The grant of a guarantee of interest was considered impolitic. It was urged that "any such guarantee would no doubt prove a great encouragement to the projectors of railways in India"; but that "it might encourage persons to embark in speculations based on no reasonable calculation of ultimate profit." It was added significantly, and with no apparent conception of the enormous indirect advantages which railways would confer on the country, that "it is not the wish, or the interest of Government to encourage any project of this nature, which does not hold out a fair prospect of moderate profit, without being dependent on the Government for its dividends." It was considered that if the Government gave land free of cost it would be sufficient evidence of the active part it proposed to take in promoting such schemes. Yet, though so little disposed to give substantial encouragement to railway enterprise, the Government of India was keenly alive to the importance of reserving the right of control over both the construction and management of railways, and even argued that the concession of free land put a railway company under such great obligations that the Government in return should have the most complete and detailed control over their administration.

These views of the Government of India were sent home to the Court of Directors of the East India Company on the 9th May 1846, and later on, in July, the Governor-General wrote a brief minute on the subject, in which he stated, that in his opinion more substantial aid than had been approved by his colleagues was needed, if companies were to be encouraged to make railways in India. He thought that the gift of land, which might be put at the value of £200 a mile, was incommensurate with the advantages to be derived from railway communication and with the cost of such works, and laid stress on the great military advantages which railways would afford, in addition to their more obvious benefits, commercially and socially. He concluded by recommending a grant of one million sterling, or an annual contribution of five lakhs of rupees (then worth £50,000) to a railway completed between Calcutta and Delhi. In October of the same year the Court of Directors issued a report on the whole question, together with a long list of lines which had been submitted to them by promoters. They agreed that the first line should be made from Calcutta to Delhi, and by the agency of a joint stock company; but the terms on which the line should be carried through were not arrived at without lengthy discussion between the projectors, the Court, and the Board of Control. The views of the latter have been described as "narrow and obstructive" as compared with the "liberal and practical" views of the East India Company. The Court dissented from the Government of India on the subject of a guarantee, which they held to be essential to the formation of the company, and recommended 4 per cent on all sums paid into the Treasury—up to a certain figure representing a cost per mile of £15,000, under the following conditions, viz. That the Court of Directors should be the sole judges regarding the expediency of granting a guarantee on sums required for extensions; that all profits should be divided between the Government and the railway company; and that a deposit of one million sterling should be paid in before the guaranteed interest should commence. These proposals were not at first agreed to unanimously, but in the end the view of the majority was adopted, and submitted to the Commissioners for India.

On the 19th December 1846 the Board of Control communicated its views to the Court of Directors. They accepted the proposal for constructing railways by means of companies, modified the terms for ultimate purchase, and objected strongly and entirely to the idea of a guarantee, or at least until the Directors of the East India Company were fully satisfied that the money could not be raised without it, and then only for a period of fifteen years. These terms were not acceptable to the promoters; but the Board of Control would not yield, and a long period of delay intervened, during which the Chambers of Commerce of Manchester and Glasgow represented the need for encouraging the carrying out of railways in India, urging that a guarantee of a minimum rate of interest should be granted in the same way as had been given to companies for the construction of railways "in various colonies of the Empire." After further discussion, and a further representation, in June 1847, from the Court of Directors, the Board of Control reluctantly consented, in view of the then condition of the money market, to raising the rate of guaranteed interest from 4 to 5 per cent and for a period of twenty-five years, and on this basis the projectors of the East Indian Railway Company agreed to make arrangements for carrying out the project.

Further discussions followed, however, upon proposals made for constructing railways elsewhere in India; and on a project for one in the Bombay Presidency, the terms offered by the Court of Directors were submitted by the promoters to Robert Stephenson and others to report on. They advised that the proposals were inadmissible, and that the directors of railway companies should not accept them. They said, on reviewing the terms, "that the practical effect would be that the Government will choose the line, combat the details of its construction and mode of working, fix the period for its completion, draw up its regulations, limit its rates of charge and its profits, reserve to itself the power of producing very serious delays, and finally withdrawing its guarantee, confiscate the works to its own use and profit." This resulted in further correspondence, until the subject was taken up by Mr. James Wilson, then Secretary to the Board of Control, and on the 19th March 1849, a despatch was sent to the Court of Directors which ultimately resulted in a grant of an absolute 5 per cent guarantee, without limit of period, and legal agreements were shortly drawn up and finally signed on the 17th August 1849. The terms and conditions will be referred to in a following chapter. Towards the end of the year a despatch [1] was sent out to India informing the Government that a company had been formed for constructing an experimental line in Bengal, with a capital of one million sterling. It was considered advisable to make the starting-point Calcutta, to carry the line in the direction of Mirzapore or Rajmahal, and to make the railway on the English narrow gauge of 4 feet 8½ inches as a double line.

Lord Dalhousie had by this time become Governor-General.

[1] Despatch from Court of Directors, dated 14th November 1849.

He had had useful experience at home in dealing with English railways, and was not prepared to accept the views of the Directors without criticism. In July 1850, dating from Chini in the Himalayas, he wrote a minute on the subject, which is well worthy of his reputation as a statesman, and shows the keen interest he had in the success of Indian railways. He objected to the proposed alignment, recommended that the railway should be taken through Burdwan to or towards the coal-fields (as has since been done), that the line should be made single instead of double, and that a broader gauge than 4 feet 8½ inches should be adopted. He was most anxious that this so-called "experimental" line should prove a success. He said that its object "is to prove, not only that it is practicable to construct railways in India as engineering works, but that such railways when constructed will, as commercial undertakings, offer a fair remunerative return on the money which has been expended on their construction, so that the public may thereby be encouraged to invest their capital in the construction of similar works in other parts of India. Such being the object of the present experiment, I am forced to the conclusion, after a laborious and anxious consideration of the documents before me, that if the instructions with which the Government has been furnished are to be strictly adhered to, if the conditions attached to the construction of the present line are not in any respect to be relaxed, there is little hope that the Government will be able to conduct this experiment to a successful issue on any one of the lines that have been indicated." He urged that there was more risk of the ultimate failure of railway enterprise in India from the discouragement which would arise from this experimental line turning out to be unprofitable, on account of the superfluous expenditure required for a double line, than from any accidents which could possibly be caused by its being made a single line. He had grave doubts, as indeed had every one at that time, as to whether railways could be made to pay in India, and on this point said[1]: "After reading everything that I have seen written on the subject, and conversing, since I have been in India, with everybody who was able to give an opinion worth having on the question of railways in India, I have come to the conclusion that no one can safely say whether railways in this country will pay or not. . . . It remains to be seen whether, as has often been the case in Europe, a passenger traffic which did not previously exist will be created by the formation of a railway. It remains to be seen whether the goods now conveyed on hackeries along the Trunk Road will be transferred to the railway."

The concluding sentences of Lord Dalhousie's minute are worth quoting in full:—

43. I have entered on the questions connected with the commencement of the experimental railway in Bengal at some length because, although it is but a small beginning, and a doubtful one as yet, I nevertheless entertain a hope that in the years to come this great instrument of improvement may be extended over all the land, bringing with it the rich and numerous benefits it is calculated to produce. Looking far before us to this possibility, I am anxious that the Government of India should early take warning from the errors which we have all committed at home in legislating for the regulation of railway works, and that so it should profit by the experience which others have dearly bought.

44. I heartily trust that the East India Company and the Government of India may hold by the principle on which they have acted in the present case. I trust they will ever avoid the error of viewing railways merely as private undertakings, and will regard them as national works, over which the Government may justly exercise, and is called upon to exercise, a stringent and salutary control. This control should not be an arbitrary right of interference, but a regulated authority, defined and declared by law, which is not to be needlessly or vexatiously exacted, but which in my humble judgment is necessary at once for the interests of the State and for the protection of the public.

---

[1] Lord Dalhousie's Minute of 20th April 1853.

A further development of our Indian railway policy is to be found in another minute by the same hand, written in 1853, which, while dealing with the general question, sketched the direction to be taken by the trunk lines. The minute is marked by great ability and breadth of view, and has been rightly regarded as a very important State paper. He believed that if the lines were judiciously selected they would be largely used by the natives, and that they would in the end be so far remunerative as to relieve the State of the onus of the guarantee. Should it prove otherwise, he held that a payment of a part of it might be "cheerfully borne" in view of the indirect advantages to be derived from railway communication. On the important question as to the agency by which they should be constructed, Lord Dalhousie held that it was advisable that railways in India should be made by joint-stock companies, under the control and supervision of the Government. He recognised that from time to time difficulties and friction might arise on this score, but that this should not be regarded as sufficient reason for condemning this system. On the 17th August 1853, the Court of Directors replied to this minute, and a large scheme of railways was forthwith approved, and surveys ordered. In assenting to the proposal to make over Indian railways to companies, they laid stress on the great need, in view of the guarantee, of strict supervision and economy in the construction of the works. The difficulties above referred to, which were anticipated as the consequence of a system of guarantee, were soon realised, and were felt, as was to be expected, more keenly in India than at home. The powers of supervision were delegated to military engineer officers, whose knowledge of construction, on railways especially, was necessarily limited, and who were not always endowed with the tact and judgment needed for dealing with the questions which arose between them and the companies' officers. The engineers of the companies originated everything, while the Government's engineers were the critics, having the responsibility of dealing with the details of projects of which they knew little, and being forced to conceal their ignorance by asking for further information or explanation. There was consequently a ceaseless cry of obstruction and delay. Both sides felt themselves unfairly dealt with, and in the end it became necessary to bring the matter before a Committee of the House of Commons (in 1857-58). This afforded an opportunity to both sides for airing their grievances. In concluding their report the Committee observed: "By a judicious adherence to the spirit rather than the letter of the contract, your Committee feel assured that arrangements may be simplified, united action for one common object secured, and railway enterprise in India may before long assume proportions commensurate with the vast commercial, agricultural, and mineral resources of that country."

The result of this inquiry was that matters went more smoothly; the position was accepted as one that had to be worked, and a desire was shown to compromise difficulties, instead of fighting over them; indeed since then there has been a marked improvement in the relations between the railway and the Government engineers. Under this system of guarantee and control, the great trunk lines of India have been constructed—the East Indian, the Great Indian Peninsula, the Madras, the Bombay, Baroda, and Central India, the Sind, Punjab, and Delhi, and the Eastern Bengal Railways, all on the standard gauge of $5\frac{1}{2}$ feet. This very important gauge question will be referred to in a later chapter dealing with its whole history and development. The system of construction by companies under guarantee was not adopted without an attempt on the part of the Government of Madras to induce the Home Government to allow an experiment to be made in that province of direct construction by the State. This was not acceded to by the Board of Control, which in replying to Madras, in 1852, urged that it was of great importance to attract British capital, skill, and enterprise to such undertakings in India, and that with this view, moreover, the system of contract was "the more eligible and conducive" to this end. They further felt doubts "whether an equally effective control over the expenses of such works could be maintained in India, under general instructions from the home authorities, as that which is now exercised through the Railway Boards meeting in London, under the constant and immediate supervision of the Court." This view was accepted by the Government of Madras, and the guaranteed company became until 1869 the recognised system for railway construction throughout India.

The provisions in the contracts for the ultimate acquisition of the lines by the State, were at the outset considered of much importance, although, as time went on, the desire to enforce these powers grew weaker. But in a memorandum written at the end of 1845 for the Madras Government by Mr. F. G. Simms, the Consulting Engineer to the Government of India, he said that the cost and construction "should not be left to the opinions of any engineers who may chance to be employed by the railway companies, as they are too frequently induced to adopt inexpensive expedients, wise or unwise, to overcome pecuniary or other difficulties which for the time may answer the purposes of the promoters of the work; because I look upon the railways of India as one vast scheme of the highest importance to the future welfare of this great Empire, and although they will be at first constructed and maintained by private companies, yet after a lapse of years will fall into the hands of Government, and become public property."

By the end of 1855 the system of railways projected by Lord Dalhousie was being actively carried out; but the outbreak of the Mutiny in 1857 threw everything into confusion, and not only was the progress of railway construction seriously impeded, but questions of railway policy, judging by the meagre record, were relegated for consideration to quieter times. The trouble of the Mutiny brought out, however, one salient advantage of the guarantee system, in so far that funds for the prosecution of the works were always forthcoming; whereas had they been purely State works, carried out by State funds, the exigencies of the time would certainly have resulted in the allotments for the railways being absorbed for more urgent necessities. The companies' engineers did excellent service at this time. When the tide of war passed over their districts, they shouldered their rifles, entrenched positions, and served as volunteer troopers; and when it had passed away, their proper work was calmly resumed. The pluck and skill shown in the defence of a house at Arrah by Vicars Boyle, with a handful of Sikh soldiers, gave a salutary and notable example to others at that time.

There would seem to have been no tendency towards any change in railway policy, or any defined doubt as to the continuance of the system of guarantee, until the year 1863-64, when various projects were before the Government for the construction of railways by companies with assistance in some form or other, and it became necessary to formulate the conditions and limits of such assistance. The most prominent of the proposals were those put forward by the Indian Branch Railway Company for the construction of lines in Oudh and Rahilkund on the basis of a subsidy of 1000 rupees per mile per annum for twenty years, for each mile open, with an additional allowance for each large bridge, land being given free to the company for a term of ninety-nine years. Mails were to be carried free, and reduced fares allowed to officers and soldiers, and for the carriage of public stores. The works were commenced on this basis in 1863-64, but prior to the execution of a formal contract between the Company and the Secretary of State. Towards the end of 1864 representations were made to the Government, that unless more favourable terms were conceded than those proposed in the original negotiations, it would not be possible to raise money for the completion of the entire system, and later on, a demand was made for a guarantee of 5 per cent on a certain portion of the capital. In replying to this in

December 1865, the Secretary of State, then Sir Charles Wood, declined to do more than advance a small sum necessary to complete one of the lines, on which advance interest at 5 per cent was to be charged. If this was not accepted, he was willing to take over the works as they stood, "at the present market value of the shares." To this the Directors responded by proposing to raise the amount required on debentures, but eventually requested the renewal of the offer of the loan, which in March 1866 was agreed to. Up to this period the Company had only succeeded in raising £200,000 out of a proposed capital of two millions, and before two months had elapsed the Company was again in difficulties, owing to the failure of a bank. Further help was asked for, which, however, was distinctly declined.

In the meanwhile negotiations had been carried on with the Great Indian Peninsula Railway Company for extensions of their system, on somewhat similar conditions to those granted to the Indian Branch Railway Company, with the similar feature of the grant of a lump sum subsidy for a term of years. The negotiations were complicated by the fact that one of the proposed lines was to run through a native state, from which it was hoped that further assistance would be derived. Proposals of the same nature were also made by the Bombay and Baroda Company. But the same difficulties arose in each case. Money for any railway in India was in fact not then obtainable in London without some form of Government guarantee, and in the end the Secretary of State had to give way. He sent to the Government of India a draft of a fresh contract proposed to be made with the Indian Branch Railway Company, and admitted that the idea of obtaining capital for Indian railways without guarantee was practically abandoned. The guarantee proposed was 5 per cent on a capital of four millions, and the profits of the line above this figure to be equally shared with the Company. The reply to this, on the part of the Government of India, was made at the end of 1867, and the important despatch in which it was conveyed was accompanied by minutes by the Governor-General Sir John (afterwards Lord) Lawrence, and the Members of his Council. A long and able note by Captain (now General Sir) E. C. S. Williams, K.C.I.E., R.E., was also sent with the despatch, in which the system of guarantee was reviewed, the principles exhibited on which aid had been afforded to railways in other countries, with an outline for a new system, and a sketch of a proposal for the construction of railways by the State itself. One point in the despatch is of peculiar interest, it being stated, among the matters of chief importance was that of making arrangements for the ultimate transfer to the Government of India of the whole of the Indian railways constructed by English capital, "with the view to the prevention of a too great investment of such capital in India."

The proposals of the Government of India may be said to have been contained in the Governor-General's minute above referred to, the principal of which were briefly as follows. That no company should be allowed very large development of its operations, on the ground that this might be inconvenient, or even dangerous, to the Government, and at the same time "proportionately inefficient." That a fixed limit should be placed to expenditure on guaranteed interest, and that the Government should fix an average rate of mileage cost, and on no account guarantee interest on any sum beyond this rate. That the companies and their servants should be regarded as the agents of the Government for the purpose of constructing railways, and that the Government be empowered to dismiss or suspend all railway servants at its discretion; that land should only be granted for 99 years instead of 999 as proposed in the new contract with the Oudh Company (formerly Indian Branch Railway Company), and the "right of entry" after that period be absolutely secured to Government; and that Government should for political reasons by degrees obtain possession of all the railways. The reply of the Secretary of State for India, then Sir Stafford Northcote, to these proposals are contained in three despatches, dated in January and August 1868. In the two first, the Secretary of State considered that it would be desirable to distinguish, as clearly as possible, between commercial and political lines; that the former should be such as would "open up districts whose natural resources are at once the largest, and the least developed," while competing lines should not be promoted, but care taken to scrutinise the grounds upon which any line is said to be in competition with another. As to such lines, he held that they should be constructed by companies, and under a system of guarantee, adding, however, that this system tended to weaken the ordinary motives to efficient management and superintendence, and he invited suggestions for additional precautions on this score. With regard to the political lines, he was "inclined to think that direct Government action might be preferable, as the guarantee system did not appear to be one admitting of indefinite extension, and that if a line had to be made on which there was a prospect of commercial loss it would be best that the Government itself should make it, so as "not to weigh down the market for railway securities by the introduction of a stock which is never likely to rise to a premium."

An important point made in the despatch from which quotation has been made, was that it was desirable, as regards the progress of future railway extension, to fix a limit to the sum that should be regarded as the annual charge to be borne on railway account, and thus "establish a system under which, in proportion as the revenues of India were relieved of the charge on account of the older lines, by their becoming self-supporting, new ones might be taken up in their place." The despatch of the 24th November 1868, to the Government of India, dealt with the views of Lord Lawrence as referred to above, expressed decided objections to the policy there sketched out, and made no further reference to the question of the construction of railways by the direct agency of the State. In March 1869, however, the Government of India, still under Lord Lawrence, took up this matter in earnest, and submitted with it a long and most able minute by the Governor-General, the ultimate effect of which was to completely revolutionise railway policy in India. Up till then the construction of railways by companies, under a guarantee, or some equally effective assistance, had been held by both the Secretary of State and the Indian Government to be, if not the most economical, the only possible way of carrying out and administrating these works. The strong common-sense of Lord Lawrence, his intimate knowledge of the country and its people, and a just appreciation of the value of the large body of engineers who were then carrying out public works under the Government, enabled him to make out an unassailable case against this, and to banish for many a year a system which at the time seemed likely to press very severely on the revenues of the Empire.

It is difficult, within the limits of this sketch, to do justice to Lord Lawrence's minute. It is, in fact, a careful and well-reasoned essay, in which the comparative advantages of the guarantee system, and direct construction by the State, are drawn with firm lines, and the conclusion is arrived at that "for the future railways should, as far as is consistent with actual and implied engagements with the existing companies, be carried out by the Government itself." Dealing with the character of the control which should be exercised by the Secretary of State over railway matters in India, he referred to the difficulties which must arise, and had probably already developed, owing to the undue influence of the India Office. He said—

I am fully impressed with the propriety, and even the necessity, of placing in the hands of the Secretary of State for India, the most complete control over the administration of India in all its branches, and I hope that nothing I am now saying will be considered as implying a desire to weaken that control. But the power exercised in England over affairs actually conducted in India, should surely be essentially one of control, and the initiation and practical direction of measures should as far as possible remain in the hands of the Indian Government. I cannot think that it is conducive to good administration to remove from the cognisance of the local authorities—for the purpose of placing it in the hands of the Secretary of State—the principal management of transactions which already involve an outlay of 100 millions sterling, and must probably extend to double that sum, and which are entirely carried out in India, and at the charge of the Indian revenues. I must ask permission to state my opinion in plain language on this very important point, to the effect that the true interests of India demand that the Secretary of State's direct action in relation to Indian railways should be exercised only so far as is essential for the prompt despatch of that part of the business connected with them, which is necessarily carried out in England; and that beyond this, his intervention should as a rule be limited to the control of the Indian authorities, on whom should be placed the same complete responsibility for railway management, both in respect to administration and finance, as is placed on them in all other branches of public business. I feel in the strongest manner that real success in the economical and efficient management and extension of railways in India can only be attained by the frank adoption of this policy.

The minute contained a careful review of the probable financial position of Indian railways, and an estimate of the amount, which was placed at two millions, that the revenues could bear as an annual charge on their account, to meet charges for guaranteed interest, land, loss by exchange, and Government supervision. An estimate of the probable future earnings of the existing lines, and of the new lines to be made, seemed to show that the country might afford to invest $3\frac{3}{4}$ millions yearly in the prosecution of railway extension, and at the end of twenty years the yearly charge on the revenues would be reduced to about one million. In estimating the net charge for interest on new lines it was, however, assumed that the rate of interest would be 5 per cent—a figure which was largely reduced as time went on, and has now become nearer $3\frac{1}{2}$ per cent. The gross average earnings of all Indian railways was estimated to reach £30[1] per mile per week after twenty years, or in 1889, and although the circumstances have materially altered since this estimate was made, and many hundreds or thousands of miles of military and famine lines have been carried out, which were not then contemplated, the actual figure has, as it happens, closely approximated to this, having been during 1891-92 about Rs.286 per mile per week. After sketching out a programme for future railway extension, following in a great measure the lines of Lord Dalhousie's minute of 1853, Lord Lawrence concluded his minute in the following terms: "Skill in engineering work implies the successful adaptation of the art of construction to varying circumstances. For a poor country, economy is one of the essential conditions to be complied with, and its requirements may be as rigid as any of those imposed by physical conditions. Wholly to reject railways for a country which is not able to support lines of the most costly description is quite unreasonable; and if, on a further examination in detail of the probable cost and returns of any of the lines, which otherwise seem desirable, the expense of lines of the ordinary gauge seems prohibitory, while lines of a narrow gauge would be financially practicable. I should consider it a most mistaken view to reject the narrow gauge line. And so with any other modification of ordinary practice. For complete success in the great operations which the Government of India has before it, broad views, and a ready adoption of all truly sound measures, whether out of the usual course or not, are essential, and it will be a source of lasting regret if the progress of this country, which of all others depends on the improvement of its means of internal communication, should be retarded

[1] Then Rs.300.

by the weight of administrative prescription or engineering prejudice."

In replying to the Government of India in July 1869,[1] the Secretary of State (then the Duke of Argyll) accepted their views. He said that whatever may have been the reasons which had led to the introduction of the guaranteed system in India, the time had now evidently arrived when "both in raising and in expending such additional capital as may be required for new lines in India, the Government should secure for itself the full benefit of the credit which it lends, and of the cheaper agencies which ought to be at its command." Surveys were ordered to be made forthwith, and in concluding his despatch the Duke of Argyll informed the Government of India that, regarded as a whole, the arrangements proposed in the three despatches under acknowledgment appeared to him to be "well adapted for providing in India gradually, regularly, and with all advisable rapidity, a fairly complete national system of railway communication." The question of the gauge upon which the new lines were to be constructed was reopened in a despatch from the Government of India, No. 51, of the 17th May 1870. They admitted the evils of a break of gauge in a country in which a railway system was approaching completion, but regarding Indian railways as being as yet in their infancy, and that a narrower gauge than the 5 feet 6 inch gauge, then in force for the main trunk lines, would better accord with the financial and economic condition of the country, they urged that what India now wanted was an extensive scheme of light lines, on which the traffic should be worked at low speeds, and proposed for a large part of the railway extension now contemplated in India "a narrow gauge track, laid on a substantial road and subway, with rails proportioned to the limited wheel loads of the improved engines now obtainable, and to the moderate speed required by the circumstances of the country."

[1] Despatch No. 42, of 15th July 1869.

This was replied to in October 1870.[1] The conclusions of the Government of India,[2] as regards the adoption of a narrower gauge for future extensions, were agreed to, and the report of a Committee appointed by the Secretary of State to consider the gauge to be adopted was enclosed. This subject is dealt with at length in a subsequent chapter. The conclusion arrived at in the end was to adopt a gauge of one metre (3 feet $3\frac{3}{8}$ inches), on which, at the date of this work, over 7000 miles of line have been constructed. The Government of India set to work vigorously, organised a new railway branch of the Indian Public Works Department, into which were drafted most of the engineers then in Government service who had had railway experience in England; and to these were added others who were available from the Staffs of the guaranteed companies, and a certain number of Royal Engineer officers. The money for this new system of direct construction by the State was raised in London by the Secretary of State on the credit of the Indian revenues. The sums expended on railway extension between the years 1870-92, the rate of interest per cent, and the rate of sterling exchange on the rupee, are given in the following table. The figures of expenditure include construction by direct State agency, and the sums spent in recent years indirectly by the State, through the agency of assisted companies, such as the Southern Mahratta.

[1] Despatch No. 72, of 26th October 1870.
[2] Then under Lord Mayo.

[TABLE

Financial Year.	Sums expended in Rx.[1] on State Railways.			Average rate of Interest for Loans.	Average rate of Sterling Exchange on the Rupee for the Year.
	From Borrowed Money.	From Revenue.	Total.		s. d.
1870-71 . .	452,748	9,569	443,179	3.98	1 $10\frac{1}{2}$
1871-72 . .	650,170	4,175	645,995	3.93	1 $10\frac{1}{4}$
1872-73 . .	1,430,047	14,863	1,444,910	..	1 $10\frac{3}{4}$
1873-74 . .	2,424,526	39,409	2,463,935	3.90	1 $10\frac{3}{8}$
1874-75 . .	3,106,430	114,481	3,220,911	3.94	1 $10\frac{1}{8}$
1875-76 . .	3,245,401	29,680	3,275,081	3.98	1 $9\frac{5}{8}$
1876-77 . .	2,965,110	38,260	3,003,370	3.92	1 $8\frac{1}{2}$
1877-78 . .	4,158,174	50,896	4,209,070	3.94	1 $8\frac{3}{4}$
1878-79 . .	3,465,221	171,782	3,637,003	3.96	1 $7\frac{3}{4}$
1879-80 . .	2,987,383	1,786,155	4,773,538	4.00	1 8
1880-81 . .	3,212,893	2,317,395	5,530,288	3.58	1 8
1881-82 . .	2,213,773	1,131,470	3,345,243	...	1 $7\frac{7}{8}$
1882-83 . .	1,883,542	347,019	2,230,561	3.97	1 $7\frac{1}{2}$
1883-84 . .	3,382,367	470,486	3,852,853	...	1 $7\frac{1}{2}$
1884-85 . .	3,526,152	1,209,958	4,736,110	3.20	1 $7\frac{3}{8}$
1885-86 . .	4,712,828	1,221,055	5,933,883	3.52	1 $6\frac{1}{4}$
1886-87 . .	5,123,105	406,635	5,529,740	3.46	1 $5\frac{1}{2}$
1887-88 . .	2,251,776	80,945	2,332,721	...	1 5
1888-89 . .	1,178,111	23,308	1,201,419	3.12	1 $4\frac{3}{8}$
1889-90 . .	2,794,458	19,734	2,814,192	2.98	1 $4\frac{1}{2}$
1890-91 . .	2,881,783	54,512	2,936,295	3.02	1 6
1891-92 . .	2,770,336	648,028	3,418,364	3.18	1 $4\frac{3}{4}$

The contracts with the guaranteed lines empowered the Government, by giving six months' notice, to acquire them on certain terms after the first twenty-five years, and one of these railways could have been taken over in 1874. During the year 1869, however, negotiations were entered into by the Secretary of State for India, and without reference to the Government of India, for relinquishing this right on certain conditions. These were in substance, that on the understanding that the State would extend the existence of the companies for a second period of twenty-five years, and would forego the arrears due by the companies for guaranteed interest, a new contract should be executed, in which it should be

[1] Rx. represents conventional sterling, assuming that ten rupees equals one pound.

stipulated that for the remainder of the lease surplus profits over and above 5 per cent should be divided equally between the companies and the Government. The intentions of the Home Government became known to the Government of India, but indirectly only, and a protest was sent by them, as soon as possible, against this policy, although, as it happened, too late to have any effect on the ultimate decision. The despatch of the Government of India[1] indicated, and in forcible language, the objections taken to the proposal. It pointed out that various considerations had made it seem desirable that the Government should acquire the guaranteed lines as soon as possible, and that the concession by the companies with respect to the disposition of surplus profits was in effect no concession at all; while, on the other hand, the surrender of arrears of interest, and of the right to acquire the lines after the first twenty-five years would mean a very serious loss to Government. There was, the despatch said, no apparent object in making such concessions. "The credit of the Government was never better; the undertakings of these companies are approaching completion: their demands on the money market have almost ceased, and their stocks are quoted at a considerable premium. It is, therefore, in vain that we seek to discover the grounds which have actuated Her Majesty's Government in this matter; and looking at the stage at which it has arrived, as evidenced by the interpellations in Parliament, we cannot but regret that no opportunity was afforded us of placing your Grace in possession of the views we entertain on this important question."

As already mentioned, this protest arrived too late to effect the decision arrived at by the Secretary of State, and new contracts on the above conditions were granted, first, to the Great Indian Peninsula Railway, and later on to the Bombay, Baroda, and the Madras Railways. It is not possible to offer the reasons which led the Home Government to adopt this

[1] Despatch No. 80, of 12th August 1870.

course, which was taken not only against the opinion of the Government of India, but in the face of facts which should seemingly have offered good grounds for a decision of a directly opposite character, viz. to acquire these lines for the State at the earliest possible date. It may be admitted that it was then difficult to foresee the enormous expansion of the Indian export trade which followed shortly after, and it may also have been deemed sound policy to sacrifice some share of the public revenues for the purpose of encouraging and attracting the investment of English capital in India. The result has anyhow been distinctly felt in the financial position of the Empire, and there can now be no difference of opinion in the matter. The loss to the State has, on the other hand, been a very material gain to the shareholders of the first two of the lines above mentioned, and as an illustration of this the figures for 1891-92 may be taken as showing the share of surplus profits of the Great Indian Peninsula shareholders, which in that year was Rs.5,187,260, and of the Bombay and Baroda shareholders Rs.1,798,260, besides contributions to Provident Funds. In calculating this surplus, moreover, the interest paid in England is converted into Indian currency at the rate of exchange named in the contracts, viz. 1s. 10d. per rupee. The amounts paid to the companies are, therefore, more than a moiety of the true surplus, after meeting interest charges, since the loss by exchange—*i.e.* the difference between 1s. 10d. and the actual rates of exchange, now much lower—is not taken into account, the whole loss falling on the Government. In any half-year during which the net earnings fall short of the interest charges, as in the case of unusually heavy debits against revenue for maintenance charges, the deficiency is borne wholly by the Government. The following table, extracted from a note by the Accountant-General, Public Works Department, shows the results to the State of the above contracts with the lines mentioned, and the Madras Railway —the only three now remaining of the older guaranteed railways—for the year 1891-92, the figures being in Rx. or tens of rupees :—

	Charges.					Gain or Loss (+ or −) to the State.
	Net Traffic Receipts.	Interest.	Surplus Profits.	Contributions to Provident Funds.	Total.	
	Rx.	Rx.	Rx.	Rx.	Rx.	Rx.
Great Indian Peninsula . .	2,272,863	1,716,453	518,726	17,004	2,252,183	+ 20,680
Bombay, Baroda, and Central India . . .	822,344	595,638	179,826	7,498	782,962	+ 39,382
Madras . . .	397,911	757,339	...	...	757,339	− 359,428
Total . .	3,493,118	3,069,430	698,552	24,502	3,792,484	− 299,366

Having decided that future railway extensions should be carried out directly by the State, no action was taken by the Government for the next ten years in any other direction, and private enterprise, whether aided or unaided, received no further encouragement during this period. The greater part of the new mileage was carried out on the metre gauge, with the intention that this should be adopted for subsidiary or feeder lines, but with a full recognition nevertheless that the main traffic routes should be accommodated by the standard gauge. The metre gauge was to carry light local traffic. For the latter half of this period the portfolio of Public Works in the Council of the Governor-General was held by General Sir A. Clarke, R.E., whose wide administrative experience in other fields greatly strengthened the position of the Government in dealing with this new development in their railway policy. A new and terribly potent element was, however, to be introduced into the question. During the years between 1874 and 1879, the country was visited by a succession of most serious and widespread famines, which, in spite of colossal efforts for relief, resulted in an appalling loss of life, and of property in field cattle, without counting the loss to the State in the remissions of land revenue. It cannot unfortunately be said that famine was a new calamity in India. In the famine of 1837, in the North-West Provinces and Rajputana, over a million lives are believed to have been lost, and perhaps double that number in the famine of 1869; while in Orissa in 1866 famine is said to have swept away one-third of the population. The famines of 1876-78 in Madras, Bombay, and Mysore are said to have resulted in the death of more than four millions of people, and the cost of relief and of remission of revenue came to fully eleven millions sterling. As was truly said by Sir Theodore Hope in a paper read before the Society of Arts in 1890, "these figures do but imperfectly indicate the loss to the people, whose savings of years were depleted, whose cattle died in enormous numbers, whose enfeebled condition rendered them an easy prey to a whole army of fatal diseases, even after actual famine had ceased, and among whom the normal birth-rate was not recovered for some years." There were two directions in which protection was obviously needed against such calamities. One was the extension of irrigation works, and the other, and the more pressing, was the improvement of the means of communication by which the surplus produce of one area could be rapidly and readily diverted to that in which famine was impending. A Famine Commission, appointed in 1880, insisted on the great importance of railways in the prevention of famine, and it became clear from their recommendations that the progress which was being made in this direction by means of State construction was inadequate to meet the requirements of the country. The Commission considered that 5000 miles of line were urgently needed, and the country could not be held to be safe from such calamities in the future until the Indian railway system could show an aggregate of 20,000 miles.

The outcome of this was the projection of large and

important schemes of famine-protection railways, but unfortunately the outbreak of the Afghan War led to the diversion of the resources of the State to another and more immediately urgent direction than that of famine protection, and it became increasingly evident that if railway extension was to be carried out with the rapidity which was necessary it would be impossible to rely solely on the operations of the Government. In June 1880 (previously to the arrival of Lord Ripon as Viceroy) a despatch had been sent to the Secretary of State,[1] in which the views of Lord Lytton and his Council were advanced as regards the provision of funds for railway extension. Its main features were that light cheap lines might be constructed on the separate financial responsibility of Provincial Governments. The Parliamentary Committee of 1879, on Indian Public Works, had, it should be observed, limited the funds to be borrowed by the Imperial Government for "productive" works, such as irrigation and railways, to 2½ millions sterling annually. In replying in September 1880, and in January 1881, the Secretary of State, then Lord Hartington (now Duke of Devonshire), thought the time had come for reverting to the agency of private enterprise in support of the direct operations of the State, and that although so far it had not been possible to attract investment without a guarantee, an endeavour should be made to attract capital "on the exclusive security of the success of the undertakings." Should, however, this prove to be impracticable, it might be necessary to offer some form of modified guarantee. The later despatch laid down certain principles to be rigidly adhered to with respect to future expenditure on productive[2] works, and the construction of

[1] Despatch No. 184, Finance, of 8th June 1880.

[2] For the inclusion of any work in the "productive" class, it was held to be necessary that there should be reasonable prospect of its paying 4 per cent on the capital invested within a maximum limit of five years from date of the line being opened for traffic. On the other hand, "protective" works were held to be such as were not directly remunerative, but were necessary to guard against future expenditure in famine relief.

railways was to be considered on "commercial principles," no new line being undertaken that did not offer fair promise of paying 4 per cent within five years of being opened for traffic. Meanwhile Lord Ripon had assumed the Viceroyalty, and was prepared to accept a vigorous policy in the extension of railways, more especially as to those which were destined to afford protection against famine.

Lord Ripon was earnestly and ably supported in this object by the financial member of his Council, then Sir Evelyn Baring (now Lord Cromer). The views of the Government of India may be held to have been embodied indeed, in his Financial Statement in March 1881. In this it was held that an outlay of 2½ millions annually on productive public works, including railways, was wholly inadequate to meet the wants of the country, that it was now necessary to abandon the hope of getting such works constructed with greater rapidity and that it was to be expected that English capital could be attracted, to some at least of the projects then proposed, without a guarantee being insisted on. He said—

> It has always appeared to me to be a remarkable fact that India—with all its magnificent and, as yet, only half developed resources, and with all the security to life and property resulting from a Government which, whatever be its objects, is at all events strong, honest, and well-intentioned—should, up to the present time, have been obliged to pledge the full security of the State in order to attract any considerable portion of the surplus capital of England. I hope that some railways afford sufficient attraction to induce private individuals to undertake their construction without the aid of Government, or, at all events, with a minimum amount of such aid. I do not question the wisdom of the policy which would permit capitalists to embark in this field.

He then proceeded to combat the objection that railways were monopolies, and should therefore be in the hands of the State, or that to concede the right of building a railway was in effect to part with one of the most productive resources in its hands.

It is true that a railway is generally a practical monopoly. The State should therefore exercise so much supervision over its working as will prevent the monopoly being exercised in a manner detrimental to the public interests. Thus the State should possess a right of inspection in order that the line may be certified by competent authority to be safe for the transport of goods and passengers. It should regulate the maximum tariff, and fix the gauge on which the line is to be constructed. It is especially necessary that a conditional right of purchase after the lapse of a certain period should be reserved. But when provision has been made for these, and some other points, which I will not now enumerate, the necessity for State interference ceases. The interests of the public do not necessarily demand that the State should create an artificial monopoly in its own favour, in respect to the construction of all railways.

As regards loss of revenue, he held that if the profits of a railway were "left to fructify in the pockets of the people," they would be more advantageously employed than would be the case were they paid to the State, with a great chance of their being employed on unproductive expenditure; while the indirect profits to the State, and to the country, resulting from railway communication, would be obtained equally well, whether railways are constructed by Government or by private agency. He was not without hope, moreover, that native capital could be induced to enter this field, and that he should regard such a movement "as an important factor in the practical education of the people. . . . If ever the natives of this country are to be schooled in the first rudiments of self-government, it is desirable that they should be encouraged to act for themselves in such matters, rather than that they should rely always upon that coercive philanthropy which insists upon doing everything for them."

Following on this statement the Government of India put forward their views in a despatch, No. 92, Railway, of the 22nd July 1881, to the Secretary of State for India. They reviewed the policy hitherto adopted in the following words: "We began with the system of guaranteed private enterprise inaugurated by Lord Dalhousie. After a lengthened trial, succeeded by an abortive attempt to encourage the expenditure of private capital by means of subsidies, this system was condemned by Lord Lawrence in a minute which he left behind when he retired from the Viceroyalty, and in which he expressed his preference for the plan of State railways constructed by Government with borrowed money. His successor, Lord Mayo, adopted this plan, and pushed it on with energy and vigour. But after a time strong objections were felt, especially at home, on financial grounds, to unlimited borrowing for public works, and of late years successive Secretaries of State, acting in accordance with the recommendations of a Committee of the House of Commons, have placed numerous restrictions upon the railway expenditure of the Government of India." They pointed out that these restrictions practically allowed no more than fifty lakhs of rupees annually for such lines as could not be classed as "productive," but which were nevertheless urgently needed to protect the country from famine. Under these circumstances they felt obliged to admit that they had no hope of being able to effect what was urgently needed, without dangerous delay, except by entrusting their railway works to private enterprise, "under a safe and reasonable guarantee." They proposed that interest granted under such guarantee should be a charge on the sum set aside for expenditure on Famine Protective Works. This despatch was followed by another,[1] in which the Government of India proposed the following conditions under which private enterprise should be again allowed to construct railways under a limited guarantee. That Government should determine the direction of lines, and, if required, make the necessary surveys; give land practically free for ninety-nine years; allow interest on capital during construction, and make up the earnings to a

[1] No. 113, of 24th September 1881.

certain percentage to be agreed on for five years after opening; retain powers over rates and fares and powers of purchase, and be repaid advances of interest by a division of surplus profits over the agreed percentage.[1]

These proposals were replied to by the Secretary of State in the following December,[2] and were not agreed to. He stated, as before, that his view of "private enterprise" was that it should be based, not on a guarantee, but "on the exclusive security of the success of the enterprise," and that it was of the essence of this policy that the proposals should not be made by the Government but by capitalists themselves. He said, "I can conceive nothing more injurious to the success of the policy of enlisting private enterprise in the development of railway enterprise in India than to lay before the public a large scheme of railways, avowedly of an unremunerative character," and as regards the proposal to employ the agency of companies for the construction of other than "productive" lines, he did not regard it with favour; but that no other agency than that of Government for such lines could be expected.

The result of this reply was to stop further development of the contemplated policy for the time; but meanwhile the portfolio of Public Works in the Viceroy's Council had fallen to Sir Theodore C. Hope, to whose marked vigour and ability the railway system of India owes much. In concert with Sir Evelyn Baring, who was still Financial Member of the Council, he drew up the terms of an important despatch[3] from the Government of India. This observed that the last formal and complete declaration on the subject of this policy by the Secretary of State was that railways should be constructed (1) by unaided private enterprise to the utmost possible extent;

[1] This new departure resulted in the floating of the Bengal Central, the Assam, and the Southern Mahratta Railways, all partly aided lines (see chap. ii.)

[2] No. 365, Financial, of 8th December 1881.

[3] No. 29, of 23rd January 1883, to Secretary of State, Department of Finance and Commerce.

(2) under guarantees of limited amount and duration, when unaided enterprise was not obtainable; (3) by the State out of borrowed money, or surplus revenue, provided they would probably pay 4 per cent within five years; out of the three-quarters of a million allowed for protective works, if they would not afford such a return on capital, and under special arrangements, if made under the actual pressure of war or famine. The Government of India pointed out how these views restricted operations which had been shown by the report of the Famine Commission to be vitally necessary, and they proposed to classify railway extensions under two schedules. They held that some limit must be assigned to capital expenditure, from funds borrowed by the State, for unprofitable lines of railway, and proposed that Schedule A should include indispensable railways, while Schedule B should include railways which, though mostly desirable in themselves, were not indispensable for protection or other urgent purposes, and might be left to private enterprise, aided only by the free grant of land. Schedule A contemplated the construction of 3837 miles of railway, including lines in progress, of which nearly the whole was "productive"; but only 1500 miles could be held to be "unproductive." Three agencies were proposed for the construction of these lines, viz. that of Government, of "Construction and Working Companies," and of private companies under limited guarantee. The despatch was accompanied by a minute by Sir T. Hope, in which, dissenting from a majority of the Council, he advocated the placing of the grants for Imperial Public Works upon the basis of a quinquennial contract, similar to what had been made for administrative purposes with Provincial Governments.

As marking a fresh epoch in the policy of the Government of India it may be well to give some extracts from this despatch, and to summarise portions of it:—

2. During the last two years the policy of the Government of India has been unsettled. We do not think that this is a matter

for surprise or for regret. In inaugurating a policy under which railways should, to some extent at all events, be constructed through the agency of private enterprise, it was almost inevitable that there should be a period of transition during which it would be exceedingly difficult to adhere to any fixed policy. It was easy to declare beforehand the broad aim which the Government sought to attain, viz. the construction of railways through the agency of unaided private enterprise. But experience alone could show how far that aim was attainable. It is now clear that the present condition of things is open to considerable objection. In the absence of any very clearly-defined principles for our guidance, each case has to be considered on its merits. The result of this state of things is that there is a risk of drifting unawares into the adoption of measures which may prove a source of future embarrassment. We have now had two years' experience of the private enterprise policy. During that time a certain number of facts have been accumulated which, we think, are sufficient to enable us to lay down a definite policy, at all events for the immediate future, say for five years.

The Government of India would not discuss the question of the principle on which railways were to be constructed in future, or whether by the State directly or by private agency. They were content to assume that the Home Government avowed a policy of constructing these works by unaided private enterprise, and, further, that the main portion of the required capital must come from England, although every facility should be given to local capitalists to subscribe. They pointed out that a public works policy in India must in a very great degree depend on the financial position, and that in face of an unstable standard of value, and the precarious position of the opium revenue, great caution was necessary before incurring fresh liabilities, especially if it should involve any increase of taxation. Indeed, they went so far as to say that they would regard increased taxation as a greater evil than relatively slow progress in railway construction, more especially in the case of railways which were not urgently needed as a protection against famine. As regards the absorption of profits from railways as a substitute for taxation, the Government of India, while admitting that much might be said against this course, considered that "the practical necessities of the financial situation" might oblige them to recognise those profits as a source of income in the immediate future.

After pointing out the directions in which private enterprise had already advanced under the new *régime* of a "limited guarantee," and that there were signs of less distrust on the part of capitalists in viewing Indian railway schemes, they urged that while it seemed likely that no difficulty would now arise in obtaining the means for constructing "productive" lines, the means for making "protective" railways seemed still quite inadequate. They held, therefore, that it was now necessary to invert the system hitherto in force. They said,—

> We consider that instead of continuing State agency for the construction of productive lines of railway, we should, for the future, as far as possible, exclude the action of the State altogether from this field of enterprise, and that, as a general rule, the Government should only undertake the construction of railways which, from their unprofitable character in a commercial sense or other causes, cannot be made by private agencies. A good deal might be said in favour of this policy from the point of view of abstract principle. It will, however, be sufficient for our present purpose if we look wholly at the practical issue which is involved. And the practical issue is this—that the adoption of this policy, for the time being at all events, will alone permit of the speedy construction of those railways which are urgently required as a protection against famine.

The despatch then dealt with the financial aspects of this new policy, pointing out that it involved a complete reversal of that which had obtained during the last few years.

> The essence of the present policy is that railways constructed by the State should, generally speaking, be self-supporting. The essence of the new policy is that the railways constructed by the

State need not, and often will not be self-supporting. It is sufficient to state the facts thus, in order to show that the change of policy will materially affect the financial position of the Government, and it becomes of the highest importance to inquire whether the change may be made with a due regard to financial prudence. It is obvious that some limit must be assigned to capital expenditure, from funds borrowed by the State, on unprofitable lines of railway. A policy which involved borrowing to an indefinite amount in order to construct such lines, must almost infallibly lead in the end to most serious financial embarrassment. The possibility of giving practical effect to the policy depends, indeed mainly, on the amount of money which it is proposed to sink in investments which are not calculated to yield a rate of interest equal to that at which the Government of India is able to borrow. This rate may be taken at 4 per cent per annum.

The proposals as regards funds for carrying out the programme as exhibited in the Schedules above referred to were, firstly, to increase the loan raised annually of 2½ millions for productive works of all kinds, including navigation, by the sum of £350,000, the whole sum being in future held available for both productive and unproductive works; and, secondly, by making arrangements with companies, involving an annual liability of £250,000, of which it was proposed that £200,000 might be hypothecated from the Famine Fund of 1½ millions. The sum of £200,000 was the estimated burden, under the worst conditions, which was to be expected on the three principal "protective" railways which were put forward. The Government of India further proposed that private companies should in future receive no other aid than that of the free grant of land, but that, on the other hand, the State should raise no claim to a share in the direct profits from such lines. They were prepared, moreover, to allow the debit of interest during construction to the capital account.

The Secretary of State replied to this on the 16th August

1883, and regarded the proposals, more especially in their financial bearing, as going far beyond what had been considered by the Famine Commission as necessary for the protection of the country; as likely to involve an annual expenditure of three times the amount (2½ millions) now authorised to be expended from borrowed money; and to cause, by such large expenditure, a rise in the price of labour and materials, which might largely detract from their financial success. He admitted, however, that the present restriction on the limit for borrowed money should be removed, or the limit extended, and that with this view the Home Government had decided to propose the appointment of another Select Committee to re-examine the policy which should be pursued in the extension of Indian railways, and with special reference to the recommendations of the Famine Commission. The views of the Secretary of State were combated by the Government of India,[1] but the Secretary of State declined to pursue the discussion, or to entertain certain proposals of private companies, pending the result of the inquiry by the Parliamentary Committee. The Government of India, however, returned to the charge, and in January 1884 again reviewed the whole position, submitting modifications of the Schedules A and B, and justifying their previous statements that the outlay proposed was neither sudden nor excessive. The proposal of Sir T. C. Hope above referred to, as regards a contract basis for the supply of funds for Public Works, was mentioned. It was said that he considered "that the profits of Indian railways should not, for a few years, be swallowed up in the general expenditure of the Empire, but should be devoted, in one form or another, to that railway extension which the country so urgently needs for its protection from famine, the development of its external commerce, the counteraction of the fall of silver, and the general enrichment of its people. In short, he would let railways breed railways. . . . For this proposal it is claimed that in addition to minor

[1] Despatch No. 269, of 24th September 1883.

technical advantages, it would promote thrift in expenditure, furnish a stimulus to increasing receipts, as similar contracts in the case of Provincial Governments have been found by experience to do, and also provide a means of railway extension sufficiently rapid, but under the strict security for financial soundness which the contract limit would entail." This proposal was not, however, supported by the Government.

Early in 1884 Sir Auckland Colvin took over the post of Finance Member of the Viceroy's Council. He was not disposed to wholly agree with the policy which the Government of India proposed to adopt. He admitted that "protective" railways must be made by borrowed money, but that a scheme of real and urgently-needed projects of this nature should be laid down, and that Government should be empowered, but not obliged by any programme, to spend on them, and not on "productive" works, so much of the borrowed capital (2½ millions yearly) as was not devoted to irrigation. Moreover, that similar conditions should apply to the utilisation of the Famine Grant, which should be expended as capital only, and not as interest. The substance of the minute was to recommend the concentration of effort on carrying out protective works, and to restrict expenditure on so-called productive works. He said, "All we can at present do for commerce is to tell it what lines it is at liberty to construct, to give the land necessary for its railways, and to see that no obstacles are thrown in its way."[1]

In the meantime the Select Committee of the House of Commons had been at work, it having commenced its sittings in March 1884, and it reported in July of the same year, making the following principal recommendations:—

1. That the evidence in favour of a more rapid extension of railways is conclusive.

---

[1] The other members of the Government dissented from Sir A. Colvin's views, and a minute supporting their position, by Sir T. C. Hope, sent home to the Secretary of State with Sir A. Colvin's minute.

2. That all the leading trunk lines with their principal feeders should be on the broad gauge.
3. That the rigid technical distinction between productive and protective lines cannot be maintained.
4. That the amount proposed to be spent on railways by the Government in the next six years was moderate.
5. That the limit of 2½ millions of borrowing fixed in 1879 might safely be enlarged.
6. That a fixed scale of expenditure should be maintained over a considerable term of years.
7. That money may be borrowed in England for schemes approved by the Secretary of State.
8. That the bulk of these lines should be made self-supporting.
9. That no portion of the Famine Grant should be hypothecated as interest on capital.
10. That railway extension should not involve additional taxation; and
11. That the Secretary of State should be responsible for deciding what amounts may with safety to the finances be borrowed for Public Works.

The Secretary of State informed the Government of India that he concurred with the general tenor of the Committee's recommendations, and made certain proposals as regards finance, to which the Government of India replied in September 1884,[1] submitting a forecast of the requirements for the next six years, and recapitulating its views and recommendations regarding the concession of certain projects to companies. To this the Secretary of State replied, fixing the sum to be borrowed yearly for Public Works at 350 lakhs of rupees absolutely, and that no expenditure in excess of this except from revenue was to be incurred. This decision and the grounds for it were communicated in a despatch, No. 148, of the 27th November 1884.

In the same year, 1884, the gauge question again came up, owing to the difficulties which were experienced in deciding upon the gauge required for each project, the decision having

[1] Despatch No. 150, of 29th September 1884.

been based, of late years, on the supposed financial prospects of the line, and the views of the Government for the time being. The Government of India communicated its intentions on the subject in a despatch to the Secretary of State in April 1884,[1] and the policy on this point then recommended was practically endorsed by the recommendations of the Select Committee of the House of Commons. This subject will be fully dealt with in Chapter V.

Another era of companies' lines, side by side with State lines, both in construction and administration, was thus commenced under Lord Ripon's Viceroyalty. It was hoped at first that railways which appeared likely to be remunerative would be taken up by companies either without a guarantee, or at most a guarantee for a limited number of years. Two small schemes were started in 1881, on a limited guarantee, and early in 1882 a larger scheme, that of the Southern Mahratta Railway Company, was started on the basis of the railway belonging to the State, but being worked and the funds being supplied by the company. A guarantee was given on the capital of 4 per cent for seven years, and 3½ per cent subsequently, together with a fourth share to the company of net profits. Later on in the same year another company, the Bengal and North-Western, was launched without any guarantee, a share in profits over 6 per cent being only reserved for Government. Other projects were under negotiation, when it became obvious that money could not be raised in England without a definite guarantee, and two important lines were launched in 1885 and 1887—the Bengal-Nagpore, and the Indian Midland—on similar conditions to the Southern Mahratta Company, but with a permanent guarantee of 4 per cent, and one-fourth of surplus profits over and above this figure. Thus the system of railway construction by the agency of companies was

[1] Despatch No. 48, Railway, 22nd April 1884, which was rendered necessary owing to the persistent efforts of the Secretary of State to force the metre gauge for adoption on what were evidently trunk lines.

practically a reversion to the policy of Lord Dalhousie, the difference being that each line was held to be State property from the outset, the rate of interest was 4 instead of 5 per cent, the State had power to fix rates and fares, and the lion's share of profits over the guaranteed figure was taken by the State. In referring to this new departure, in a paper read before the Society of Arts in June 1890, Sir Theodore Hope was of opinion that this system of using both State and companies' agencies worked well, and was well suited for a permanence, in so far that State debt and State establishments could be kept at a moderate level, that there would always be some railways, which, for military or other reasons, it was desirable that the Government should keep in its own hands; while there were others, with which a company could most conveniently deal. Another advantage which could have been claimed, was that the two systems introduced a healthy rivalry between State and companies' lines, both in cheapness of construction and in subsequent working.

An important feature in railway policy, relating to rates and fares, may here be briefly touched upon though dealt with at greater length in a subsequent chapter. The through opening of the Rajputana Railway, metre gauge, which belonged to the State, led in 1881 to a representation from the Calcutta Chamber of Commerce to the effect, that low rates were being charged to Bombay, and in consequence that traffic was being diverted to that port which formerly found its way to Calcutta. On this an assurance was made by Government, that the through rates from the common point, Delhi, should not be lower to Bombay than to Calcutta. Meanwhile the Secretary of State had had his attention drawn to the matter at home, and in March 1882,[1] a reference on the subject was made to the Government of India. The Secretary of State held that "the natural course of traffic on two lines, proceeding from the same place to ports on different sides of the continent of India,

[1] Despatch No. 41, Railway, of 1882, to Government of India.

should not be interfered with by any idea of adjudicating on the rivalry between them, and that the advantages due, either to geographical position, or other circumstances, should furnish no reason for imposing on either artificial restrictions, in the shape of enhanced rates in order to produce an equal return of profit on the capital of both." In replying to this, the Government of India disclaimed any intention to "adjudicate" in the rivalry between the two ports, but affirmed that their orders had been passed on the principle that a line with cheap fuel and easy gradients can afford to carry goods at a lower mileage rate than one not possessing these advantages, and that to keep the rates on the former at a level with those on the latter, would be prejudicial to the country served by the more cheaply-worked line. It was their desire, they said, "in the interest of the country generally, that all rates should be reduced to the lowest limit which will give a fair profit, and this cannot be attained by the adoption of uniform mileage rates on all lines." To this view the Secretary of State (Lord Hartington) objected *in toto.*[1] He said "that to attempt to proportion rates on competing lines to the supposed aggregates of the factors of cost of transport on each is impracticable, and would not be desirable if it were practicable," that it should be left to the managers of lines to fix such rates as they might deem most advantageous, and that the interest of trade and of the railways would be better served by accepting the legitimate consequences of competition. To this the Government of India responded by the issue of a circular letter, embodying and accepting the view of the Secretary of State. At the same time, it is not surprising that the Government of India, as the owner, or potential owners, of all the Indian railways, should have viewed with anxiety, or even alarm, the outbreak of a war of rates which threatened to imperil their financial results; but it would be now readily admitted that the remedy they then proposed to adopt was one

[1] Despatch from Secretary of State, No. 132, Railway, of 19th October 1882.

that was equally impracticable and impolitic; while that which was accepted, on the advice of the Secretary of State, was, and has been proved to be, the sound one.

An important outcome of this correspondence was, that it led to a consideration of the question of the agency by which certain groups of lines could be most properly and economically worked. The State lines, as completed, had hitherto been made over to State officials to be worked without consideration as to their bearing or position with respect to adjacent or connected railways, and it seemed advisable, both on this account and with the view of economy, to review the position, and if necessary to make over the working of some of these lines to companies. Any rearrangements in this direction were necessarily complicated by the terms of the contracts with the guaranteed railways, and no alteration in their working agencies was possible until their contracts expired. The first move was made in 1884 by the making over of the Rajputana-Malwa metre gauge system—a State concern—to the Bombay, Baroda, and Central India Railway Company on a lease, or working agreement for a term of years, the State being assured of a fixed percentage on the capital cost of the line, and taking a large share of surplus profits over and above this. In taking this step the Government of India expressly declared that it was in no way due to its being recognised that State management was inferior to that of a company; but that in substituting private agency, under due control, for that of the State, it was probable that incentives would be created towards more vigorous and economical management, and that it might be expected that the State, whether directly or indirectly, would not be a loser by the arrangement. In contrast to this, about the same time the contract of the Eastern Bengal Railway expired, and was not renewed; the line was acquired by the State, and made over for working to State agency, which was then administering a large metre gauge system in connection with it. Later on similar action was taken in the purchase of the Sind and

Punjab Railway, and in its adoption, under State management, into the north-eastern frontier railway system. Other cases of the same sort have been dealt with on similar lines after due consideration of the circumstances, the general tendency being perhaps towards the making over of State lines to be worked by companies' agency on working agreements.

In 1879 the Government considered it desirable to convene a conference of railway officers of both State and companies' lines to discuss and determine certain questions of importance which had arisen in the working of Indian railways. This, the first, conference met in January 1880, and since this conference others have been convened, and with great benefit to the administration of Indian lines. The same year saw the institution of a Provident Fund for servants employed on State railways, all employés being obliged to subscribe to it, and voluntary subscriptions to a certain extent allowed besides. Government gave depositors the same rate of interest as was allowed in the State Savings Banks, and as an inducement to employés to take an interest in the economical administration of the line they were engaged on gave them an annual bonus from net profits. This fund enabled the Government before long to abolish the pension system for railway servants.

Brief reference must here be made to the policy of Government in the matter of military railways. The importance of the railway system in India for military purposes was naturally recognised at the outset, and great stress was laid on this in Lord Dalhousie's minute of 1853. But until the outbreak of the Afghan War, at the end of 1878, no comprehensive views had been taken of the interconnection of our frontier communications, nor any programme laid down for railway construction for purely or mainly military objects. This must be attributed in some measure to the pressure of famine troubles for several years previously, and the severe tax they imposed on the resources of the State. The Afghan campaign revealed, however, the need, not only for improved means of moving troops along our frontier, but for improvement in the connections and capabilities of existing lines leading from our military centres. The value of railway communication during this campaign was vividly illustrated in the case of the railway which had been rapidly pushed across the desert to the mouth of the Bolan Pass, where one train, in a day of sixteen hours, was found to do the work which it would have required 2500 camels to do in a fortnight. Up to the year 1883 no very definite policy had been pursued in dealing with military or frontier railways, but during the Viceroyalty of Lord Ripon this question was taken up seriously, and a definite programme, which was estimated to cost over five millions sterling, was submitted to the Secretary of State in 1884. The Government of India proposed, though not unanimously, that this outlay should preferably be derived from borrowed funds, on a separate and distinct loan, which should be discharged within thirty years by terminable annuities and a sinking fund. The scheme received the approval of the Home Government, but exception was taken to the financial proposal. The Secretary of State admitted that such works were both urgent and exceptional in character, but that, nevertheless, their cost should as far as possible be met from revenue, and that for such purposes borrowed money should only be had recourse to when funds from revenue were exhausted. He was, however, prepared to allow an extension to the limit of the annual sum borrowed for public works, and decided to raise the figure from 2½ millions to 350 lakhs of rupees in conformity with the recommendations of the Parliamentary Select Committee of 1884.[1]

The result of this decision was a correspondence between the Government of India and the Secretary of State on the financial bearing of their railway policy. One point which arose in this bears strongly on the general question of the construction of railways by the direct agency of the State, and

[1] At an exchange of 1d.–4d. to the rupee the 350 lakhs are now considerably less than 2½ millions.

deserves particular notice. The attention of Sir T. C. Hope, the Member of the Viceroy's Council for Public Works, had for some time been drawn to the serious public inconvenience, and even positive pecuniary loss, which resulted from the way in which funds for railway construction were provided by the Finance Department, and in 1883, as already mentioned, he had concluded that the only satisfactory way of meeting this difficulty was that an informal agreement, or contract, should be made for five years with the Public Works Department, and that within the limits thus fixed to leave this Department a free hand in utilising to the best advantage the funds placed at its disposal. This had not met with approval; but in 1886 Sir T. C. Hope took the opportunity of referring to the subject again on an intimation from the Secretary of State that certain considerable lapses had been allowed to occur in the railway grants. He pointed out that neither at home nor in India was there an adequate appreciation of the fact that uncertain supplies, of either funds or materials, must certainly lead to such lapses, and that it appeared to be considered that such supplies could be turned on or off "as readily as water from a tap." He showed that the procedure by which stores were obtained from England for State railways frequently involved delays, which in turn generally implied lapses of the grant for the year; that these lapses were not necessarily regranted in the next year, and in consequence the programme of construction of a line was thrown out, works might have to be suspended in order to provide money for stores arranged for in the previous year, or, as might happen, material might arrive at the port of destination and no funds be available to meet the cost of transit to the works. Thus money had to be withdrawn from some other work, and its programme disorganised, the only certainty in the vicious circle being that of waste of time and money in one quarter or another. He dealt earnestly, moreover, on the effects of sudden withdrawals and expansions of funds according to the financial or political position at the time. He said, and most truly, "Large works, such as railways, cannot profitably be executed by driblets. Once started, economy is best secured by keeping the establishments at their full working power by supplying materials in a regular flow at the time they are actually required, and by completing successive sections as an aid to the rest. Starting and stopping work from time to time spasmodically; suddenly discharging labour carefully collected and trained, and as suddenly endeavouring to re-collect it; keeping highly-paid staff partially or wholly unemployed for months; at one time sending out material which there are no funds for utilising, at another suspending field work for want of material; and operating throughout on uncertain and fluctuating resources—this is a mode of business which no mercantile firm could pursue with impunity, or would even contemplate seriously."

The soundness of these views could scarcely be denied by those who were in the least degree conversant with the nature of railway operations, and it may be assumed that they would have been regarded with more favour by the Government of India as a whole had the country and its finances been free from sources of serious embarrassment. Among these actual and potential famine may be said to have held the first place; while secondly, the possibility at that time of war with Russia entailed a new and evidently prolonged outlay on works for the defence of the Empire. But the great and increasing difficulty of the Government lay in the fluctuation in the exchange value of silver, the standard of the currency. Had there been any reasonable hope of finality in this it could have been accepted as a heavy but transient burden, to be met temporarily by retrenchment or increased taxation, or by both; but the Government could not but recognise that it was more likely to increase than to decrease, and that no prudent system of finance could, in the face of this difficulty, justify their entering into any undertaking which should bind them to a heavy and regular annual expenditure on public works. The table on

p. 28 shows the fall in exchange between the years 1870-71 and 1891-92.

For some years the financial difficulties of the Government had been ominously increasing, both on account of the fall in the exchange value of silver, and from the necessity, then fully recognised, of expending large sums yearly in works for the defence of our north-western frontiers. Thus the guarantees in sterling, given to the Indian Midland and Bengal-Nagpore Railways, were most reluctantly assented to, notwithstanding the urgency which appeared to attach to them as famine protective lines. Indeed it had seemed to Sir Auckland Colvin, then Financial Member of Council, that the increasing obligations of the State would render it necessary to impose fresh taxation to meet them, and to this step there were grave difficulties and objections. On this point the Secretary of State in a despatch to the Government of India, dated 29th July 1886, observed that while he did not in the least overlook the importance of extending the railway system in India, both for the purpose of providing additional means of protecting the country against famine and for developing its resources, he said that he must impress upon the Government that even these unquestionable advantages might be too dearly bought if they were compelled, in order to meet their expenditure, to resort to increased taxation; adding that measures which might have seemed highly desirable, when there was a fair prospect of a surplus of revenue, must be suspended in the changed condition of affairs. In spite, however, of these views, and of their bearing on the immediate position, the grant of a 4 per cent sterling guarantee was eventually made to the Bengal-Nagpore Company in February 1887, on similar terms to the contract of the Indian Midland Company. It was allowed, nevertheless, that unless the position materially improved—a contingency which in no way seemed probable—no further assistance to private enterprise could be given in this shape, and that unless some other system could be found by which English capital could be attracted to railway construction in India, the extension of these works must, for the future, depend on such allotments as could be provided by the State from revenue or from the fixed amount of the annual loan for public works. In December 1887 the portfolio of Public Works in the Viceroy's Council was assumed by Sir Charles Elliott, K.C.I.E.

It became necessary to seek some new form in which the requisite assistance or encouragement could be given to the English investor, while not involving the incubus of a guarantee. After some considerable negotiation, the new departure took the shape, in 1889, of an agreement on the part of the Government with the Delhi-Umballa-Kalka Railway Company, in which the latter was to construct a line in connection with the East Indian Railway with the grant of free land only; but on the condition that on the completion of the railway the line should be worked by the State for 50 per cent of the gross receipts. In October of the same year the Government of India addressed a lengthy despatch to the Secretary of State,[1] in which a programme was sketched for future railway extension. In this despatch only casual reference was made to the possible co-operation of private enterprise, whether in the direction above referred to or in any other, and appeared to contemplate future operations as being mainly the result of direct State agency. In November the Secretary of State (Viscount Cross) in a despatch, No. 132, Railway, in acknowledging the receipt of the programme above mentioned, gave a very definite expression of the views of the Home Government as regards the employment of companies on Indian railways. He pointed out that the steadily increasing receipts on these concerns fully justify the anticipation that further extensions, if judiciously carried out, would yield "a fair return" on the capital invested. He agreed with the conclusion which had practically been adopted by the Government of India and his

[1] No. 14, Railway, of 1889.

predecessors that the choice between direct State agency and that of companies must depend on the circumstances of each case, that while generally the multiplication of agencies should be avoided, both might still be employed, but that financial conditions should predominate in arriving at a decision on this point. He was disposed, however, to think that it was expedient to as far as possible enlarge the scope afforded by railways in India for private enterprise, and thus diminish the burdens and responsibility of the Government, promote decentralisation, and encourage the spirit of emulation which would result from a variety of management. He therefore held that "in the case of projects for which the requisite capital can be provided, and the working conditions arranged on reasonable terms, the plan of employing companies in the construction, and still more in the working of railways, possesses certain recommendations that will frequently make it expedient to give that agency the preference." The continuance of the system of guarantee, whether for a short or long period, was plainly objected to; but a hope was expressed that other means, then under consideration, might be found by which the requisite aid might be given to companies, and reference was made to an idea of advancing money to them from a sum of ten millions which had recently been raised on the authority of Parliament for special application to railway extension in India. A company was to raise one-third of the cost of a line, the remainder being advanced by the Government in India, and interest on the company's share of the capital was to be a first charge on the net earnings of the line. The despatch further contained a suggestion for the institution of Local Boards, in connection with the administration of Indian railways, from whose advice marked benefit might be expected. A reference was also made to the question of gauge, and the Secretary of State recorded his concurrence in the recommendation of the House of Commons Committee of 1884 on this subject to the effect that all leading trunk lines should be on the broad ($5\frac{1}{2}$ feet) gauge, while the metre gauge as a rule should be confined "to tracts where that system is already in successful operation, and to local lines where the traffic is likely to be so light that the cheapness of construction more than counterbalances the undoubted disadvantage of break of gauge."

The views of the Government of India on the above-mentioned despatch were given in March 1890[1] (Lord Lansdowne being Viceroy). They fully agreed that the multiplication of agencies was an evil to be avoided, and more especially as regards working companies which were "always exposed to the temptation of trying to divert traffic into their own lines, and to block other lines by prohibitive rates." This evil it was hoped to minimise by the creation of a Railway Commission; but it was considered that there would always be the danger of a small company occupying the most remunerative part of a tract of country, and thereby increasing the difficulty of providing for the extension of a line to portions likely to be less productive. A proposal made in the Secretary of State's despatch was referred to, which was to allot a certain area to each trunk line, and require all extension within that area to be made by such line. This was agreed to as being eminently sound in theory. "Its effect would be to discourage purely competitive lines, to give the benefit of railway communications to the greatest extent of country with the least possible expenditure, and to economise working expenses by concentrating the traffic of a country on a railway system adequate for it." It was, however, pointed out that although this principle might be readily adopted on a blank map, it was a different matter to apply it in a case where, as already in India, railways had been constructed with disregard to it, and thus making it impossible to define the natural sphere of each system. The financial difficulty was, moreover, no light one, in so far that a scheme might be submitted by a company which had funds but had

[1] Despatch No. 55, dated 25th March 1890.

not the claim to the territory, while on the other hand a company which held this right might not be in a position to find the funds. On the question of gauge, the Government of India alluded to proposals then before them (to which reference will be made farther on) to reserve certain areas for each gauge, and stated that although the evils of break of gauge had as yet been little felt in India, it was to be expected that as the railway system increased and became "closely interlaced" the inconvenience would become so sensible as to render a large expenditure justifiable in order to alter the gauge on some lines.

The financial proposals made in the Secretary of State's despatch did not meet with approval from the Government of India. They held that the assistance thus given would secure none of the advantages which were to be expected from private enterprise, and that it was in fact nothing less than a sterling guarantee on a company's share of the capital in another form. The condition that the State should be required to advance so large a proportion of the capital seemed to the Government of India to be likely to lead to serious difficulties in the event of war or famine, which would impose serious strain on the finances, and thus render it impossible to meet the requirements of a company. The Government might consequently be exposed to claims on account of the stoppage of the works. The ideal of private enterprise in Indian railways, in the view of the Government of India, was that a company should require nothing more than the free grant of land; but they were not prepared to support the creation of companies "which would have a very limited interest in the concern from which they take their name, which would contribute only a small portion of the capital at an unnecessarily high rate of interest, yet on what is really absolute security, and which, for the rest of their capital, would have to draw, from the Government Treasury, funds in the management of which the State could thereafter have but little influence, and from which it would probably get a very poor return." They considered that rather than raise funds in such a way, for expediting railway extension, it would be better and safer to increase the borrowing powers of the Government of India than to enter into arrangements with private companies which would pledge the supply of money to them without reference to the state of the finances at the time.

Meanwhile negotiations had been in progress between the Secretary of State and the South Indian Railway Company, on the expiration of the contract of the latter, for the basis of a new contract, under which the lines then forming the system were to be taken over on a working lease by a new company, which was also to find capital for extensions. Ultimately, in November 1890, the contract was executed on conditions very similar to those which had been sketched in the Secretary of State's despatch above noticed. The Company was held to be formed primarily for the purpose of working, managing, and maintaining the existing lines, and to raise one million sterling as capital for the purpose of extension, this sum being held to be equivalent to 140 lakhs of rupees, and the interest on this, at 3½ per cent for three years, and thereafter at 3 per cent, to be a first charge on the net revenues of the line. The second charge on the receipts was to be interest at 3 per cent on the Government share of the capital, *i.e.* the original cost of the line, while any surplus over and above these charges was to be divided in proportion to the capital subscribed by the Government and the Company. The contract to be for twenty years, and at its expiration or determination the Company's capital to be repaid in London, in sterling at par. As may be gathered from the sketch already given of the views of the Government of India, these terms were considered by them to be too advantageous to the Company; but in this the Secretary of State felt unable to agree, holding that under the circumstances less favourable terms would have led to the failure of the negotiations. Early in 1891 the Secretary of State, Lord Cross, returned to the subject,[1] and expressed his views generally as regards the employment of the agency of companies. He said that the policy which had dictated the action taken as to the South Indian Railway Company, was in effect that of his predecessors, and with this he was in complete accord. He was not disposed to discard the agency of companies, "which had been so largely employed by the State from the first introduction of railway communication into the country," adding that on "various substantial grounds, some of them not less important than immediate financial considerations," it was expedient to continue the employment of companies in both the construction and working of railways in India. It was at the same time evident that the terms and conditions on which this policy was to be carried out must vary according to the circumstances of each project, the state of the money market, and the aspect of the finances of the country, and that only in this sense were negotiations for new lines to be regarded as constituting a new departure. He concluded by stating that if the encouragement of private enterprise was to be confined to the offer of terms upon which, under certain conditions, it might be impossible to negotiate, railway extension from this source must be indefinitely postponed, or the whole burden must devolve on the State.

This despatch was replied to by the Government of India in October of the same year.[2] They repudiated any intention of pressing for the exclusive employment of direct State agency, while on the contrary they would cordially welcome the co-operation of companies, but that this might be obtained at too high a price, and in this sense private enterprise as properly understood would not be secured. They had no desire to employ State agency further than to secure adequate employment for their existing establishments, which they believed,

[1] Despatch No. 16, Railway, of 5th February 1891.

[2] Despatch to Secretary of State, No. 107, of 14th October 1891.

moreover, were fully as efficient as those which were employed by companies.

At this point this sketch of railway policy in India must be brought to a close, the later developments being noticed in another chapter. It should be observed however, that the discussions referred to in the preceding pages, as to the conditions on which the employment of companies should be encouraged, did not imply that there was any cessation, or even material diminution, in the expenditure on railways by the State itself. In the year 1892-93 about 310 lakhs were expended by Government under this head, and in part from revenue, on new lines, while about eighty lakhs more were devoted to new works and improvements on existing lines. The demand under this latter head is in fact growing heavier year by year, and already trenches severely on the strictly limited funds available annually for railway expenditure.

If the salient features of this brief sketch be passed in review, it will be seen that there have been three distinct phases of policy. From the beginning up to the year 1869, the construction and working of railways was left entirely to companies under some form of guarantee. From 1870 to 1880, on the other hand, nearly all new lines were constructed by the direct agency of the State and with State funds; while from the latter year up to the present time, the operations of both the State and of aided companies have gone on together. The proposals made in 1883 by the Government of India, which have been referred to at some length, were to lease the productive lines to private enterprise, while the unproductive lines were to be carried out by the State either directly or indirectly. To a great extent this policy has been adhered to; but until a stable figure of exchange can be attained for our Indian currency, it must be acknowledged that the assistance of private enterprise on any large scale is not to be reckoned upon without a guarantee in some form or other. Thus so far the expectations of 1883 have not been realised. For the future the very serious financial difficulties in which the Government now finds itself forbid the hope of any continuous or forward policy. It cannot afford to give definite assistance to private enterprise, and the day seems at hand when the expenditure of the State itself must be greatly restricted. The outlook can in fact be improved in one way only, viz. by the establishment of a stable sterling value for the rupee.

CHAPTER II

GUARANTEES AND ASSISTANCE

IN the previous chapter an outline has been given of the phases through which the policy of the Government of India has passed in dealing with their railway system, from the beginning to the present day. It is necessary, however, to give a more detailed description than that sketch affords of the character of the assistance which it was deemed necessary to concede to private enterprise in Indian railways, and the nature of the co-partnership, and the control, which was reserved for the State in the contracts. Whatever may have been the changes in the attitude of the Government towards the promoters of companies, for constructing or working railways, no intention has been shown to relinquish or diminish the rights of the State to share, either immediately or in future, in the profits of each undertaking, or to weaken its powers of control and supervision. The initiation of this policy may perhaps be properly attributed to Lord Dalhousie, who before he became Governor-General, in the early days of Indian railways, had had exceptional opportunities of observing the ill effects of the supineness of the Government in England, in its relation to railway enterprise, and who showed a clear determination to avoid this mistake in India. In accepting the co-operation of companies in the commencement of these works, and in the grant to them of a guarantee of interest on their capital, he exercised the right of the State to direct their operations, and to require that their development should be carried out on definite and well-considered lines. The advantages of this course, to both the investor and to the general public, has been incontestable; it has protected the shareholder at home from the mistakes of injudicious and inexperienced agents, and has enabled the Government to have its railway system designed with due regard to the interests of all classes.

The earliest agreements with companies under guarantee are dated in August 1849, and were between the Secretary of State for India and the East Indian and Great Indian Peninsula Railway Companies. The prolonged negotiations which preceded their completion have been noticed in the preceding chapter. The first recorded proposal was made in December 1844, by Mr. (now Sir) Macdonald Stephenson. The Government of India were at first opposed to any form of guarantee, while on the other hand the Court of Directors of the East India Company were of opinion, in which they were undoubtedly right, that money could not be raised in England for the purpose without aid in this, or some other equally tangible form. The outcome was on the whole, and in the light then available, on the prospects of railway enterprise in India, a fairly equitable one. The Government relieved the shareholders of all risk, gave them some expectation of profit over and above the guaranteed interest, and in return claimed reasonable powers of control and the right of purchase. The following are the principal conditions of these contracts:—

The Government would determine the route to be followed, and had power to alter or extend it.

Land was provided by Government for all works on a lease for ninety-nine years.

The necessity and expediency of all works was to be certified in writing to the Company.

The Government had power to determine the number, speed, and times of running of trains, to approve the fares leviable, and to require a reduction of these when the line paid over 10 per cent.

Entire control and superintendence was reserved for Government over the servants of the Company, and free access stipulated for to all books, papers, and accounts, together with the appointment of an unpaid Government Director who had power of *veto*.

The expenditure of the Company to be submitted to Government for approval and sanction, and only expenditure so approved to be carried to the Capital Account.

Gross receipts to be paid into Government Treasury.

Interest at 5 per cent per annum, to be paid to the Company on capital paid into the Treasury, for ninety-nine years.

A reserve fund was to be instituted for making good deterioration, the net profits of the line being applied in the first instance towards the repayment of interest to Government. The accumulated interest debt was to bear simple interest only, at the rate of 5 per cent per annum, and when the profits exceeded the amount payable on the guarantee, one-half of such excess was to be credited to the Company, and the other half to be applied firstly towards payment of interest on the debt, and then towards the extinction of the debt itself. When the debt and interest had been discharged the Company was to take the whole of the surplus net receipts.

Provision was made for the carriage of mails and postal servants free of charge, and for the carriage of troops and military stores at reduced rates.

At the expiration of the term of ninety-nine years the land and works to become the property of Government, the rolling stock and other movable property being paid for at a fair value.

The company might voluntarily surrender the line after completion, on giving six months' notice, when the Government would refund the capital outlay.

The Government had the option of purchasing the line within six months after the first twenty-five years, or first fifty years, the sum to be paid being the full amount of the value of all shares and capital stock, calculated on the mean market value in London during the preceding three years.

In case of default by the company in finding capital, or in the execution of the works, in working the line, or in any other way, the Government could, on giving three months' notice, take possession of the line on payment of the capital outlay within six months, less debts. Moreover, if the line was not properly maintained when open, the Government had power to do what was necessary, and to deduct the cost from the sum due for guaranteed interest.

Instead of repaying capital directly, the Government was empowered to commute this by granting annuities, payable half-yearly, for the remainder of the term of ninety-nine years, the rate of interest to be used in calculating the annuity to be the average rate of interest during the preceding two years received in London on public obligations by the Secretary of State for India.

Finally, the Government bound itself to promote such legislation as might be necessary to enable the company to fulfil the objects of the undertaking.

The instructions of the Court of Directors were very explicit as to the exercise of the powers of the Government in respect to the supervision over the companies under this contract. They required that this control should not only be effective, but even minute, extending both to the operations of the companies during construction, and after the lines had been opened for traffic. The rules laid down for the guidance of the inspecting officers of Government, who were then, and have since been termed "Consulting Engineers," were drawn up on very definite lines, which were briefly as follows:—

All questions of general importance were to be referred for decision to the Government, and under these were to be included the general direction of each line, the position and the general arrangement of stations and works. After such sanction was given the Consulting Engineers had powers to deal with details.

All designs, estimates, and indents, whether for works or for establishments, were to be approved by the Consulting Engineers, who could reduce the amounts of indents, or require designs, or proposed operations to be modified; with the stipulation that the agent of a company could, if dissatisfied, refer matters for the decision of the Government.

The proper exercise of such powers, in the interest both of the State and of the Company, demanded a capacity for judicious compromise on both sides—conditions which unfortunately were seldom fulfilled. The railway officials objected to what they considered over-interference, demurred to giving detailed designs and estimates, discussions and delays occurred too frequently, and in the end a Committee of the House of Commons was appointed, in 1857-58, to inquire into "the causes of the delays that were alleged to have occurred in the construction of Indian railways." These delays were classified as follows :—

1. Those arising from Governmental supervision at home and in India.
2. Those incidental to the execution of extensive and complicated public works under such circumstances in a distant country.
3. Those produced by political causes, such as insurrection and mutiny.
4. Those arising from the natural difficulties which the face of the country presents.

The Committee arrived at the conclusion that, although some cases had been brought forward in which the control of the Government had been productive of vexation and annoyance to the railway officials, no very material delay could be charged to this circumstance. They held that the Government had acted wisely in giving over railway enterprise in India to companies, that a guaranteed interest was indispensable to induce capital to embark in such undertakings, and that in order to protect the State from undue expenditure control was not only requisite, but valuable, in the interests of the shareholders themselves. At the same time, the Committee thought that under a system complicated in its character, and necessarily somewhat cumbrous in its machinery—a system, moreover, the greatest defect of which lay in the facility it afforded for the evasion of responsibility—a clear and distinct definition of the duties, responsibilities, and extent of jurisdiction of all heads of departments, and those under them, was essentially requisite for its smooth and successful working; always assuming that due care was taken to entrust discretionary power only to men who were to be relied on or competent to distinguish an effective general control from too minute an interference in detail. They concluded by expressing their belief that what was needed was a judicious adherence to the spirit rather than the letter of the contract. The effect of this inquiry was distinctly beneficial in improving the relations between the railway officials and the Government officers. There was a marked improvement in expediting the disposal of business, a feeling of mutual respect and confidence arose on both sides, and, to quote the words of one who had full opportunity of observing the improvement in these relations, "the officials of the company learnt that the (consulting) engineers with whom they have to deal are competent as well as practical men, obliged to be so from the very nature of the duties they have always had to perform, and that no captious opposition or unfair criticism was to be anticipated from them."

Having noticed the first practical difficulties in working the system, reference must be made to what were ere long recognised as the advantages and disadvantages of the guarantee system on wider issues. It has been stated that in 1853 the Government of India, as represented then by Lord Dalhousie, was in favour of it; but he was nevertheless impressed with the necessity of seeing that the sums to be guaranteed should be based on sufficient data, as regards the cost of the works, "well and economically" carried out, and that some provision should be made to ensure the completion of a line within some period to be named, recommending, however, that the terms should be liberal, both as regards time and money. These views were not definitely adopted in subsequent contracts made by the Home Government, but later on, in a despatch, No. 2, of the 29th November 1858, Lord Canning, then Viceroy, again referred to the great need for restraint on the capital outlay. He said "that in any future contracts involving a guarantee an essential element should be, that previous to the commencement of work a thorough and critical estimate should be made of the whole line with its works, from actual survey and inquiry—exactly such an estimate, in fact, as would be required by a company in view of inviting tenders in England for a lump sum contract, but embracing the cost of engineering establishment; that this estimate should be subjected to the criticism of our officers, under the injunction that a liberal spirit is to be exercised in this criticism; and that after adding a handsome margin to this for contingencies, the gross sum, and no more, should be the amount on which the Government guarantee interest." The then President of the Viceroy's Council, Sir J. P. Grant, took a stronger view. He objected to the dual management, and especially to the financial basis of the system. He said that it really implied "the raising of money by a special public works loan, but under conditions the most disadvantageous possible for the public, who must be taxed for the payment"; that the money was not raised at the lowest market rate, and that instead of repayment being at the option of the borrower (the Government), this could not be done, whatever the loss might be in keeping it; while the lender could at any time reclaim it, or an equivalent annuity, whatever the financial position of the Government might be at the time." The Finance Member of Council, Mr. S. Laing, writing in April 1861, also recorded an opinion against the system, on the grounds that the management was non-resident and that the data as to first cost and probable traffic being so uncertain, the companies looked almost exclusively to the guarantee. He considered that these two factors went far towards neutralising all the advantages of private enterprise, and that although, as a general rule, and under ordinary circumstances in commercial matters, joint-stock management must be held to be greatly superior to that of a Government, yet that this advantage could not be claimed when the real company was 5000 miles away and the guarantee absolute. The shareholders had their 5 per cent whatever happened. This was probably all that they expected, and consequently no adequate motive existed for restraining the outlay on the works.

On the other hand, the system offered advantages which, although brought less to notice, were nevertheless clearly recognised by the Government. The one which stood out most prominently, and especially during the troubles of the Mutiny period, was that neither the political nor financial position of the Government had any effect in curtailing the supply of funds for the purposes of railway extension. On the faith of the guarantee, the companies found money without demur or difficulty, and for a definite purpose only; while had the capital been raised as a Government loan, for distribution to the companies, there was every likelihood that it would, on more than one occasion of financial stress, have been diverted to other more urgent public necessities. To quote the words of an officer,[1] writing in 1868, who was well qualified to offer an opinion: "This advantage will be acknowledged by all, but can only be fully appreciated by those who have seen with dismay canals almost useless for want of distributing channels, roads entirely so from the absence of bridges, and buildings half erected falling to ruin for want of a roof. The steady and unfluctuating supply of needful funds is a great and decided benefit, for which Indian railways have to thank the guarantee system. Had they been constructed on funds raised by a direct Government loan the Indian railway system would

[1] Colonel E. Davidson, R.E., *The Railways of India.* 1868.

not in all probability have been half completed by this time, instead of being nearly finished as it is."

Another, though less obvious, advantage of the system was to be found in the probability that the holders of shares in railways in India would be led to take a wider and more definite interest in Indian affairs, and in the general progress and welfare of the country. Moreover, the operations of the companies introduced a new and much-needed non-official element, from which a freshness and independence of opinion was derived on many matters. The railway engineers were always a welcome addition to the centres of Anglo-Indian life, and in the stormy days of the Mutiny their vigour, pluck, and readiness of resource made them prominent figures in the struggle, and formed a by no means insignificant addition to our strength. Yet, curiously enough, the presence of the non-official element was still regarded with some amount of jealousy and suspicion even then; and in drawing attention to the possible dangers that might arise from the overgrowth of English companies in India, the Government laid stress on the necessity for their having power to summarily dismiss railway officers whose action might be held "to endanger the peace and security of the country." The companies' officials had in fact for many years to feel themselves regarded as necessary evils, as being in the country to a certain extent on sufferance, and having to tread warily in their relations with the natives and with Government functionaries as such.

Regarded from our present standpoint, the terms of the guarantee appear to be unduly onerous on the Government; but it has to be borne in mind that India was then an almost unknown country to the English investor, that the Government was not in a position to carry out such works itself, and that there was a desire to attract English capital into the country. The guarantee for a term of ninety-nine years applied to all money paid into the Government Treasury and expended with the sanction and approval of the Government.

When the capital account thus sanctioned was closed, which was then considered both possible or desirable, so much of the subscribed money as was not required for the undertaking was to be returned to the companies. The contracts provided that the amount advanced by Government on account of the guarantee was to be eventually repaid from the future profit of the railways, and under the following arrangement. Net receipts were to be paid into the Government Treasury. If they amounted to less than the sum due for guaranteed interest, an addition had to be made from the revenues of the country to make up that sum. If they amounted to more, half the excess was to be added to the shareholders' dividend, and the other half applied to the repayment of monies previously paid by the Government for guaranteed interest; while if the receipts did not suffice to meet the cost of working and maintenance, the deficiency was charged against the guarantee. When the whole arrears due to Government under the guarantee had been repaid (with simple interest), the companies were entitled to the whole profits. Many years elapsed before any one railway earned a dividend equal to the guaranteed figure, and there is still one that has not yet accomplished it.[1] The result was that enormous arrears of interest due from the companies accumulated, and in the end were remitted on the drawing up of fresh contracts, under which the Government assumed a larger share of future surplus profits.

By the end of the year 1859 eight companies had been formed for the construction under guarantee of nearly 5000 miles of line, with a capital of 52½ millions, and the works were being vigorously prosecuted. The largest concern at that time was the East Indian Railway Company, with a capital of nineteen millions. It had already been noticed that the employment of so many different agencies implied the existence of a more expensive and complicated machinery than if the

[1] The Madras Railway.

Government had retained these works in its own hands; and moreover that so many companies involved unnecessary expense in the administration in England, while they were liable to create a competition amongst them for materials and freight, which would unduly raise prices. But the policy at the time was to encourage so-called "private enterprise," and at the same time to assign such limits to the sphere of each concern as would tend to prevent the creation of inconvenient monopolies. The fear that the competition between the companies for materials and freight would enhance the cost of these transactions was perfectly justifiable. The material to be sent out from England for each mile of railway may be taken at an average of 250 tons, representing for 5000 miles a total of 1¼ million tons, which in the four years 1855-58 gave freight to 2518 vessels; and as the export trade of India was then in its infancy, compared with its present figures, and as ships were only sent out for return cargoes, it may be supposed that this unusual demand for carriage to India must have led to abnormal rates. No difficulties had been experienced up till the end of 1860, in the raising of capital by the guaranteed companies, and considerable balances had been accumulated to their credit, but the troubles of the Mutiny period had forced on the Government the necessity of making heavy loans in the English market, and this had the effect of seriously interfering with the financial operations of the companies. This difficulty became at one time so acute, that it was in contemplation to raise funds through the direct agency of Government, and to guarantee no further projects until the lines then sanctioned had been completed. Fortunately, the additional difficulty of exchange did not then exist; the sterling value of the rupee stood at 2s., while the rate under the contracts was 1s. 10d. In the following year, however, the condition of the money market improved considerably, the sound financial position of India was accepted with more confidence by the public, the value of railway securities rose steadily, and Government was relieved from the need for raising money on behalf of the companies. The crisis which was then happily tided over has, however, a significant bearing on the relations between guaranteed companies and the Government of India, or indeed of any Government, under similar political conditions. The suspension of extensive railway operations, at a certain stage of progress, would materially injure the Government, the companies, and above all the public. A large outlay might remain unprofitable, and much positive loss might be incurred, in leaving the works unfinished.

Except under the subject of rates and fares, to which reference will be made in another chapter, no material addition to the railway policy in India can be traced up to the end of 1863. An important question then arose as to the proper distribution of outlay by the companies, between capital and revenue. A clause in the contracts provided that a charge to capital might be made for such "additions, alterations, and improvements" as, having been made with the approval of the Government, "are properly chargeable to capital." This left matters in a very indefinite form, and as soon as the lines began to feel the incidence of maintenance charges, it became necessary to define what "properly chargeable" meant. After a full discussion of the question, and after ascertaining the practice which commonly prevailed on English railways, the matter was decided by a despatch to the Government of India, dated the 9th March 1864, from Sir Charles Wood, then Secretary of State for India, the rulings in which have continued in force on Indian railways up till now. Some extracts from this despatch are worth quoting.

7. I think it advisable, however, to take this opportunity of laying down some general rules, which may be of assistance in enabling you to decide questions of charging expenditure to Capital or Revenue.

8. There can be no doubt that the expense of an additional line of railway, of the doubling of an existing line, of the

original construction of any work, including that of those intended to be only temporary, as well as of all additions to existing work, ought to be charged to Capital Account.

9. When new lines form a junction with an existing railway, the expense of the junction and all its concomitant appliances of stations, sidings, signals, etc., is properly chargeable to Capital Account, and the cost should be divided in such proportion as may be fair, between the two companies for whose mutual and joint benefit the junction is made.

10. The cost of additional stations and of any important building not previously contemplated, which is added to an existing station, should be charged to Capital Account.

11. The cost of maintaining, in a proper condition, the works when completed, must be charged to Revenue Account; but when any extraordinary casualty may occur, such as the destruction of a bridge by flood, the case must be regarded as exceptional, and the cost of construction or replacement must be charged to Capital or Revenue, or divided between them, as may be deemed proper, according to the circumstances of the case.

12. In relaying rails, if the original rails have proved too light, and additional strength in weight of iron or steel be required, the Capital Account should bear the difference between the cost of the new and improved rails and that of replacing the old rails by rails of a similar character, Revenue being chargeable for relaying and all other expenses. The same principle should be applied to replacing by iron sleepers those of wood originally laid down.

13. In the locomotive stock, the Capital ought to bear the first expense of any addition which may be made to the existing stock, and of any important improvement or alteration which may be made in the same, as well as of all machinery which is absolutely new, and not merely in replacement of old; but all repairs and less important alterations of the existing stock of engines, carriages, and waggons already paid for, and handed over for working

purposes, should be charged to Revenue. The rolling stock and plant after being once paid for from the Capital must be kept up by Revenue to its full complement.

14. In no case should the cost of mere appurtenances of stock, after the opening of a line, or of a change such as the substitution of one mode of lighting for another, whether in engines, carriages, stations, or signal-lamps, the cost of which has already been paid for out of Capital, be admitted as Capital expenditure. These properly belong to the Traffic Revenue Account.

The despatch then went on to deal with the old difficulty as to the closing of the capital account of a line, and pointed out that finally to close such an account, either at first opening or at any given period, was practically impossible, inasmuch as to do so would imply that the utmost requirements for its future working had been duly provided for. This could never be the case, "as it is invariably found that the traffic upon a railway steadily and progressively increases long after its opening, and therefore to finally close the capital account of Indian railways, and prevent the application to them of any additional capital, must be fraught with injury to all parties, whether guarantors or guaranteed." The despatch concluded by saying that these rules were not intended to interfere with the arrangements which had been made with each company, by which the cost of maintenance for a certain period after opening was allowed to be charged to capital.

Two attempts had been made on a small scale previous to the years 1863-64, to raise capital for railway extension in India without a guarantee, viz. by the Indian Branch Railway Company in Northern India, and by the Indian Tramway Company in Southern India. Their endeavours had met with but small success, and a lengthy correspondence resulted, between the Government of India and the Secretary of State, as to the possibility or otherwise, of constructing railways with assistance from the State, in some other form than that of a guarantee, which it had been virtually decided should not be extended farther than was necessary to complete the main trunk lines. After much discussion and deliberation it was decided to encourage the construction of lines on the standard ($5\frac{1}{2}$ feet) gauge, by the grant of land free of cost, and a maximum subsidy of £100 a year, per mile open, for twenty years from the date of opening. This system was to involve no other interference on the part of the Government than was necessary in the interest and for the safety of the public, while it made it incumbent on the projectors in their own interests to complete their works economically and rapidly; a limit of time being fixed, failure within which to open a line carried with it a reduction of the period for which the subsidy was payable. At first this proposal seemed likely to be received favourably by the public, but it was doomed to early failure, as it was found that these terms were not liberal enough for the then feeling in the money market at home with regard to Indian investments. Modifications which were proposed of this system of subsidy had no better success. There was in fact still ample opening for investors in India and elsewhere, on a guarantee of interest, and it seemed to be understood that any investment out of England, at that time, must be assured, without fail, of a return of 5 per cent. Thus after negotiations between the Secretary of State and two companies, extending over the years 1864-67, the Secretary of State addressed the Government of India in March 1867,[1] informing them that it had been found necessary after all to revert to a guarantee of 5 per cent, and a contract on this basis was drawn up with the Indian Branch Railway Company for the construction of railways in Oudh and Rahilkund.

The principal differences between this contract and the former contracts with a guaranteed company were briefly as follows:—

1. Estimates were to be formed for the cost of the works, and

[1] Despatch No. 18, Railway, of 23d March 1867.

if the Secretary of State should, after perusing them, not desire to co-operate further with the Company in the proposals made, the contract could be terminated on repayment of cost of the surveys, and the money which had been paid in by the Company to be refunded.

2. The rate of exchange was altered from 1s. 10d. to 2s.
3. The grant of land was in perpetuity, instead of being only for ninety-nine years.
4. The Company to fix rates and fares within maxima, which should be settled by the Secretary of State, such rates being reduced if the net earnings exceeded 10 per cent on capital, so as that profits should not exceed this figure.
5. The State could purchase the line at any decennial period, after twenty years, instead of only after twenty-five and fifty years.
6. The guarantee was absolute on all, instead of only on approved expenditure.
7. The Company was to be subject to any future enactments for the regulation of railways.

In replying to the Secretary of State in December 1867,[1] the Government of India, then under Lord Lawrence as Viceroy, accepted the necessity for reverting to the guarantee system, but took exception to the views of the Secretary of State and to the terms of the contract, and held in substance that no company should be allowed the opportunity of a very large development, because this might be inconvenient, and even dangerous, to the Government on account of the responsibility for interest, and at the same time the company might be proportionately inefficient. That a fixed sum should be stated as a limit to expenditure on guaranteed interest, extension of capital being only allowed as net receipts reduce the actual charge. That the Government when considering new projects should fix an average mileage rate of cost, and determine that it will not guarantee interest on any sum exceeding this. That the companies and the servants should be required

[1] Despatch No. 125, of 3rd December 1867.

to look on themselves as the agents of the Government for the purpose of constructing railways according to its wishes, and that they must understand that no interest will be given on outlay made "under the virtual dictation of companies and their engineers." That Government be empowered to dismiss or suspend all railway officials at its discretion. That land should be granted for ninety-nine years, and the right of entry, after that period, secured to Government. That it was politically dangerous, and might be very embarrassing to Government, to allow very large capitals to be invested in guaranteed railways in India, and that the Government should either by special contract or actual purchase ultimately obtain possession of all such works. That the method proposed in the contract for the repayment of the interest guaranteed was open to objection, in so far that instead of dividing surplus earnings over 5 per cent between the Government and a company until the debt was extinguished, either the whole surplus should be taken by the State until the debt was paid, or that the half surplus be taken by the State absolutely and permanently; but preferably that the State should take the whole surplus till the debt was paid, and the half surplus thereafter permanently.

Replying to this in 1868,[1] the Secretary of State (Sir Stafford Northcote) stated his inability to concur in these views. He said that it was essential, in working the guarantee system, that the confidence of the investing public, or, in other words, of the "money market," should be secured; that "due regard should be paid to the constitution of joint-stock companies, as regulated by Parliament"; and that if a certain class of railways in India is to be constructed by the agency of guaranteed companies, such terms must of necessity be given as will attract them, and not such as would repel them from entering into contract. He felt certain that no company would consent to look on itself and its servants as the mere agents of the Government, liable to removal or suspension at its pleasure,

[1] Despatch No. 90, of 24th November 1868.

and that no reputable engineers would take service with a company under such conditions. As to the view of the Government of India, that large companies might be politically dangerous or embarrassing to Government because of the responsibility for interest, he pointed out that if the Government became the owners of the railways it would be by means of borrowed capital, and that the responsibility would only be in another form. Generally, this despatch held that the terms of the contract with the Oudh and Rahilkund Company (formerly Indian Branch Railway Company) had no important defect, and that if more stringent conditions had been enforced higher terms would have been needed; while in the opinion of the Secretary of State, the political and military advantages of the Indian railways would have been so far cheaply purchased even had they been more costly, and that he was not disposed to hinder their extension by the exaction of too onerous terms.

This divergence of opinion between the Home and Indian Government, on issues which the latter then thought of great importance, led, there can be little doubt, to a rapid development of the views of the latter as regards the construction and administration of railways by the direct agency of the State. A tendency had already been shown in this direction in previous communications, and had been so far favoured by the Secretary of State as to lead him to agree to this policy being adopted for political lines only. Before leaving India, in 1869, Lord Lawrence wrote a minute, dated 9th January of that year, in which he boldly and most ably advocated the relinquishment of the guarantee system, and the construction by Government itself of all future railway extensions. His views were endorsed by his successor, Lord Mayo, and accepted by the Duke of Argyll, then Secretary of State. A more detailed account of this phase of railway policy will be found in another chapter, and it is sufficient to say that for the next twelve years the guarantee system lay in abeyance, so far at least as the initiation of any new company. The introduction of the metre gauge dates from this period, and is dealt with in the chapter on this subject.

Between the years 1874-79 a series of disastrous famines had visited India, and on these followed the Afghan War. The great difficulties experienced in sending food with sufficient rapidity for the relief of scarcity, and of moving troops towards the frontier from our military centres, led the Government of India to the conclusion that more rapid progress was needed in railway extension, and that it might be possible to supplement the efforts of the State by enlisting the aid of private enterprise again, but without the assistance of a guarantee. In January 1881 the Marquis of Hartington (now Duke of Devonshire), then Secretary of State for India, addressed a despatch to the Government of India, in which this policy was approved, on the basis of capital being subscribed "on the exclusive security of the success of the undertaking"; but that if this should prove to be impracticable, it might become desirable to consider whether some modified form of guarantee could be adopted, such as, with respect to time and to the rate of the guarantee, would give the shareholders "a real interest in the efficient and economical administration of the railway." This was in effect the proposal of Major E. Baring (now Lord Cromer), who was then Financial Member of the Viceroy's Council. It happened that the time was favourable to this new departure. The credit of India was good, money was plentiful in Europe, and capitalists were ready to take up investments in almost any direction. The result of this was that a scheme of apparently a very promising nature, in Bengal, was taken up on the above basis by an eminent firm of financiers, and the Bengal Central Railway Company was formed in London in 1881. Before describing the terms of the agreement with the Secretary of State, it will be advisable to go back a little and notice a very important step which had just previously been taken in regard to the largest of the guaranteed companies.

The Government of India had the right in 1879, under the contract with the East Indian Railway Company, to acquire that line, and it was decided to carry out this operation. The negotiations terminated in an arrangement by which the Government availed itself of the right to purchase the whole undertaking by the grant of annuities, and made over the working of the line to a new company on a new contract. This contract is dated the 22nd December 1879, and the terms of the purchase were based mainly on the provisions of the original contract. The capital stock amounted to £26,200,000, and the company was entitled to be paid either in cash, at the average price of the stock during the three previous years, or by an annuity for seventy-three years equivalent to it. The average price of the stock was taken at £125, so that the total amount, if payable in cash, amounted to £32,750,000. The Government, however, preferred to make the payment in the shape of an annuity, and one of £5 : 12 : 6 was allowed in lieu of the £125. At the same time the company was allowed to defer a portion, leaving £6,550,000 in the hands of Government to be regarded as the capital of the new company, on which they receive 4 per cent interest in the first place; and secondly, one-fifth of the net profits after providing for working expenses and other charges. Under this arrangement the Government secured an agency for working the line which had been eminently successful in the past, and in giving up one-fifth of the net profits to the new company it was considered that the line was "likely to yield more satisfactory results than the best conceivable official management without that stimulus." The arrangement, moreover, had the prominent advantage of redeeming the whole cost of the line in a period of seventy-three years. Under the new contract the Government has full powers of control, the company being bound to work and maintain the whole system to the satisfaction of the Government, to give running powers for the stock of other lines, and to construct auxiliary or branch lines upon terms to be agreed upon. The term of this contract is for fifty years, but the Secretary of State or the company may terminate it at the end of the twentieth, or at the end of any succeeding fifth year, on giving two years' clear notice.

It may be well to notice briefly the price that the State has had to pay (in the shape of one-fifth of the net profits of this concern) by availing itself of the agency of the new company in its administration. The following table shows the sum paid yearly to the deferred annuitants, and the rate per cent received by them, including the 4 per cent stipulated under the contract:—

Year.	Amount in Rx.[1] paid as Fifth Share of Net Profits.	Rate per cent in Sterling received by Deferred Annuitants.
	Rx.	£ s. d.
1880	177,269	6 4 6
1881	206,386	6 12 4
1882	178,807	6 4 6
1883	210,772	6 12 6
1884	129,298	5 11 5
1885	178,229	6 0 0
1886	159,593	5 16 0
1887	173,477	5 17 0
1888	127,834	5 6 6
1889	91,534	5 0 6
1890	114,258	5 6 0
1891	275,021	6 17 3
Average . .	168,540	5 19 2½

The Government of India has thus paid on the average the sum of Rx.168,540 yearly on the assumption that a Board of Directors in London is better able to work the line, and to make it more fully successful than if worked by its own railway administration in India, from which, as it happens, the present principal officers of the company have been obtained. This question need not here be discussed. It will be referred to in a subsequent chapter.

[1] Rx. represents conventional sterling at ten rupees to the pound.

Reverting to the scheme of the Bengal Central Railway, it may be mentioned that it was based on surveys and reports prepared by Government officers, from which the prospects of the line were shown, as it ultimately proved, too confidently, to be exceptionally good. The prospectus of the promoters adopted the facts and figures of the Government reports, which were made public without reservation, and on the faith of these a Company was formed as stated, in 1881, to carry out the scheme, the money being subscribed twice over. The terms of the agreement with the Secretary of State were briefly as follows :—The direction and location of the line to be subject to the approval of Government, and the general character of the works to conform with the established standards of Indian broad gauge lines. Land to be given free of rent for ninety-nine years. The Secretary of State to pay 4 per cent on the capital deposited with him until withdrawn for the purposes of the Company; and until the opening of the "primary" undertaking throughout, or until June 1886, the Secretary of State to advance to the Company such sums as, together with the net earnings of the line, should give the company 4 per cent on the capital withdrawn for expenditure. All sums so advanced to be repaid with simple interest at 4 per cent by appropriation of half the net earnings above 5 per cent on the capital. The Secretary of State to have power to purchase the line and its equipment at the end of thirty years, or fifty years, from the 1st January 1882, on giving one year's notice, and paying £125 for each £100 of stock. At the end of ninety-nine years the works and buildings of the line to become the property of the Secretary of State, who should pay the value of the rolling stock and movable property. Rates and fares to be within a maximum to be fixed by Government, and in case of failure to run at least one train a day, the Government to have power to take possession on repayment of the capital expended. Until all advances had been repaid by the Company their accounts to be audited by an officer appointed by Government.

The Government of India was informed of this agreement by a despatch from the Secretary of State dated 11th August 1881, in which it was stated that the aim in the negotiations for the contract had been "to avoid all unnecessary interference with or control over the affairs of the Company, and to secure for the Government only such powers of supervision as will protect the interests of the State in respect of the power of purchase, and the repayment of the advances for interest made while the line is being constructed." It was expected that this railway would be the forerunner of many to be launched on similar terms, and indeed had the anticipated traffic on the line been even approximately realised, this expectation might have been fulfilled. Unfortunately, however, for both the Government and the Company, the line turned out to have been misjudged as a lucrative one, and its ill success from the first and subsequent troubles were a source of serious embarrassment to both parties, and eventually destroyed the confidence of investors in lines which were not supported by more tangible forms of assistance. The later phase of the Company was that the Government had to submit to a new contract (in 1887), granting a sterling guarantee of 3½ per cent on the capital expended, or likely to be expended, while the sum due for arrears of interest was cancelled. Shortly after the launching of this Company another, the Rahilkund and Kumaon Railway, was started on a similar basis, and in 1882 a larger concern, the Bengal and North-Western Railway, was floated without guarantee, the Government giving the land and allowing 4 per cent to be paid from capital for a period not exceeding five years. The shares of both of these concerns were taken up readily at first, though ere long fell in price; but the energy and ability of the Company's agent in India and the absorption by the latter of the Tirhoot State Railway has completely changed their position, and at date the shares are at a considerable premium.[1]

[1] It should be mentioned that in the contract of the former of these lines

In accordance with the views already mentioned, a despatch was sent from the Government of India, in July 1881,[1] to the Secretary of State, in which the urgent need of enlisting private enterprise in Indian railways was insisted on, the then financial position of the country showing that there seemed no hope of it being possible to carry out all the needed extensions to protect the country from famine by direct Government agency, and for such projects as were approved, it was proposed to give "a safe and reasonable guarantee," *i.e.* limited in amount and duration. It was considered that each concession should be dealt with on its own merits, so that there should be the least possible burden on the finances, and at the same time to give companies the greatest possible interest in the working of their lines; while a preference was indicated in favour of a low rate of interest for a longer time than for a high rate for a shorter term. The first important result of this change of policy was the creation in 1882—the contract being dated the 1st of June of that year—of the Southern Mahratta Railway Company, which was to take over works already commenced in the Deccan for famine protection, and to carry out a large system of metre gauge lines designed for this object. The contract of this Company with the Secretary of State was on an essentially new basis, and except in one important particular, to be mentioned hereafter, may be regarded as the prototype of subsequent agreements of the same nature. It embodies, in fact, two distinct functions for the Company. On the one hand the Company is an agency for raising a certain sum of money, viz. three millions sterling, for the Secretary of State, on which he guarantees interest, during a fixed period for construction of 4 per cent, and thereafter of 3½ per cent. This sum was to be made over to the Secretary of State, and

a small subsidy of Rs.40,000 yearly is given by the State, and in both contracts the Government shares equally with the Companies in net profits when the line has paid 6 per cent to the shareholders.

[1] Despatch No. 92, Railway, of 22nd July 1881.

in the words of the contract, "all moneys paid by the Company under this section shall belong absolutely to the Secretary of State, who shall not be deemed a debtor to the Company in respect thereof." The above-mentioned sum was in effect a loan raised by the Company for the Secretary of State on a guarantee of interest. Subsequent clauses of the contract stipulate that the Company shall construct certain railways, and that for these purposes the Secretary of State shall provide the requisite funds (Clause 29), and that all receipts whatsoever of the Company, exclusive of the interest payable on the capital raised by it, should be paid into a Government Treasury. Having constructed the lines, the Company (although it is not specifically so stated in the contract) was to work them, and from the net earnings (Clause 42) three-fourths were to be taken by the Government and one-fourth by the Company. On this point it is to be particularly noticed that the above clause contains no condition for a first charge against gross earnings to provide for interest on capital paid by the Secretary of State; and that the Government has to reimburse itself on this account from the three-fourths' share of the net earnings of the line. This perhaps too liberal condition has not been repeated in subsequent agreements with other lines, it being stipulated that net earnings shall mean that gross earnings have been first charged with sums due for interest paid by the Secretary of State on the capital raised by the Company. The justification for the concession made to the Southern Mahratta is to be found in the fact that the lines to be made by it were essentially for famine protection, that they could not be expected to be remunerative for many years (they have not yet paid 3 per cent), and that the money loss to the State was to be accepted as the necessary price for securing the protection of certain large districts from famine. This system of railways is in fact State property, the Company being merely an agency for working it under stringent conditions as to maintenance, supervision, and power over rates and fares.

In 1883 another new departure was made in assisting private enterprise by granting to a small concern, the Tarkessur Railway Company, a very favourable working arrangement for a branch to be made without guarantee on the capital. This branch, twenty-two miles in length, was to take off from the East Indian Railway (a State line), and the nature of the agreement accorded to the Company is practically that the line is worked and maintained by and at the percentage of working expenses of the home line, and of the net receipts one-fifth is taken by the working company and four-fifths paid to the Tarkessur Company, less a charge of 5 per cent on the gross receipts for use of rolling stock. This small Company has been eminently successful, but its success has been due to exceptional circumstances, viz. firstly, to the very favourable terms for working; secondly, to the unusually heavy passenger traffic on it, and thirdly, to it having been a very cheap line to construct. Its promptly profitable career has, however, given a great impulse to this form of State assistance, and several other schemes have been proposed, and one important one, the Delhi-Umballa-Kalha Railway, carried out on similar terms, while later on, as will be noticed subsequently, this has become the recognised basis for assistance in the construction of branch lines by independent companies.

Two projects of great importance had been put down in the list of "protective" famine lines to be carried out, if possible, by private enterprise. One was the Bengal-Nagpore line, running from Nagpore through a highly productive part of the Central Provinces, to a point (Assensale) on the East Indian Railway, and the other a system of lines through Central India with junctions at Agra and Cawnpore, and terminating on the Great Indian Peninsula Railway at Itarsi. Negotiations for placing these schemes in the hands of companies extended over a considerable time, and eventually, viz. in October 1885, a contract was executed with the Indian Midland Railway Company for the latter of these projects. The terms of the contract were generally similar to those of the Southern Mahratta Railway above referred to, the Company being the agents for raising a loan for the Secretary of State, and at the same time allowed to construct and work the lines mentioned in the contract. The rate of interest on the capital raised was, however, increased to 4 per cent for the whole period of the contract; but the first charge on the earnings, after paying working expenses, is devoted towards payment of interest on the capital, and the net earnings over and above this are, in the first place, to be applied to the repayment of interest not repaid, and of the residue, if any, of the surplus, three-fourths were to be paid to the Secretary of State and one-fourth to the Company, "free from all control." All money so payable to the Company was to be paid in India, and the receipts of a year, and not those of the half year, were to be the basis of calculation. It was, moreover, distinctly stipulated (Clause 56) that the line as and when completed was the property of the State, together with all the movable property of the concern. Stringent clauses have been inserted as to supervision, the maintenance of the line, powers over rates and fares, the audit of accounts, the definition of "working expenses," the working of other lines, the grant of running powers to other lines and other facilities, and other minor conditions of control. The Secretary has power to terminate the contract at the end of the year 1910, or of any succeeding tenth year, on twelve months' previous notice, or by default on six months' notice. On termination of the contract, the Secretary of State is merely bound to repay such capital as shall have been provided by the Company, and in such case the Company is bound to relinquish possession of the whole line, land, and movable property of the concern. The subsequent contract (in March 1887) with the Bengal-Nagpore Railway Company was couched in precisely similar terms.

Both the above-mentioned Companies, and the Southern Mahratta, have, perhaps for want of a better means of defining their character, been termed "assisted" companies, as opposed to the "guaranteed" companies; but as will be seen, the term "assisted" does not properly explain their relation to the Government. Their contracts might, in fact, have been in two documents instead of in one—the first representing the terms on which the Companies raised a certain sum of money for the Secretary of State for India at a certain rate of interest, and the other being an agreement for constructing certain lines, and subsequently working them on lease for a definite period, and on certain conditions of copartnership with the State. The railways constructed by these Companies have been carried out by them merely as agents and disbursers for the Government. The lines belong to the Government. As regards the capital raised, these Companies are as much "guaranteed" as the older ones; but, on the other hand, the terms under which they work the lines are greatly more advantageous to the State than those of the older contracts under the guarantee. It may be added, that in each case the Government could have raised the necessary funds itself at a considerably lower rate of interest, but was debarred from this course by the restriction of its borrowing powers by the House of Commons Committee, referred to elsewhere. There were, moreover, other causes which made it appear desirable to entrust these lines to what has been called "private enterprise." The expression "enterprise" is scarcely applicable in such a case, if it is intended to convey an implication of risk. There could be but little risk in lending money to the Government of India at 4 per cent, together with a definite prospect of an addition to this in the future from surplus profits; while the high price the shares have steadily held in the London market effectually disposes of any such view of the investment.

The financial stress due to exchange, to the heavy outlay imposed on the country for frontier defences, and other causes, became so serious in 1885 that the lines above mentioned would certainly have been deferred much longer had it not been that they were regarded as being of the greatest importance as famine protective works. The negotiations with the promoters of the Bengal-Nagpore Railway extended over something like four years, owing partly to the impossibility of meeting the terms required by the Company in the face of the existing obligations of the Government.[1] The urgent necessity for the line led, however, in the end to the acceptance of the new burden; but it was then practically acknowledged that India could no longer afford to face the cost of further sterling guarantees, and that unless some other means could be found of attracting English capital, railway extension in India must for the future depend on what could be effected from the annual State loan for Public Works. The solution of this difficulty was offered in 1889, by a proposal to make a line 162 miles in length in connection with the East Indian Railway, between Delhi and Kalka, on terms based on those above referred to of the Tarkessur Railway, but embodying conditions giving greater control to the State and a share in surplus receipts. The contract with the Secretary of State stipulates that the Company shall make the line on being given land free, and that the Government of India will undertake to work it and maintain it at 50 per cent of the gross receipts. A second agreement made between the Secretary of State and the East Indian Railway Company (which is working a line now belonging to the State) provides that this Company shall work and maintain the Delhi-Kalka Railway for 48 per cent of the gross receipts, which shall include the provision of rolling stock. The State thus receives 2 per cent of the gross receipts as a direct contribution, in addition to its share in the surplus profits from the East Indian Railway. The 2 per cent may be held to represent the cost of Government supervision and control.

It is as yet too soon to estimate the future of this form of

[1] Also greatly to discussions with the Secretary of State as to details of construction.

assistance to private enterprise in Indian railways, but so far as can be judged from the present position in the market of the Delhi-Kalka shares there does not appear to be much likelihood that it will offer sufficient attraction in its present shape for the investment of English capital. The primary conditions of the success of a project, started on similar terms, must be in the careful and judicious selection of the line on the advice of persons intimately acquainted with the tendencies of trade in India, and with the details of railway working, so as to be able to afford a close and reliable estimate of receipts and of the cost of working the traffic. Another almost equally important condition is, that there shall be no ambiguity or obscurity in the provisions of the agreements, especially when, as in the case of the Delhi-Kalka line, or indeed in any other started on similar terms, those agreements are threefold, or between three parties, whose interests are not in complete harmony. Their interests are, in fact, in line, so to speak, in one direction only, viz. in making the new railway the most effective and remunerative dividend-paying machine. But with this aim in view both the State and the working company show a not altogether unreasonable inclination to force the new company to provide funds for the improvement of the line—a course for which the shareholders have not shown much appreciation, and hence difficulties have arisen which unfortunately have tended to throw some discredit on the arrangement.

For some years previously a large and important scheme had been under investigation for a system of metre gauge railways, on the east of the Bramaputra river, with the object of connecting Assam with the old but now rising port of Chittagong on the Bay of Bengal. As soon as the project was complete, if not before then, the Government of India was approached by promoters under the intention of forming a company for the carrying out and working of these lines. By this time the Government had found its financial position so seriously affected by the loss in exchange, and the outlook in the future so unpromising, that it had been forced to the decision to refuse to entertain any proposals which involved a sterling guarantee. In consequence of this, endeavours were made to obtain capital for the scheme in London on the basis of the concession of waste lands along the line, and the grant of mining rights in an area adjoining the projected railway, which was supposed to be rich in minerals, more especially coal. These attempts, however, were not successful, it being impossible to satisfy investors or financiers on the conditions imposed on this form of assistance, and it was found necessary to again consider the grant of a guarantee. In the meanwhile, the Secretary of State had received offers in other directions, and eventually, though in opposition to the views of the Government of India, a company was formed in London in 1892 under an agreement of a somewhat novel character. Premising that the cost of the whole scheme might be about 5½ millions sterling, the company was to raise the sum of 1½ millions in shares of £10. On this the Secretary of State guarantees interest at 3½ per cent during construction, or until June 1898, and thereafter at 3 per cent until the determination of the contract. The balance of the funds necessary for constructing the line is to be found by the Secretary of State, and net surplus profits are to be divided between the Government and the company in proportion to the capital supplied by each. Under the contract the line belongs to the State. The capital account is to be debited with all sums advanced as interest by the Secretary of State, and, after deductions for contributions to a provident fund, the interest charges are to be a first charge on the net earnings of the line.

New conditions, which have been for some time under consideration, have recently been issued[1] by the Government, for encouraging investment in the construction of branch and feeder lines, on the basis of their being worked by the railway

[1] Resolution No. 924, Railway Company, of 15th September 1893.

with which they are connected. The main features of these conditions are as follows:—(1) The free use of such land as may be required for the undertaking; (2) the provision of rolling stock, and the maintenance and working of the new lines by the main line administrations; (3) the free use of surveys made at State expense; (4) the carriage of stores and materials on favourable terms; and (5) the grant of a limited rebate from the main line earnings towards ensuring to the shareholders in the new lines a dividend of 4 per cent per annum on approved capital expenditure. In addition to this, it is proposed, if legal powers can be obtained, as to which there is not likely to be any difficulty, to allow interest to be paid from capital during construction at the same rate, viz. 4 per cent. In offering these conditions, the Government of India has distinctly laid down that no concession will be given for any project unless it is shown to have reasonable prospect of financial success, and in any case all plans and estimates must be approved by the Government. These terms practically ensure a minimum return of 4 per cent on capital invested in such lines, while there is no restriction as to the maximum return, or any stipulation as to division of surplus profits over and above a certain figure with the State. It is consequently anticipated, and with good reason, that such concessions will offer considerable attraction for English capital, and in a form which involves no risk whatever. It should be added that the Government reserves the right of purchase of such lines at the expiration of twenty-one years, and thereafter at successive intervals of ten years, at twenty-five years' purchase, based on the average net earnings for the five years immediately preceding the purchase, provided that the price shall not exceed the total capital expenditure by more than 20 per cent, and shall not be less than the capital expenditure. Purchase may be also made at the expiration of fifty years on payment of the actual capital outlay.

CHAPTER III

STATE CONSTRUCTION AND ADMINISTRATION

It was shown in the first chapter that the construction and workings of railways in India was at first entrusted to guaranteed companies, and that it was not until the year 1867, under the Viceroyalty of Lord Lawrence, that the objections to their policy were distinctly formulated and seriously discussed. Endeavours had been previously made to induce the investment of English capital in Indian railway schemes on less onerous conditions than that of a guarantee, in the form either of a lump sum or annual mileage subsidies, accompanied by the free grant of land. It was soon found, however, that only a feeble response was to be expected to such conditions, and in such cases as took shape, notably in that of the Indian Branch Railway, it eventually became necessary to revert to the guarantee as the only means of securing the completion of the works. The cost of the guaranteed railways up to this time had, for sundry reasons, largely exceeded the original estimates, while the anticipations of traffic had as yet not been realised, and with the result that there was a steadily increasing charge on the revenues on account of interest. It thus became urgently necessary for the Government to review its position, and, if the requirements of the country in the extension of the railway system were to be fulfilled, to determine the nature of the agency by which this should be effected, and the financial measures which would be involved. In December 1867 a despatch on the subject was submitted to the Secretary of State for India,[1] accompanied by minutes by the Viceroy and the members of Council, to which was added an able and exhaustive note on the guarantee system by Captain (now General) Sir E. C. S. Williams, R.E., and also a note by Colonel (now General) C. H. Dickens, R.A., then Secretary to the Government of India in the Public Works Department. General Williams' note would deserve lengthy notice. It discussed the advantages and disadvantages of the guaranteed system in India, sketched the systems under which railways had been promoted by the State in other countries, submitted proposals for a new system for encouraging railways by State aid in India, and referred, though in brief and cautious terms, to the desirability of an experiment being made in the construction of railways by direct State agency—a proposal which, although at the time wholly opposed to authoritative opinion in India, was destined to see early fruition. Neither in Lord Lawrence's minute, nor in those of any of his Council, is there any mention of this policy; all that was insisted on, and with practical unanimity, was that action should be taken towards the ultimate acquisition by the State of all the railways, and that this aim should be steadily kept in view.

In replying to this, in two despatches of the 16th and 24th January 1868, the Secretary of State for India (then Sir Stafford Northcote) dealt with the question of State construction in the following terms: "You have recently come to the conclusion that the guarantee system should, so far as regards irrigation works, be superseded by a system of direct Government agency. The reasons for this decision, however, are not applicable in the case of railways, as the question of possible interference with the land revenue does not here arise. At the same time, there are other considerations which ought not to be lost sight of. The main objections to guarantees, in connection with railways, are that they tend to weaken the ordinary

[1] Despatch No. 125, Railway, of 3rd December 1867.

motives to efficient management and superintendence, and recent disclosures as to the state of the works on the Great Indian Peninsula line afford new proofs that there is much room for apprehension on this score. I am therefore anxious to know whether any, or what additional precautions, can in your opinion advisably be taken to secure good workmanship under the guarantee system, which, in spite of its obvious defects in certain particulars, I am disposed to regard as upon the whole the one best adapted for the extension of one class of railways, viz. the commercial. For the political class, I am inclined to think that direct Government agency might be preferable." This declaration did not seem likely to advance matters or to lead to any immediate or material change of policy; but later on, in the same year,[1] the Government of India in referring to negotiations then in progress with certain companies, in which some important points in connection with State control were involved, expressed a hope that the question of direct action by the State would be regarded in a broad light, and not merely from that relating to its bearing on the money market. They said that "such a point of view is no doubt important, but at present its importance is in some sense of a minor order. There is no doubt that the Government could raise money for railway undertakings and make all other necessary arrangements without the intervention of companies at all." They also pointed out that in the arrangements with capitalists, and in the details of contracts, the Government of India were not given sufficient opportunities of offering opinions, while the practical working of them had to be carried out in India.

A change in the Ministry placed the Duke of Argyll in power as Secretary of State early in 1869, and in March of that year the Government of India addressed a despatch to the Home Government,[2] in which they openly and strongly advocated direct construction by the State. Lord Mayo had

[1] Despatch No. 122, Railway, of 15th August 1868, to the Secretary of State.

[2] Despatch No. 24, Railway, of 15th March 1869.

then became Viceroy; but before leaving India, Lord Lawrence had recorded a minute, dated 9th January 1869, in which he showed his complete conversion to this policy. In this he urged, that under the guarantee system of construction, the Government was liable to a permanent and probably increasing charge for interest, the burden of which was accentuated by the fact that under the existing arrangements the Government could derive no profit from the most successful railway, while it bore the whole loss of those which did not pay; that there was, in fact, no set-off of profit against loss in the Government share in these transactions. "The whole profit goes to the companies, and the whole loss to the Government." He said that he was "thus led to ask what are the reasons which should induce the Government to accept the position in which it is placed by the present system of railway construction? . . . Can it be really essential for satisfactory progress that such a distribution of losses and gains should continue, and is there any sufficient ground for placing the State in so false a financial relation to the construction of railways as that under which the former must bear all loss, and cannot possibly obtain a set-off by any gain? These questions involve the discussion of the character of the agreements which have till now been entered into with companies for the construction of railways in India, and the policy under which these works are entrusted to companies in preference to being executed by the direct agency of the State."

He urged that the issue was, whether the agency of companies afforded any such special convenience or advantage to the State as to justify the Government in giving them terms which were alike unsatisfactory in a financial and administrative point of view, and that the only possible reply could be in the negative. He foresaw that a doubt seemed likely to be thrown on the expediency of direct Government action as regards the presumed incapacity of the Government to carry out and manage such undertakings. But on this point he, at least, felt no hesitation. He pointed out that the history, so far, of the operations of guaranteed companies had given illustrations of management as bad and as extravagant as anything which the worst opponent of Government agency could suggest as likely to result from that system, and that the best conducted and cheapest of these lines had been carried out entirely under departmental management, *i.e.* without the intervention of contractors, in a way that, in short, differed in no respect from that which was followed on Government works under the Public Works Department. With reference to the Indian share of the work, he was satisfied that "under a reasonable system" the Government could at least secure as great ability to carry out the works, and with no greater outlay. The experience of twenty years under the guarantee system had shown, in the opinion of Lord Lawrence, that there was no reason to expect that the Government could derive any financial advantage in obtaining the capital for railways through the agency of companies, unless they could carry out the works and manage the lines very much more cheaply than could be done by the Government through its own agency. His own view was that the latter course would be the most economical to the State, and that the Government had already at its disposal a sufficient number of officers who were both qualified in railway work and in local experience; while he saw no adequate reason for supposing that if Government deliberately borrowed money for railway purposes only, there need be any necessity for stopping operations on every occasion of financial difficulty.

The despatch above referred to, from the Government of India, was practically based on Lord Lawrence's minute. He said, "We assent to these views, and to the arguments on which they are based. The conclusion opposed to direct Government action in such matters, which has been most commonly adopted till the last few years was doubtless justified by the circumstances of the time in which it was formed, and we are very far from questioning the great value of the work actually performed by companies in the prosecution of railways in a period of undoubted difficulty. But the whole conditions of the problem have since changed, and in this, as in numerous other matters of great public importance, modified methods of action are necessary to meet the altered circumstances of the time. . . . Although we thus desire to substitute as far as possible, in the future extension of railways, the direct action of the State for that of companies, it is yet proper that we should consider the cases in which companies may, from any causes, be again entrusted with the construction of new lines." They pointed out that there were two fundamental conditions which it was desirable to impose on a company, viz. the limitation of the financial responsibility of the Government, and the protection of the public against the possible evils of an authorised monopoly. The first mainly affected the operations of construction, and the second those of working the lines. The key-note of the whole despatch was that unless railways could be constructed more cheaply than had been the case hitherto, further extension would soon have to be stopped, or the finances of the country become seriously disordered. It insisted on the paramount importance of a very strict limitation of first cost, and the views of the Government on this point are worth quoting. "An extravagantly-constructed railway is permanently a financial failure. To a poor country like India this lesson is of exceptional importance. Here the needful capital for railway construction can only be obtained at the risk and under the guarantee of the State. An unsuccessful railway is therefore a public burden. Resources which might otherwise be applied to the extension of material or administrative improvements are permanently diverted to provide for the payment of interest on capital which has been misapplied, and remains unproductive. Even in a country of such extraordinary wealth and productive power as England the wasteful expenditure of railway capital has become a serious evil, and it may be affirmed with the most complete certainty that if India cannot manage to provide itself with railways which shall so far pay, or at least to cover the ordinary rate of interest on the necessary capital, the progress of railways must very soon be stopped, or the finances be brought into a condition of extreme disorder." It was shown that the average cost of Indian railways, single line, had up to that time reached about £17,000 per mile, while the income of the very best line had then barely risen to a figure sufficient to pay the guaranteed interest, 5 per cent, and that the average was about 3 per cent. They pointed out, moreover, that the lines already made, or in course of construction, occupied the best fields for railway enterprise, and that it could not be expected that further extensions then contemplated could do as well. They were confident that by making suitable arrangements, the cost of railways could be largely reduced; that it was no longer necessary to look to England for guidance in railway construction; and that they might now, "with complete propriety, claim the same degree of discretionary power in dealing with the administration and construction of Indian railways as is exercised in relation to all other branches of the administration and all other classes of public works." They further urged that the proposal to make over the profitable or "commercial" lines to companies, and to leave the unprofitable or "political" lines to the State was unfair and unpracticable, and concluded by saying that unless the necessary conditions, as regards economical construction and management, could be secured in arrangements with companies, it was desirable that in the future their agency should be altogether dispensed with for the construction of Indian railways.

The Government of India addressed the Secretary of State again on this subject in March 1869,[1] drawing attention more particularly to the serious liabilities which were being incurred by the State under the system of guaranteed companies; that the State was bound to pay a fixed rate of interest to the

[1] No. 28, of the 22nd March 1869.

shareholders, whatever the cost of the line, or whatever the character of the management might be; and that while the Government only was seriously interested in securing economy, no substantial co-operation in this direction was to be hoped for from the companies. Attention was also drawn to a very serious phase of the company system, viz. that the Government of India was by degrees losing its power of control over them, in so far that its decisions were not accepted as final in India, but were habitually referred to the Boards of Direction in London. The position of companies was compared with that of the Government in plain terms. It was urged that the former "have only to supply the capital, and to *receive* their interest from the Government, whatever be the outlay, and whatever be the results of the undertakings," while on the other hand, the Government had "to *pay* the interest on the capital in full, and to be satisfied with the partial set-off derived from the net profits. To the shareholders it is comparatively unimportant whether the first outlay is strictly confined to what is necessary or not. Their capital is an investment, the return from which is guaranteed under all circumstances; and even, in some cases, wasteful outlay may be directly advantageous to them, as leading to the creation of a stock which may be sold at a premium." This despatch reopened up the question of gauge, and held that too much importance had been attached to uniformity in the case of a country like India, where the distances were very great, and the centres of population far apart. For passenger traffic in India the evil of a break of gauge was, they considered, of no moment; while in the case of goods traffic the cost of transhipment between lines of different gauge would not exceed the cost of transport over ten miles of railway, and the practical inconvenience would amount to no more than would be represented by this charge. The financial considerations against the adoption of the broad gauge throughout the country they held to be insuperable, but otherwise they would have wished to adhere to a uniform gauge.

The Duke of Argyll, then Secretary of State, replied to this on the 15th July 1869. He held that whatever may have been the strength of the considerations which had led the Government twenty years before to entrust the construction of railways in India to companies under guarantee, he was prepared to agree with the Government of India that the time had now arrived to take up a fresh position and to "secure for itself the full benefit of the credit which it lends, and of the cheaper agencies which ought to be at its command." As a whole, the proposals in the despatches above referred to were assented to, and the necessary surveys ordered to be made forthwith. He recognised, however, that the success of the proposals would depend in great measure on the "character of the machinery" created for the purpose of giving effect to them, and asked for detail on this point. One important feature of this despatch was in the acknowledgment of the inequality of the position between the guaranteed companies and the Government, in the division of net profits (above the guaranteed rate of interest), and in the assent to the proposal of the Government of India, that in future these profits should be divided with the Government, and the right to require the repayment of guaranteed interest should be abandoned. The various lines which had been proposed by Government were reviewed in detail, and generally approved, and those to be taken up in the first instance were to be dealt with on their relative importance, and "by the supply of labour to be obtained without detriment to agriculture, or to the progress of other public works."

The very important question of the gauge for the extensions of the railway system which were here contemplated is dealt with at length in Chapter IV; but it may be stated that while the Government was prepared to carry out the trunk lines on the broad gauge of 5½ feet, it proposed to make all subsidiary lines on the gauge of one metre. Following out this idea, it was then decided that the lines intended mainly for military purposes, on the western and north-western frontiers, would amply serve commercial and political demands if made on the metre gauge. This was at first assented to by the Secretary of State, but was strongly opposed by Lord Napier of Magdala, then Commander-in-Chief. The decision of the Government arrived at in 1871 was, however, at first carried out, on both the Indus Valley and the Punjab Northern Railways. Very strong opposition was soon shown in England, and persistent representations were made to the India Office that no saving worthy of consideration would result from the adoption of the narrower gauge. To this agitation the Secretary of State (the Duke of Argyll) deferred, and allowing the question to be reopened, the Viceroy (Lord Northbrook) and his Council recommended that both the lines above referred to should be made light broad gauge, *i.e.* with rails of 60 lbs. to the yard, basing their recommendations on the military and political bearings of the case. Early in 1874 the Duke of Argyll, while urging that he still considered that the metre gauge would have sufficed for these lines, gave way to the arguments adduced, but proposed a permanent way on the broad gauge of 45 lbs. to the yard. To this the Government of India demurred, and on being considered again by Lord Salisbury, who had then become Secretary of State for India, the proposals of the Government of India were accepted. A similar but less important controversy took place at this time as to the gauge for the system of railways which, passing through Rajputana, was to connect Delhi with Bombay, but the metre gauge was eventually adopted.

The original intention as to the character of these lines was, that they should be cheaply, yet solidly constructed, and this has been consistently and thoroughly adhered to. The "pioneer" American line is, for many reasons, impossible in India. The climate generally, the intensity of the seasons, the profusion of vegetable and insect life, and the general want of suitable timber, forbids, both on the score of first and of ultimate cost, the rapid and temporary construction which in the Western States of America is equally possible and economical. During the Viceroyalty of Lord Mayo an impression became prevalent that if the American system could be adopted, matters would get on faster and the money go farther, and the Government was consequently led to engage the services of an able and experienced American engineer, in order to ascertain what amount of foundation there was for this view. After remaining two or three years in the country this gentleman (Mr. Miller) gave it as his opinion that the conditions of railway construction in India differed entirely from those in the United States, and that practically he had little or nothing to object to as regards Indian methods or designs, which in fact he readily adopted in the works he carried out in India.

The metre gauge lines were started with a formation width (in bank) of 12 feet, increased subsequently to 14 feet, and latterly to 16 feet, with 2 to 1 slopes, carefully trimmed and grassed. The permanent way was laid at first with Vignolles section rails of 36 lbs. to the yard, spiked to transverse wooden sleepers, 6 feet long by 8 inches by 4 inches. Later on the weight of rails was increased to 41¼ lbs. (steel), and for roads with heavy traffic to 50 lbs. The State lines on the broad or standard (5½ feet) gauge were laid at first with a 60 lbs. rail, which was latterly increased to 75 lbs., and will shortly be 85 lbs. as the standard, with 100 lbs. rails for heavy inclines, on which engines of exceptional character are required. In every case the lines have been unusually well ballasted—an essential condition in a country where the heavy rainfall is confined to four or five months in the year, and where timber sleepers would be otherwise exposed to rapid destruction from white ants. In view of the failures that occurred on one of the earlier guaranteed lines, special care was taken in the design and execution of masonry, and all girder-work was specially designed to types for certain fixed spans, being of rivetted work throughout, and all being rigorously tested before being passed for traffic. On small spans the road was carried on transverse sleepers, resting on the top flanges, and secured by hook-bolts. The works at stations were reduced to a minimum, and were in fact almost too cheap and incommodious. All the lines were single, and at ordinary crossing stations a loop-siding and short "lay-by" for loaded or damaged vehicles was all that was provided. At first, none of the lines were fenced, and all engines were consequently fitted with "cow-catchers." The axle loads of metre gauge engines did not in the beginning exceed 6 tons and that of waggons 4 tons, and both coaching and goods stock was four-wheeled, and fitted with central buffer and coupling combined. The minimum radius of curves was fixed at 100 metres, or say 335 feet. Latterly, as will be seen from the list of standard dimensions in the Appendix, the loads have been increased, and the ordinary four-wheeled waggon now carries 12 tons gross with a tare of about 3 tons, while bogie stock is in use on many lines. The average distance between stations averaged about 8 miles, and except at large stations the whole of the station staff were natives. The lines were, and still are worked under the "line clear" system, whereby the station-master at say A cannot start a train to B until the station-master at the latter has replied in the affirmative to a telegram asking if the line is clear, and on receipt of this message the fact is written on a form and handed to the driver of the train to be despatched. Speeds on the metre gauge were at first limited to 15 miles an hour, but at present mail trains run between stations at about an average of 25 miles an hour. On these trains European or Eurasian drivers are generally employed; but on goods and mixed trains natives (mostly Mussulmans and Parsees) are now largely employed in this capacity. They are found to be perfectly competent within a certain range, and while steady and sober to a far greater degree than the European or Eurasian, their emoluments need not be more than one-half of what is necessary for the European. Their weakness lies in an insufficient knowledge of English, and in want of "head" and judgment in positions of difficulty.

The new and important venture upon which the Government of India had thus been launched, involved both the collection and organisation of a large railway staff, and the determination of suitable machinery for control and supervision. As regards staff, a large and rapidly expanding department of Public Works offered a valuable nucleus of engineers, who could claim railway experience at home, and who, at the same time, had the great advantage of a knowledge of the country, the people, and the language. They were strengthened by some officers of the Royal Engineers, by direct recruitment from England, and by some officers from the guaranteed railway companies; and, on the whole, work was commenced under very promising conditions in this respect. Each line was placed in charge of an engineer-in-chief, the work being divided into "divisions," of from fifty to sixty miles in length, on each of which was the divisional engineer, with generally two assistants. They carried out the works as a rule themselves, by means of petty contractors or task work, although, in a few instances at first, large schedule contracts were given to European contractors. The arrangements for the general direction and control of these lines were rendered somewhat complicated by the fact that at that time the Local Governments had considerable powers in influencing the administration of the guaranteed lines, and that, consequently, it was deemed advisable that they should have even greater influence over the operations on State railways. The intention of the supreme Government was, however, that the control of both systems should eventually be centralised, and that the arrangements should tend towards this. The views of the Government of India were embodied in a resolution in 1871.[1] In this it was decided that the Consulting Engineers for the guaranteed lines, who until then had been associated with the Local Governments, should in future come invariably under the orders of the Government of India, and that in addition to

[1] Nos. 1883-1901, Railway, of 29th September 1871.

their present duties, they should exercise some measure of supervision over a portion of the new State lines. The remainder would be supervised directly either by the supreme Government or the Local Government concerned. These arrangements were not destined to continue in force very long, nor indeed was it intended that they should. Further reference will be made to this point.

In the same year, 1871, the Government of India appointed as their Consulting Engineer for State Railways Mr. G. L. Molesworth, Mem.Inst.C.E.,[1] to whose marked abilities, experience, and judgment their success is largely due. In June 1872 Mr. Molesworth, after visiting all the lines then in progress, submitted a report in which the character and prospects of the projected State railways were discussed, and suggestions made as to their design and method of construction. He was of opinion that the adoption, for subsidiary lines, of the metre gauge, was a wiser course than that of making light lines, for light loads and slow speeds, on the standard gauge. He was supported in England by Mr. (now Sir) A. M. Rendel, as adviser to the Secretary of State in the provision of English material, and who, as one of the original proposers of the new gauge, and from his commanding position in the profession, has afforded invaluable service to the Government. The direction of the new lines was left largely at first in the hands of Mr. Molesworth; but it was evident that with the mass of technical detail to be disposed of at the outset, it was impossible to give adequate attention to general administration, as regards establishment, funds, stores, etc., and that the division of responsibility was showing a bad effect on the progress of the works. It was clear, moreover, that the volume of business in connection with both the State and the guaranteed lines, required some additional and special organisation in the Public Works Branch of the Government of India. Two courses were considered, one the appointment of a Director for State railways,

[1] Now Sir Guilford L. Molesworth, K.C.I.E.

who would be empowered to deal independently with the bulk of the references, and who would refer minor technical questions to the Consulting Engineer, or that a Board of Direction should be constituted, the members of which would be selected for their special qualifications in the different branches of railway working and construction. The former course was eventually adopted (in April 1874), the first incumbent being Lieutenant-Colonel E. C. S. Williams, R.E.[1] This appointment was necessarily one of great importance, requiring exceptional judgment and ability—qualities which fortunately were amply shown in the new Director. The initiation and organisation of a new branch of the public service, the supervision and control of extensive works all over the country, the arrangements for the working of open lines, the management and proper disposal of a large staff, and the judicious apportionment of the funds provided, involved duties which, with the steady expansion of operations, became apparently too heavy for one person. Consequently, in 1877, it was deemed necessary to increase the number of Directors, by dividing the country "into systems," each in charge of a Director, and to add further a Director of Stores. The length of open line at the time was little more than 650 miles, the lines under construction about 1200 miles, and those under survey about 1100, and it would appear now that the increase was rather beyond what was really requisite; in fact these appointments were not approved by the Secretary of State, though not wholly for this reason. The correspondence which ensued on this subject ended, in September 1879, in the appointment of a Director-General of Railways, with a Deputy and Assistants for certain branches of the work. This post was combined with that of Deputy-Secretary to the Government of India in the Railway Branch of the Public Works Secretariat, while as Director-General the office carried powers similar to those which had been accorded to the Directors of

[1] Now Lieutenant-General Sir E. C. S. Williams, K.C.I.E., Government Director of Indian Railways at the India House.

the four "systems" as regards State lines. He was further charged with the supervision of the guaranteed lines, which were under the immediate control of the supreme Government, and had powers of sanction with regard to these lines similar to those pertaining to the Governments of Bombay and Madras. There was to be no alteration in the system then existing, as regards railways which were under Local Governments, either as to their powers or relations with the supreme Government; but a time was approaching when this point was to become a source of frequent discussion with the Home Government. The officer first appointed to the post of Director-General under these new conditions was Major-General J. S. Trevor, R.E.

The duplication in one and the same official, of functions which might in some respects be regarded as antagonistic, implied that the position was one of considerable difficulty; but in spite of its anomalous conditions, it has on the whole worked well, while it would have been scarcely feasible, without a very radical change of system, to have introduced any better arrangement. As Director-General alone, the duties were sufficiently heavy and responsible to have satisfied the most eager worker. He was charged with the direction of the surveys for new projects for State lines, the supervision and criticism of these projects when under preparation, the general control of the works and the establishment of them when in progress, and of the lines open for traffic. As Deputy-Secretary to the Supreme Government, on the other hand, instead of being an independent executive officer, with wide powers and direct responsibilities, he found himself acting merely as the mouthpiece of the Government of India, and thus not infrequently corresponding with himself as Director-General, and controlling and even criticising his action in that position. The explanation, and perhaps the sufficient justification for this dual appointment, was found in the more rapid disposal of business, in the curtailment of office establishment, and in the need, under the existing conception of the status of the

Director-General, of his being in close connection with the central Government. In this dual capacity it was a matter of some delicacy to decide in which of them it was desirable to take action, a distinct line having to be drawn between the views of the individual, as the executive functionary, and the collective opinion of the body representing the Government of India. In according approval to the creation of this appointment, the Secretary of State held, nevertheless, that it would not be necessary to continue it for any considerable time. He looked forward to the early probability of the Government of India being able to free itself, as far as possible, from direct executive functions, in regard to the railway system, and that eventually the construction, control, and working of the State lines would be made over to Local Governments. He thought that this should be the declared aim of the Supreme Government, that thus the functions of the Deputy-Secretary, as Director-General of Railways, would be "progressively restricted," and that the necessity for this separate office might possibly cease altogether. At this time, out of a total of about 8000 miles of State lines, either under construction or open for traffic, about 1800 miles were controlled by Local Governments, and it appeared to the Home Government that further decentralisation in this direction was not only possible but that it was out of the question, "that the railway system of a tract as large as the greater part of Europe, could be satisfactorily managed by a single central authority"; while efficient control over the details of railway administration on the part of the central Government was impossible, in view of the enormous and constantly increasing burden of other administrative duties. All that seemed necessary was to lay down general rules, and having settled questions of principle, the duties and responsibilities of supervising the management and controlling expenditure should be left to local authorities.

The Government of India did not find it possible to give their entire acquiescence or immediate effect to the course thus indicated; but early in 1888 measures were adopted, which were directed, as far as was then possible, towards fulfilling the intentions of the Home Government, but which did not materially diminish the duties or the responsibilities of the Director-General. The blot in the proposals or intentions of the Secretary of State was one of an essentially practical nature. It had not been seen that in order to obtain efficient supervision and control, in a matter so special and technical as that of railway construction and administration, it would be a necessary condition that duly qualified officers should be attached to Local Governments for this duty. It is not clear that this was fully recognised at the time, even by the Government of India; nor was it indeed possible to provide for its proper fulfilment, in every case, without adding unduly to the cost of a provincial establishment. The weakness of local supervision, unaided in this respect, has been prominently shown in several ways, and in some important cases; indeed so marked has been the evidence of this defect, that it has recently been in contemplation, on the grounds both of economy and of sound administration, to revert in great measure to a centralisation of authority in the conduct of operations on State lines. It may, however, be regarded as probable, that before many years have elapsed, the growth of private enterprise, and the making over of the working of all, or nearly all, the State railways to companies, may effect a considerable reduction in the scope of the functions now exercised by the Director-General, and that consequently the appointment may ere long disappear. It must be, however, admitted that there was ample justification for the principle insisted on by the Secretary of State; for the earlier years of the administration of State railways showed an almost morbid desire to centralise supervision over the most trivial details. Every work had to be designed to certain types, irrespective of local conditions; the dismissal of subordinates, or even menial native servants, was forbidden without sanction from headquarters, alterations of rates or designs had to be referred in the same way, and as an instance of the extent to which this interference was carried, it is on record that the question of the "write-off" of three broken lamp glasses was not thought unworthy of disposal by the Supreme Government. A very great change has been effected of late years in this respect. Both the Engineer and the Manager have now very extended powers, with results which are in every way satisfactory, while the saving in delays, in correspondence, and in friction, is equally noticeable.

Up to the period of the introduction of State railways nearly every appointment under the Government in India implied that, subject to good conduct, continuous service was to be looked for, and the grant of a pension or gratuity on retirement. The new departure, on what was essentially a commercial undertaking of great magnitude, rendered it necessary to resort to recruitment on a different basis for employés of all ranks, whose services could certainly not be engaged for an indefinite time, and to offer employment to men obtained from England on short term covenants of from three to five years; while to men—mostly natives—engaged in India, the conditions of discharge were fixed at one or, at most, six months' notice. Such service was to carry no claim to pension on retirement. The promulgation of rules to this effect led, naturally and speedily, to the recognition of the danger, especially in India, of enlisting large numbers of men to whom no other inducements were offered towards zealous or at least good service, than the hope of preferment, or the renewal of an agreement, and thus it appeared to be politic to afford to such employés some regular system of saving, and to encourage this by some contribution from the earnings of the concern in which they were engaged. This led to the institution of a State Railway Provident Fund (in 1880), under the regulations of which every European employed on the new footing was obliged to contribute one-sixteenth, and every native one-thirty-second part of his salary to the Fund. To this the State added a contribution in the shape of one-half of 1 per cent of the net earnings of the railway each half-year, to be distributed amongst the contributors in proportion to their compulsory deposits, and the aggregate bonus so granted was not to exceed the contribution (compulsory) of the said period. In case such bonus was, on the other hand, considered insufficient, the Government declared its willingness to specially consider the matter. No money could be withdrawn from the Fund, except on the decease of the contributor, or on his leaving the public service, although under special circumstances money might be withdrawn temporarily, but had to be replaced in the Fund by small additional deductions from salary. In addition to compulsory deductions, voluntary subscriptions might be made to the Fund, on which interest was given, under Savings Bank Rules, at 3¾ per cent per annum. The effect of this Provident Fund has been in every way satisfactory and salutary, and has been beneficial both to the State and to the servants to whom its provisions apply. It has given men a definite interest in the success of the undertaking they are engaged on, it has relieved them in great measure from the anxiety inseparable from the terms of their service, and has afforded the State some degree of security for economical working and conscientious service.

An important feature in the administration of Indian railways was established shortly after the appointment of a Director-General, in the shape of the assembly of the first of a series of conferences of railway officials, delegated from both State and guaranteed railways. The powers of control which could be claimed by the Government over the latter, under their contracts, did not include the right to interfere in minor matters of detail; while in those in which it would have been possible to decide and to insist on, it was wisely held to be impolitic to take action without eliciting the opinions and advice of those who had to work under such rulings, and whose hearty concurrence it was in every way desirable to enlist, in view of the interest which the State had in the successful results of these lines. It was, moreover, necessary that methods which had been adopted on State lines should be discussed and reviewed before a tribunal of experts, and, above all, that, as far as possible, an approach to uniformity of system in all essential points should be aimed at on all railways. The first meeting, in 1880, was eminently successful, and was presided over by the Director-General of Railways. A code of general rules was agreed to for the working of all lines, agreements were come to as to the interchange of rolling stock, and for recording charges for shunting and other miscellaneous engine service, proposals were discussed for the adoption of uniform classification of goods, and rules were agreed to for the preparation of half-yearly statistics. This latter point has been a salient and unique feature in Indian railways, and their value has been amply recognised both by railway officials and the general public, for whom the figures are compiled and tabulated in the annual reports of the Director-General. An obvious advantage of these conferences has been that of the personal knowledge and *rapprochment* between the railway officials, and the possibility of free discussion of most points. The introduction of the Government as an owner and operator of railways produced a keen and healthy rivalry between their officers and those of the companies, and many a difficulty which seemed insuperable to one side or other has been "thrashed out" at these meetings, and a decision arrived at and eventually adopted by both sides. In the earlier years of the State lines their working compared somewhat unfavourably with that of the older ones, partly on account of the rigid centralisation, to which reference has been already made, but largely owing to the incomplete state of the new lines, the want of rolling stock, and the poor and difficult country they passed through compared with the general character of the guaranteed lines. The Government of India were assailed from more than one direction on this point, but resolutely defended their own men, urging that time must be given for due development; that it was unfair to compare results by the percentages of working expenses to gross receipts on lines which were being operated under such unfavourable conditions; and that the true criterion should be "whether the traffic had been moved with punctuality and despatch, and whether the net earnings of a line bear a reasonable proportion to its capital cost."[1] Without criticising this somewhat untenable doctrine, it may be safely asserted that the State official has amply vindicated the attitude then taken by the Government, and has shown that when given free scope and responsibility for results, he has been able to work as cheaply, and generally offer returns quite as satisfactory, as those of the older railways; while of late years those lines have drawn their principal officers from the staff of the State railways.

The changes of policy, which have from time to time been forced on the Government, have led to a variety of shapes in the growth of the Indian railway system. The list of the lines now open, with the mileage for each gauge, is given in the Appendix, which also shows the different conditions as to ownership, and the agencies by which each line or groups of lines are being worked at present. In this we see State lines worked by the State, State lines worked by companies, guaranteed lines, assisted lines, lines owned by native States and worked by them, and lines similarly owned but worked by separate agencies. The conferences, to which reference has been already made, have done much towards introducing some degree of uniformity in what may be called traffic questions in this medley; but until quite lately no steps had been taken in this direction in the almost equally important question of assimilating the practice of these different railways in the construction of their rolling stock. In 1889, however, this want was at length clearly recognised by the Government, and

[1] Despatch to Secretary of State for India in 1880.

arrangements were made for the annual assembly of a Committee of Locomotive and Carriage Superintendents, at which representatives would be found from all the principal lines, including those of the State. The functions of this Committee, which was to meet at some large railway centre (varying each year), were defined as follows, viz.: "That it should deal with all matters relating to the mechanical improvement of locomotive and carriage stock, and the design, construction, running, and repair of the same; to determine what standards shall be adopted; to arrange for such experiments as may appear desirable; to publish papers of professional interest, and generally to consider and report upon all technical, administrative, or financial questions connected with rolling stock, workshops, station machinery, etc., which may be proposed by the members themselves, or by the Government of India." The decisions of this Committee are determined by the votes of the members, the voting power of each being based upon the number of axles in his charge. It is, however, understood, and is noted on the annual reports of the Committee, that all its decisions are subject to the approval of the agents, Boards of Directors, or other authorities for individual railways, and of the Government of India in all cases. The expenditure in connection with their meetings, the cost of experiments, models, and publications, is met by contributions from each line represented, in proportion to its mean open mileage for the year. Designs accepted by the Committee are divided into three classes, viz.:—

1. Absolute standards.
2. Provisional standards.
3. Approved designs.

The first is a design or dimension, the general adoption of which is prescribed by a Government order, such as automatic brake connections, or dimensions between centres of buffers. The second, or provisional standard, is a design or dimension, recommended for adoption, but which needs further trial to warrant its general acceptance by a Government order. The last, an approved design, covers that of a design or pattern approved by the Committee as a good example of the best practice in India up to date, and, as expressed in one of the reports, it was expected that "from time to time for each class of vehicle fresh designs will be added to the 'approved' list, and designs which may be superseded will be removed." Thus it is hoped that by degrees the differing types and patterns on Indian railways will be reduced in number, inferior or absolete designs will be gradually eliminated, and year by year *each* line in India will conform more nearly to the practice which by the common consent of *all* lines has been determined to be the best.

Until the institution of this Committee, each railway had been working pretty well on the isolated views and opinions of their Workshops' Superintendents for the time being, with the result that the tendency of their practice was more towards the multiplication and divergence of types than otherwise. In a small country, or in one more particularly in which facilities for the interchange of stock is not of vital importance, this evil would not demand the close attention of the Government; but in India, with its vast distances, its constant liability to famine and frontier wars, both of which may involve the sudden and extensive movement and massing of stock of all kinds from perhaps one end of the Empire to the other, it was a matter of great moment to the Government of India to endeavour to introduce order into approaching chaos. The exigencies of military operations particularly required, moreover, that carriage and waggon stock should be adapted, as far as possible, to the proper transit of troops, material of war generally, and animals (not excluding elephants), without materially affecting their utility for the purposes of the public; and that stock should be also of such design as would be suitable for movement over the heavy grades and sharp curves on the frontier railways. In this, and in other directions, the Committee has already done most valuable work. The results of their meetings are compiled in the Technical Section of the Public Works Department, which is in charge of the Consulting Engineer for State railways to the Government of India, and from whence the annual report is issued, and the decisions of the Committee brought to the notice of the Government. This Technical Section is another extremely useful feature in the administration of Indian railways. It has been instituted with the intention of making it a centre for information on all technical questions in connection with Indian railways, of preparing and issuing types and standard dimensions of all kinds, and of editing and publishing original papers or translations on subjects of special interest.

Brief notice must be made of another feature of interest in the State administration of Indian railways, *i.e.* in the formation of a Railway Service Corps for military operations. The first movement in this direction was made in 1874, when it was proposed that an attempt should be made to train a company of native sappers on State lines to serve as engine-drivers, mechanics, and platelayers in case of need. Little, however, resulted from this, and later on, in 1887, a proposal was considered for forming military companies of railway staff from volunteers from European regiments serving in India. To this the military department gave full support, and arrangements were made with a view of forming a corps for service on the frontier; but difficulties of a legal nature arose against this proposal, and it eventually fell through. Previously to this, in 1885, in a despatch[1] from the Secretary of State on the subject of the taking over and working by the State of all the frontier lines, it was suggested that on such of those as had more particularly military or political objects it might be desirable to have them worked by a corps of this kind, on somewhat similar conditions to those which obtained in

[1] No. 10, Railway, of the 22nd January 1885.

Germany, France, Russia, and elsewhere. The Government of India foresaw, however, "the insufficiency for the object in view" of putting any one part of the system in exclusive charge of a corps of this kind, and proposed, as an alternative, that all the European staff on the amalgamated frontier railways, then owned and worked by the State, should be required, as the conditions of their engagements, to become volunteers, under the Indian system, and from them should be taken a picked body of men and officers, who should be enrolled, under advantageous conditions, for service either within or beyond the frontiers. This proposal was the one eventually adopted with the concurrence of the Home Government,[1] the corps while employed in the field being recognised as combatants, and "entitled to share in the privileges of that position." Subsequently the scope of the scheme was enlarged, so as to include natives for subordinate work and volunteers from other railways, to take the place on the frontier lines of the Railway Service Corps. Nominal rolls of all volunteers, both European and native, are now recorded, and the numbers and class of men entered show a very useful, or indeed invaluable, addition to the military strength in case of serious frontier trouble.

Generally speaking, it may be said that the administration of railways by the direct agency of Government has, in all the essentials of working, differed in no material degree from that which has characterised that of the companies' lines; indeed it has been the aim in many directions, on the part both of the State and the companies, to assimilate their methods. In contrasting the results on both, it must be borne in mind that the lines in the hands of the guaranteed companies covered the best ground in respect of local and through traffic, while those constructed by the State directly, or those carried out under "assisted" terms indirectly, have

[1] Despatch from Secretary of State, No. 11, Railway, of 4th February 1886.

been designed either as feeders, as lines for military or political purposes, or for the relief of possible famines. The certainty of an adequate return on the capital expenditure on these railways was but in few cases expected, but indirect advantages, of scarcely less importance to the State, were their first recommendation. It might even be held that the Government had originally no definite intention of obtaining anything more from their railways than the interest borne on their capital cost, and that in the event of any greater return than this the excess might be surrendered in the shape of reductions in rates and fares. Of late years, however, very serious fiscal and financial difficulties have arisen, due to a variety of unforeseen causes, but mainly induced by the fall in the exchange value of the currency, with the natural or inevitable result that the Government has been forced to regard their railway receipts as a very considerable source of Imperial revenue, and that the State railway manager has been stimulated to keep as keen a watch on net profits as the most zealous employés of the companies' lines. This point will be referred to more fully in the concluding chapter.

CHAPTER IV

HISTORY OF THE GAUGE ON INDIAN RAILWAYS[1]

IN 1845, two private associations under the designation of the "East Indian" and the "Great Indian Peninsula" Railway Companies[2] were formed in England; but the projectors found it impossible to raise the necessary funds for their proposed schemes without the assistance of Government. The application for this aid led to a protracted discussion; and it was not until 1850 that any practical commencement of railway construction took place in India. Early in 1849, it was determined to assist these Companies by guaranteeing to them a certain fixed rate of interest on their capital expenditure, and the deeds of contract with both Companies were sent out to India towards the close of the year. Paragraph 13 of the transmitting despatch runs thus: "With respect to the weight of rails and gauge of line to be employed on these railways, we are disposed to recommend those used by the North-Western Company here, namely, a gauge of 4 feet 8½ inches, and a weight of rails of 84 lbs. to the yard, as combining the greatest utility and economy." At that time Lord Dalhousie was the Governor-General, and Mr. W. Simms, C.E., the Consulting Engineer to the Government of India for Railways. The despatch was duly considered in India. The Consulting Engineer for Railways reported on

[1] The first portion of this chapter is largely a reprint of one on this subject in the Administration Report on Indian Railways for 1880-81, by Colonel W. S. Trevor, R.E., then Director-General of Railways in India.

[2] Mr. J. Danvers' Report on Indian Railways to end of year 1859.

the subject, and the Governor-General recorded a minute, both of which were transmitted to the Court of Directors with a despatch recommending that a gauge of 6 feet be adopted for Indian railways.

Mr. Simms recorded his reasons for recommending a wider gauge than 4 feet 8½ inches as follows :—

The wider gauge of 5 feet 6 inches, which I would recommend for adoption, will give 9½ inches more space for the arrangement of the several parts of the working gear of the several parts of the locomotive engines ; and this additional space will be more needed in India than in Europe, not only on account of the machinery itself, but it would lower the centre of gravity of both the engines and carriages, the result of which would be to lessen their lateral oscillation, and render the motion more easy and pleasant, and at the same time diminish the wear and tear.

The lowering of the centre of gravity, consequent on the adoption of the wider gauge, appears to me of great importance for another reason, namely, the fearful storms of wind so frequent at certain seasons of the year, and I think it very probable that in one severe nor'-wester, not to mention such hurricanes as that of 1842, the additional 9½ inches of width might make all the difference between the safety and destruction of the trains ; and one such accident attended, as it doubtless would be, with great loss of life, would probably retard the progress of the railway system in this country very considerably.

The following extract from Lord Dalhousie's minute refers to the question of gauge :—

32. The Court of Directors have recommended at the same time the use of the narrow gauge of 4 feet 8½ inches for the railway about to be constructed. Although the letter of the Court recommends, but leaves to the Government of India to determine, as to the gauge which should be adopted on this occasion, I consider the question to be one of such moment as to deserve a careful consideration and an authoritative and conclusive decision by the highest authority connected with the Indian Empire, who

alone can have access to that full information and extended experience which would make such a decision really and satisfactorily conclusive.

33. The British Legislature fell unconsciously, and perhaps unavoidably, into the mischievous error of permitting the introduction of two gauges into the United Kingdom. The numerous and grievous evils which arose from that permission are well known, and will long be felt throughout all England. The Government of India has it in its power, and no doubt will carefully provide that, however widely the railway system may be extended in this Empire in the time to come, these great evils shall be averted, and that uniformity of gauge shall rigidly be enforced from the first. But I conceive that the Government should do more than this, and that now, at the very outset of railway works, it should not only determine that any uniform gauge shall be established in India, but that such uniform gauge shall be the one which science and experience may unite in selecting as the best.

34. At one time this question was much before me; and although I should not myself attempt to offer an opinion on so vexed a question, yet I may venture to form one on the recorded views of men competent in every way to judge. The evidence which has been given before the Gauge Commissioners in 1846, and evidence which has been given from time to time before the Committees of Parliament, backed as it has been by very high authority abroad, is, I venture to think, sufficient to show that the narrow gauge of 4 feet 8½ inches (a measurement adopted originally at haphazard and from the accident of local circumstances) is not the best gauge for the general purposes of a railway, and that something intermediate between the narrow gauge of 4 feet 8½ inches and the broad gauge of 7 feet will give greater advantages than belong to the former, and will substantially command all the benefits which are secured by the latter.

35. The circumstances which have been brought forward by Mr. Simms in his report, applicable especially to this country, strengthen the reluctance which I feel to introduce the 4 feet 8½ inches gauge into India without a very deliberate reconsideration of the question with reference to India, under the direction of the Honourable Court, by the Board of the East Indian Railway

Company. I should not have felt satisfied that I had done my duty if I had not brought this question pointedly under the consideration of the Court, requesting them formally and finally to determine whether a wider gauge than the 4 feet 8½ inches ought not to be established in India, and whether the gauge of 6 feet which was recommended by engineers of eminence in England, and which was preferred also, if I recollect rightly, by M. de Pambour, should not be introduced on the experimental line in Bengal, and at the same time on the line which is in course of construction at Bombay.

In reply to this despatch, the Court of Directors were "disposed to think" a gauge of 5 feet 6 inches was the most suitable, and communicated that decision to the several Indian Railway Boards in London.[1] This decision did not coincide with the views of the authorities; and Major J. Pitt Kennedy, who had succeeded Mr. W. Simms as Consulting Engineer for Railways, suggested that further reference to the Court of Directors might be made. To this Lord Dalhousie assented, recording his opinion in a minute. The referring paragraphs are as follows:—

2. It does not appear from the despatch of the Honourable Court whether their determination to fix the gauge at 5 feet 6 inches was the result of any deliberate inquiry, or whether the figure was merely indicated as a mean between the extremes of the present narrow gauge and that which I took the liberty to suggest. If the Honourable Court have fixed upon 5 feet 6 inches for the Indian gauge on high recognised authority, and adhere to it, of course the Government has only to obey. But if it is not the case, the Court will pardon the importunity which, for their own present and future interests, urges them to take other counsel before they issue a peremptory mandate on this important point.

3. I know of old that particular figures have been fixed upon originally for a gauge, and for others proposed in substitution of it, without the author of the proposal being able to give any reason

[1] Despatch No. 46, from Court of Directors to the Government of India, dated 4th December 1850.

whatever for selecting the particular dimensions he has specified. The original narrow gauge of 4 feet $8\frac{1}{2}$ inches was adopted for no other reason than because it happened to be the width of the colliery tramway on which locomotive power was first tried. When a general alteration was proposed, I recollect it being said that the principle on which one gentleman proceeded was to take all the different gauges, strike the average, and propose the figure that resulted as the best universal gauge. But I think that many good reasons were formerly given for the superiority of a 6 feet over the broad and narrow gauges, and I feel confident that many more could be given why that gauge should be selected for India, in preference to either of the original gauges, or to the one now selected by the Honourable Court.

4. At all events, if formal inquiry has not been entered into, I earnestly request the Honourable Court to permit the question to be so far reconsidered as to receive such reports and evidence on the subject as are suggested by Major Kennedy in the 15th paragraph of his present report. If this is not in accordance with the resolution of the Honourable Court, I shall much regret it; for I think that those who come after us will see cause to lament that the originators of this great system in the East did not profit so much as they might have done by the errors of their predecessors in Europe.

A communication to this effect was made to the Court of Directors,[1] but the recommendation to increase the gauge to 6 feet was not assented to, the Court of Directors saying that their decision had been "arrived at after a very careful consideration of the subject, and with the best opinions that we could obtain. That decision having been communicated to the railway companies who have entered into contracts for the execution of works, and for the provision of materials on the presumption that it is final, it would lead to much inconvenience and expense if any alteration were now permitted."[2]

[1] Government of India to the Court of Directors, No. 3, dated 7th March 1851.

[2] Court of Directors to Government of India, No. 45, dated 20th August 1851.

This decision was accepted by the Government of India, and the 5 feet 6 inches gauge was adopted as the standard gauge for the trunk lines in British India.

Early in 1857, the Court of Directors received several proposals for the construction of railways through Rahilkund and through the then newly annexed province of Oudh. The Court conceived that the time had come for ceasing to grant guarantees, and anticipated that the companies would have no difficulty in raising the necessary funds, with only moderate assistance from Government. These proposals were referred to the Government of India for a full report on the system of communications in that part of India, and suggesting that the kind of railway required should be distinctly indicated.

The Government of India suggested that, in preference to giving any more guarantees (the Court of Directors having intimated, meanwhile, that their expectations regarding the raising of money in the English market without a guarantee were unfulfilled), the State should undertake to build its own railways in Oudh.[1] Lord Stanley, who was Secretary of State when this matter came up for decision,[2] was not of opinion that Government should build its own railways, although he did not object to Government doing so on a small scale, such as connecting its iron works at the foot of the Naini Tal hills, etc., to the trunk lines. This policy was reiterated by Sir C. Wood, who succeeded Lord Stanley as Secretary of State, and the surveys for railways in Oudh were conceded to certain railway companies. The various proposals were reviewed in a note, dated 7th September 1861, by Lieutenant-Colonel H. Yule, then Secretary to the Government of India for Public Works. As regards the gauge, Colonel Yule remarked :—

> The results of the cattle-draught line as here exhibited are more precisely favourable. Were the enterprise destined to remain

[1] Secretary of State to Government of India, No. 16, of 24th February 1859.

[2] Despatch from Secretary of State, No. 106, of 29th October 1859.

purely local, this might therefore be preferred. But such a line is not capable of great development; a large traffic derived from a wide extent of country would choke it, and demand an amount of live and dead stock excessively unwieldy and unmanageable.

If the cattle line were adopted, I adhere to the view expressed in 1855, that the gauge of the great railways should be altogether discarded. I can see no object in adopting it sufficient to compensate for the great additional weight which it will involve. Nay more. I would now extend the same views to the light locomotive line. I do not dispute for one moment that the great primary network of continental railways should be of one gauge. But we propose here quite a different style of work. Is it worth while, on account of the necessity of transhipment at two eventual points of contact—one of which will probably be on a great river (the Ganges at Cawnpore) likely to remain unbridged for a generation, and therefore a break in any case—to give up a great economy? In the English gauge controversies there was no separation, either in character or locality, between the lines of different gauge. It was but the predilection and practice of one set of engineers pitted against those of another set, on lines of the same character constantly interlacing. I must at the same time apologise for venturing such an opinion after the views of Government and of Lord Dalhousie have been so strongly expressed the other way.

The views were adopted by the Government of India, for in December 1862, when Mr. J. E. Wilson, the Agent for the Indian Branch Railway Company, reported to Government that he was "prepared to enter into definite arrangements for the construction of the roadways and the laying down of light railways thereon" in Oudh and Rahilkund, the Government of India, in passing orders on the reference, laid down the following conditions as regards the gauge:—

The first point that calls for remark is the gauge, to which you make no special allusion. . . . His Excellency in Council is of opinion that it will be essential to insist on the adoption of the standard Indian gauge of 5 feet 6 inches in the case of all railways that are intended to form portions of main lines. But when the lines proposed are designed as *bonâ fide* tramways, that is, feeders to the main system but not essential parts of it, and when the expected traffic may warrant the outlay necessary for the formation of a full gauge line, the Government of India will sanction, as it has already done in the case of the Nalhati line, narrow gauge light lines, as a temporary expedient, on the conviction that such lines will be replaced by full gauge lines of a more substantial character whenever the development of the traffic renders such a change advisable. Where such narrow gauge lines are sanctioned, it will therefore be an advantage that they should be of the lightest and most economical description compatible with safety and the necessary degree of permanence, in order that there may be the least possible difficulty in the way of the change when it has become expedient, and that there may be no doubt as to their temporary and provisional character, and no risk of their being permitted to grow into a system which would compete with the system constructed on the standard or national gauge.

A slight digression here is necessary to give an outline of the objects of the Indian Branch Railway Company, and how they were affected by the question of the gauge. Of all the numerous companies that were projected for building light railways in India, this was the only one in Northern India that actually did proceed to make lines in India.[1] The original projector of this Company was Mr. J. E. Wilson; and it was his desire to lay light lines of railway on existing roads, but on a narrower gauge to that on the trunk lines, and thus act as feeders to the trunk lines. This idea seemed the only feasible method by which a large network of light railways could be spread over India; it was welcomed by Lord Canning as a probable solution of a most difficult problem, and was heartily backed by him during the latter months of his stay in India.[3]

[1] P. W. D. Pros., June 1864, No. 61 E.

[2] *Ibid.*, January 1868, No. 24.

[3] Lord Canning was succeeded by Lord Elgin on 12th March 1862.

The first offer made by this Company was to construct a light line of 4 feet gauge on a road which the Government of Bengal were just completing between Nalhati station on the East Indian Railway and Azimganj, situated on one of the effluents of the Ganges and on the road to Murshedabad. This line was actually made without a guarantee, was opened for traffic on the 21st December 1863, and is still working on its original gauge. It was, however, bought by the Government in 1868, and has since been relaid to the standard gauge.

This Company then desired to make a light line between Cawnpore and Lucknow and other lines in Oudh and Rahilkund, and they actually did complete the Lucknow-Cawnpore line. The Company, however, found that they could not raise sufficient capital to continue their ventures, and appealed to the Secretary of State for a guarantee. This was eventually given, and the Indian Branch Railway Company merged into what is now known as the Oudh and Rahilkund Railway Company. But before permission to construct the Lucknow-Cawnpore line was given, the views of the Indian Government had considerably changed. Lord Elgin's Government would hear of no narrow gauge railways, except in such detached and fragmentary sections as held out no promise of being ever worked remuneratively from the heavy cost of the independent establishments. Indeed, it seems that Mr. J. E. Wilson himself had changed his ideas, for it is stated that he "readily accepted the 5 feet 6 inches gauge for all his lines," etc. This is to be found in the note written on the whole matter by Colonel Strachey immediately after Lord Elgin's death, and in which is embodied, as far as was known, Lord Elgin's opinions in the case.

Sir C. Trevelyan, in a minute dated 4th September 1863, also recorded a strong protest against making either light railways or railways on any other but a uniform gauge. The following extract refers to the question of gauge:—

I have always been of opinion that a fallacy is involved in the idea of light railways. The railway experience in England is greater than that of any other country. For many years after our railway system commenced, there was a constant craving after a cheaper kind of railway. Project after project appeared for the formation of light railways or tramways, but they were all dropped. Atmospheric and other eccentric forms of railway were attempted; but, however specious the light railway principle might be, there was something in it which always led to its being abandoned on close examination; and it never arrived even at the dignity of an experiment. Cheap agricultural railways are now being made in various parts of the country, but they are all solid, full-gauged railways, quite capable of bearing the rolling stock of the main lines with which they are connected, and their cheapness arises only from their being single lines; from the landed proprietors asking moderate rates for their land, because they are convinced of the advantage to them of the railways; and from the Parliamentary expenses having been reduced to a mere trifle.

Experience is so much better than theory, that I will not waste time in endeavouring to account for these results. The fact seems to be that a metalled road is a cheap medium of communication, and so also is a solidly constructed railway, but that a railway which is constructed in such a manner that it will not admit of the full application of the power of steam is not an economical medium.

The practical difficulties in the way of converting a narrow gauge into a full gauge railway are so great, that I look upon the power which it is proposed to reserve to the Government of ordering such a conversion to be entirely illusory. Earthwork, bridges, rails, rolling stock, all have to be constructed on a different scale for a narrow and medium gauge, and, as observed by the Honourable the President, in the event of conversion, a small section of the earthwork and ballast and some buildings will be all that would be saved.

The "longitudinal" line, of which the Indian Branch Railway Company desires the concession, is no branch but a main line more than 500 miles long, passing through some of the richest and best populated provinces of the Empire. Even the branches to Cawnpore and Koorja, connecting this line with the East

Indian, are so important, that the Government very properly stipulated that they should be laid on the standard gauge. The commonest foresight, therefore, requires that the main line as well as these branches should be laid on the standard gauge; and if the Branch Railway Company obtains the concession, it must change its name and concentrate its efforts on the construction of an entire system—main line and branches—on the splendid field which will be placed at its disposal. The Indian standard gauge is 5 feet 6 inches. The gauge fixed upon by a Government Commission for the Irish railways as the smallest which could with advantage be adopted was 5 feet 3 inches.

The negotiations with the Indian Branch Railway Company were reported to the Secretary of State in April 1864 (Sir J. Lawrence, Governor-General), and the despatch was accompanied by all the notes and minutes that had been written in Lord Elgin's time. The arrangements made by Lord Elgin's Government were assented to generally; and the following extracts from the despatch will show that a gauge narrower than 5 feet 6 inches was deprecated, unless nothing better could be got without a guarantee :—

13. In contemplating the construction of light railways of the 5 feet 6 inches gauge, Lord Elgin had never intended that the *engines* of the heavy lines should run on them. It was well understood that in England engines of one company are rarely run on the line of another, and that the practical working of railways is not compatible with such a system of interchange of engines, and that all that is ever requisite is the interchange of waggons and carriages. A 5 feet 6 inches gauge light line was accordingly considered to mean a railway capable of carrying at a moderate speed the ordinary passenger and goods vehicles in use on the Indian main lines.

14. Having these views, Lord Elgin authorised an arrangement being made with Mr. Wilson, by which the character of the Oudh and Rahilkund lines was to be defined, by declaring that the maximum load per wheel should be 3½ tons, and the maximum speed 15 miles an hour. This will allow of the ordinary waggon

and passenger stock of the East Indian Railway running over the Oudh lines whenever the Ganges bridges are finished. To these arrangements of Lord Elgin we give our complete assent.

. . . . . .

29. It only remains to us to call attention to two minutes of Sir Charles Trevelyan, in the arguments of which we have been unable to concur.

30. In his first minute, dated 30th September last, objection is taken to the construction of narrow gauge and light railways. So far as the present proposals are concerned, the question of narrow gauge lines does not arise. But we are not prepared to recede from the position before taken up by the Government of India in respect of such lines, viz. that when nothing better can be got, and with due provision for their resumption and conversion into full gauge lines when the traffic calls for the change, the Government may without objection aid such lines, in each case determining the amount of aid with reference to the objects to be attained.

31. As regards light lines, very nearly the same remarks will also apply. As soon as the Government gives up the system of guarantee, and abandons all right or desire to interfere in the management of railway companies' affairs, it ceases to be in a position to decide whether a line shall be constructed of rails of one class or another. Such a matter is essentially one for the company to determine. What the Government can do is to decline giving assistance, unless certain terms are offered by the companies, as the companies can refuse to accept the assistance offered if it be too little to satisfy them. The Government of India has adopted the conclusion that a 5 feet 6 inches gauge line, of such a character as will admit of the carriage and waggon stock of the great lines going over it at a moderate speed, will probably be for many years to come sufficient to meet the requirements of the country, and this general standard it has taken as the *minimum* for the full gauge lines. . . .

It may be here remarked that the Indian Tramway Company had been allowed to build a line between Arconum and Conjeveram in the Madras Presidency on a gauge of 3 feet 6 inches. This line was 19 miles in length, and was opened to traffic on the 8th May 1865. Proposals to convert this gauge into the 5 feet 6 inches gauge and extend the line to Cuddalore and Pondicherry were made at intervals between 1866 and 1868. The Madras Government recommended in 1869 the extension to Cuddalore; but when the nature of the country through which the extension would have to pass was considered, that Government could "not recommend any departure from the present (3 feet 6 inches) gauge on which the line from Arconum to Conjeveram has been laid." In 1868 this line was included in the 3 per cent guarantee accorded to the Carnatic Railway Company, and in turn was in 1874 absorbed by the South Indian Railway Company under their 5 per cent guarantee. Its gauge was converted to the metre in July 1878.

A minute was recorded in 1869 by Sir John Lawrence, reviewing minutely the whole question of railway extension. It is dated the 9th January 1869, three days before Sir John Lawrence made over the high office of Viceroy and Governor-General of India to Lord Mayo. Little time was lost by Lord Mayo in reporting to the Secretary of State on the subject of railway extension in India, and in March of that year a series of despatches was sent home advocating the immediate construction of several lines of railway—some by the agency of companies, and some by direct State agency. The policy advocated was that an extension of railways was absolutely essential to the proper development of the resources of India; that the finances of India could not bear the burden of the proposed additional railways if constructed on the same expensive principle as had hitherto ruled; that Government was quite capable of making its own lines, and that as it could raise money cheaper than a company, to make its own lines was the more economical proceeding; that the position of several of the proposed lines was such as did not demand a first-class standard railway, and that either a lighter construction, or a narrower gauge, or both, could be adopted with economical advantage; and that Government, possessing its own railways, would be capable of exercising on the spot a more efficient and economical management than if administered by a Board of Directors in London. The Duke of Argyll was then Secretary of State for India, and he approved of Lord Mayo's proposals almost in their entirety.

The introduction of the metre gauge as the gauge for certain railways in India may be said to have arisen from this correspondence. The following portions of the correspondence [1] are those that bear on the question of a narrower gauge than the standard gauge of 5 feet 6 inches:—

42. There is only one other point to which I wish to refer. If there is one thing which comes out in more prominent relief than another in connection with railway construction in all parts of the world, it is this, that those lines are financially successful in which the capital accounts are kept down to a low amount, and those are unsuccessful in which this has not been accomplished. The lesson we should learn from this is, that the character of the line and the amount of expenditure upon it should be regulated as far as possible by a proper consideration of the possible returns, and not more than is essential by any preconceived ideas of what is the best standard form of railway to adopt. I regard it as the extreme of infatuation to lay down any absolute rules to regulate the modes of construction of railways in a country so vast, so various in its natural features, and so poor as India. Still more mistaken is it to apply to India rules essentially based on the wants of England, which is probably the country in the world from which India most widely differs. England, of all others the richest, the most populous, the most celebrated for its manufactures, the most addicted to commerce; an island of small size in a highly advanced state of civilisation, where despatch is of extreme importance and time equivalent to money; England of all countries is the last which we should take as our model in these things. In one respect certainly, but only in one, can I admit

[1] Sir John Lawrence's Minute, dated 9th July 1869.

that English standards are applicable—let all workmanship be thoroughly good of its kind, and every part of the construction permanent and suited to what is required of it.

43. Skill in engineering works implies the successful adaptation of the art of construction to varying circumstances. For a poor country, economy is one of the essential conditions to be complied with, and its requirements may be as rigid as any of those imposed by physical conditions. Wholly to reject railways for a country which is not able to support lines of the most costly description is quite unreasonable ; and if, on a further examination in detail of the probable cost and returns of any of the lines which otherwise seem desirable, the expense of lines of the ordinary gauge seems prohibitory, while lines of a narrow gauge would be financially practicable, I should consider it a most mistaken view to reject the narrow gauge line. And so with any other modification of ordinary practice. For complete success in the great operations which the Government of India has before it, broad views and a ready adoption of all truly sound measures, whether out of the usual course or not, are essential, and it will be a source of lasting regret if the progress of this country, which of all others most directly depends on the improvement of its means of internal communication, should be retarded by the weight of administrative prescription or engineering prejudice.

Again, discussing the question [1] of a line of railway between Pondicherry and either Madras or Arconum, the Government of India wrote :—

27. Although we are far from opposing the adoption of a narrow gauge railway when circumstances seem to indicate that proper financial results cannot otherwise be obtained, we are not inclined to acquiesce in the expediency of constructing short lengths of railway on a gauge different from that in common use. If narrow gauge lines are to have a fair field, they must be given a sufficient development to render the cost of shifting goods from their waggons to those of adjoining broad gauge lines unimportant

[1] Despatch to Secretary of State, No. 25, Railway, dated 11th March 1869.

in relation to the freight for the average distances over which the goods are carried. We do not think that this condition can be properly complied with, unless 100 or 200 miles at least of a narrow gauge system is constructed, and short of this we should not view favourably a proposal to execute narrow gauge lines in a country so easy as that immediately south of Madras. The known desire of the French Government to obtain a railway connection with Pondicherry by a line of the full Indian gauge should, we think, have much weight in the decision come to on this question; and on the understanding that the outlay will be kept down to the sum valued in the estimates that have been made, about £7000 per mile, we are clearly of opinion that the 5 feet 6 inches gauge for this railway should be adopted, as far at least as the point from which the line to Pondicherry would leave it.

In calling the attention of the Secretary of State to that portion of Sir John Lawrence's minute extracted above, the Government of India wrote:[1]—

19. The considerations which have led us to these conclusions also indicate that, under the conditions in which India is placed as to the provision of capital for railways, if it appears to be financially impossible to carry out railways on the full 5 feet 6 inches gauge, the Government should not hesitate to accept any other system of construction which will afford a practical means of extending these works. It is quite well known that perfectly useful and satisfactory lines have been carried out on a much narrower gauge, and it would be evidently unreasonable to reject the provision of such railways if they afford evidence of being profitable, while broader gauge lines, from their greater cost, could not be undertaken with financial propriety. These remarks more particularly apply to the more thinly-peopled and hilly tracts of the Peninsula and Central India. Across these Provinces, main lines on the full gauge have already been carried, giving communication between Bombay and Madras on the one side, and Bombay and the North-Western Provinces on the other; and whatever advantage is to be obtained by the possible transfer of the

[1] Despatch to Secretary of State, No. 28, Railway, of 22nd March 1869.

rolling stock of the north to the south of British India has thus been secured. For the further extension of the network of railways, no hesitation should be felt in accepting whatever system of construction is proved to be economically the best suited to each case.

20. We are disposed, as we indicated in our last despatch on this subject, No. 25, dated 4th March, to consider that too great importance has been attached to the value of uniformity of gauge beyond certain limits. That there are many conveniences in uniformity of gauge is, of course, evident, and in a compact, densely peopled, and highly-civilised country like England differences of gauge have been proved by experience to be inconvenient and are highly undesirable. But the inconveniences, where the distances to be gone over are very great, all the centres of population and trade are far apart, as is commonly the case in India, are of a secondary character. For passenger traffic, changes of vehicles, if not frequent, are a very minor objection, and are commonly enforced on passing from the lines of one company to those of another in every country. For goods, changes of vehicles represent a certain additional charge for loading out of one set of waggons into another. This charge will commonly not exceed the cost of transport for 10 miles of railway, and the practical inconvenience is no greater than that which would have been caused by such an addition to the distance over which the goods had to be carried.

21. The advantage obtained from any facilities of construction of locomotives for a broad gauge must be set off against the corresponding facilities of construction of the road and works for a narrow gauge; and where the traffic is likely to be light and the cost of construction high in comparison to the net profits, the balance may readily rest with the narrow gauge line.

22. It would always be our wish to conform to the 5 feet 6 inches gauge, if the financial objections to it were not insuperable; but we shall hope to receive your approval to our considering it an open question, when the prospects of the returns from any contemplated system of lines are not satisfactory, whether such lines might not be constructed on a narrow gauge, say 3 feet 6 inches instead of the ordinary broad Indian gauge.

The Duke of Argyll's despatch in answer to these despatches

from the Government of India makes no direct reference to the question of gauge, but merely remarks, in assenting to the principles enunciated, that the Secretary of State "concurs generally in your reasoning, and in the more important conclusions at which you have arrived."[1] A few months before this despatch was written, the Secretary of State had sanctioned the execution of a railway between Lahore and Rawalpindi as a State undertaking; and in this despatch he gave sanction to the commencement of a line down the Indus Valley, one from Delhi and Agra to the Sambhar Lake, another from Kulburga to Hyderabad (Deccan), and a fourth between Karwar and Hubli. It was on the question as to the proper gauge to be adopted on the Indus Valley and the Lahore-Rawalpindi lines that the battle of the Indian gauges was fought. As soon as the Secretary of State had given his sanction to the Government of India building its own lines of railway, Lord Mayo took up the matter in strong earnest. He wrote to America to obtain the services of an engineer who had had experience of the construction of light lines of railway, and a gentleman was selected and arrived in India.

The question of gauge for certain lines was also immediately taken up.[2] The propriety of adopting a narrower gauge, and thus reducing the first cost, for many branch railways, which were never likely to become through routes of communication, and the fact that lines on a gauge of 3 feet 6 inches had been adopted with more or less success in Norway, Queensland, Chili, and in the Madras Presidency, led the Government of India to think that such a gauge might well suffice for such branches as those from the main lines to the salt works at Sultanpur (near Delhi), to the salt works at Pind Dadan Khan in the Punjab, and for any lines that might be made in Burma. As sufficient information on the subject of cheap lines was not in the possession of the Government of India, the Secretary

[1] From Secretary of State, No. 42, dated 15th July 1869.

[2] Despatch to Secretary of State, No. 111, Railway, dated 16th October 1869.

of State was asked to obtain the best professional opinions of the day on the whole subject. The brief was worded as follows :—

> We do not desire that any absolute standard narrow gauge should be fixed, as the peculiar features of very difficult country may make such an extremely small gauge as that of the Festiniog Railway desirable in rare instances. At the same time, we are fully sensible of the disadvantages of a variety of gauges, even when the lines are not in connection, especially in the matter of obtaining stock and material; and we therefore should wish to ascertain what is considered by the highest authorities in England on such a subject to be the narrowest gauge compatible with carrying a passenger and goods traffic—say such as exists on an average branch line in England, at a speed of say 12 miles an hour—with efficiency and economy, the line being supposed to be constructed through country which presents no especial engineering difficulties and gradients not steeper than 1 in 100. Of course the economy of first construction must be duly considered and weighed against possible increased charge for working.

Before any report was received in answer to this request, the Government of India made a further representation to the Secretary of State,[1] recommending the more extended use of a narrow gauge for railways in India,[2] and making a distinct proposal that the Indus Valley and Lahore-Rawalpindi lines should be constructed on a gauge of not more than 3 feet 6 inches. The most serious objections to the use of a narrow gauge which had been felt in times past were "based on the practical difficulties met with in the construction, working and maintenance, in the repair of engines, and in the economical designing and safe working of the vehicle stock." But these objections had been overcome; the evidence which the Government of India had collected of the working of narrow gauge lines in other countries, and the interesting reports on

[1] To Secretary of State, No. 51, Railway, dated 17th May 1870.

[2] *Ibid.*, No. 52, Railway, dated 17th May 1870.

the Festiniog and on the Mid-Wales Railways which the Secretary of State had sent out to India,[1] clearly showed that the above objections to a narrow gauge had now been removed by the skill of the manufacturer, and there was abundant evidence to prove that a line could be constructed and stocked so as to carry, on a gauge of from 3 feet to 4 feet in width, all the traffic that was likely to seek any of the secondary lines yet to be constructed in India, if not indeed the traffic of the trunk system.

The proposal of the Government of India was, therefore, to divide the railway necessities of the country of India into two classes, and make a broad distinction between the railways hitherto constructed and which formed a connected system of trunk lines along the great political and commercial routes, and those lines which were about to be taken up and which were of secondary importance in the network of railways designed to open out the resources of India. These secondary lines, as proposed, were very extensive, and formed systems in themselves; and believing that if built on a smaller gauge the demands for traffic would be amply met, and a large saving effected in the initial cost, the Government of India came to the conclusion that substantially built narrow gauge lines were all that were necessary. The following paragraphs of the first despatch (No. 51, Railway) above quoted give the views of the Government of India:—

7. In easy country the saving in first cost of a narrow gauge line, compared with a line on the standard gauge, will be comparatively small. But in difficult country this saving may be increased very considerably, in some cases enormously, by the adoption of steep gradients and sharp curves, which have an important bearing on the location, and therefore on the outlay on the formation. By their introduction deep cuttings and high embankments are avoided with the heavy works necessary for passing the natural drainage through the latter. We may

[1] From Secretary of State, No. 23, dated 13th April 1870.

eliminate the effect of the gradients from this discussion as applicable alike to all gauges; but the economy in construction resulting from the adoption of sharp curves in a hilly country will be generally admitted, though it must also be admitted that, with the introduction of specially constructed engines and vehicles, sharp curves can be combined with retention of a wide gauge. There can, however, be no doubt that the narrower the gauge, the sharper are the curves possible; for whatever special construction be applied to the rolling stock, it is applicable to the stock of all gauges alike.

8. Apart, however, from all question of the saving that thus admits of being directly estimated, we are of opinion that the practical declaration involved in the adoption of a narrow gauge, that we are determined in all things to suit ourselves to the requirements of the country, and not to waste a rupee in perpetuating a standard of railway in excess of these requirements, merely because it exists in certain parts where it may, or may not, be suitable, will lead to economies in many indirect ways, the aggregate of which will be important, and will contribute towards the earlier consummation of the extensions already admitted to be required.

9. Firmly convinced of the sufficiency of a narrow gauge to carry the traffic of our secondary lines, and fully satisfied that an important economy must ensue in the aggregate over the whole extension system, we should fail in our duty to India if we hesitated to advocate the adoption of gauge narrower than the present standard. Whether that gauge should be 3 feet or 3 feet 6 inches is comparatively a matter of detail. As at present informed, we should regard 3 feet 6 inches as the maximum width that should be adopted. An early decision on the point is called for, so as to admit of timely arrangements being made for rolling stock, and we should be glad if your Grace would determine it after communication with the best authorities on the subject.

The Government of India in this despatch clearly indicated its desire to have good substantial lines of a narrow gauge than to have light lines with slow speed on the standard 5 feet 6 inches gauge. Not that a high speed of forty or fifty miles an hour drawn by heavy engines with a wheel-load of seven tons was ever intended on the narrow gauge lines, but the Government of India thought that the lines should be substantial enough to bear locomotives with a wheel-load of four tons and to stand a maximum speed of 25 miles an hour.

The Government of India proposed to make the whole length of line from Karachi to Lahore, and eventually on to Peshawur, on a narrow gauge. This involved converting about 319 miles between Karachi and Lahore, which was already opened to traffic, to the narrow gauge. The reasons adduced are given in the following extract from despatch No. 52, Railway, dated 17th May 1870:—

The present position of affairs is doubtless well known, but it will be convenient to describe it here. From Karachi to Rawalpindi a line of railway has been sanctioned, and there is little room for doubt that its extension to Peshawur will follow. The total distance by this route from the sea to Peshawur is 1080 miles, of which 320 miles [1] in two sections, separated from each other by 500 miles, have been constructed and stocked on the standard gauge, and are now being worked. Of the intervening 490 miles, the section between Mooltan and Kotri of about 300 miles in length has been surveyed, and the estimates are now under preparation. Of the section from Lahore to Peshawur, construction is just commencing on the 100 miles between Lahore and Jhelum, on the understanding that the rails will be laid on the Trunk Road to the standard gauge; beyond Jhelum, as far as Rawalpindi, the surveys are approaching completion. Between Kotri and Mooltan, and between Lahore and Jhelum, the country presents no features which would demand, on the score of economy in location, the adoption of a narrow gauge

	Miles.
[1] Karachi to Kotri	105
Mooltan (Rajghat) to Lahore	214
Total	319

in preference to the standard gauge. Beyond Jhelum the country is extremely difficult, and the improvements and diversions of the Trunk Road requisite to admit of rails being laid upon it must entail a heavy expense, which will be reduced the narrower the gauge and the sharper the curves adopted. In brief, the country is such as to indicate distinctly a narrow gauge for the 170 miles between Jhelum and Peshawur. Lahore, it should be added, is the north-west terminus of the standard gauge trunk lines from Calcutta and Bombay.

3. We have no hesitation in saying that were it a question of the section between Lahore and Peshawur alone, we should at once dismiss from consideration all idea of anything but a standard gauge line. The ordinary traffic on this route, with the exception of salt from the Pind Dadan Khan mines, is so small, that any railway of the smallest gauge or lightest rails would carry it. Commercially, the line has little to recommend it. Politically, it is of the highest importance, and in consequence, may, on emergency, be exposed to the demands of a heavy extraordinary traffic. To adopt a different gauge, then, from the lines terminating in Lahore would involve the necessity of maintaining a large stock in inactivity, so as to be prepared for the emergency. This would be a constant source of outgoing, in addition to the loss of interest on the capital sunk.

4. The question has, however, presented itself whether, as the gap between Mooltan and Kotri of 500 miles has yet to be constructed, the necessary reserve of stock might not be secured by adopting a narrow gauge for that line. It is true that the country is such that the saving by the adoption of a narrow gauge line would not, as respects the reduction that may be feasible in the works, be so great as in other parts of the plains of India; but there can be no doubt that, in a sparsely populated country like Sind, every possible reduction in the amount of work to be executed should be taken advantage of. There would, however, be a saving which, over 500 miles, may amount, it is roughly estimated, to £200,000, apart from any further saving which may be possible in stocking the line, or by using a light description of permanent-way. The adoption of a narrow gauge on this gap would, however, necessarily involve the relaying of the Sind and,

as far as Lahore, of the Punjab line on the same gauge. These lines are at present laid with rails of from 65 lbs. to 68 lbs. per yard, chiefly on timber sleepers, about 70 miles of the Punjab line being on iron bowls. The rails are heavier than would be required for the improved stock of the narrow gauge, but, together with the stock at present working over them, can be utilised elsewhere. The consent of the railway company would, of course, be necessary; but looking to the probable diminution of their capital account that would result from the laying of these lines with the lighter rails, and to the obvious advantage of uniformity of gauge throughout the Indus Valley, we apprehend that a proposal to this end would not prove unwelcome. The first opportunity under the contract of Government purchasing these undertakings is as yet remote; but it might suit the shareholders to surrender them in anticipation if the proposal were not regarded with favour. The difference of value between the old and new rails and stock should more than cover the cost of relaying.

5. Believing then that, irrespective of any saving in first cost by the use of a lighter description of permanent-way, the adoption of a narrow gauge would lead to a large saving on the cost of the 170 miles of line north of Jhelum, to a by no means insignificant saving in outlay on 500 miles between Mooltan and Kotri; also that lighter rails on a narrow gauge may be substituted on the existing railways in the Indus Valley without additional outlay, we would urge your Grace to accept the recommendation contained in our telegram already referred to, that a narrow gauge should be adopted for the entire line of railway from Karachi to Peshawur. As a light description of permanent-way may be combined with a broad gauge, we have not adduced the saving from its adoption in support of the narrow gauge, but we may mention that we estimate the saving by the use of lighter rails at about £400 a mile over the 760 miles of new line to be constructed. With light rails on a broad gauge, special engines, it should be noted, would be required. The poor returns hitherto realised on the Sind and Punjab Railways and on the Indus Flotilla do not justify our forming any sanguine expectation of an early remunerative traffic on the Indus Valley Railway, even when completed so as to form a through line of communication, and afford an

additional reason, if needed, for keeping down the outlay both on first cost and on working to the lowest possible limits.

On the 28th June 1870, probably after perusal of the above despatch, the Duke of Argyll sent the following telegram to Lord Mayo :—

> I am carefully considering narrow gauge question. Many objections raised. What does Lord Napier think regarding Indus Valley line on military interests involved?

The answering telegram was sent on 9th July 1870, and was as follows :—

> Lord Napier gives his opinion as follows: "Because nearly one-third of the line from Karachi to Lahore is laid and working on the broad gauge; because of the comparatively easy country of the remaining two-thirds; and especially because of the advantage of accumulating rolling stock of other lines for military emergencies, I am in favour of completing the Indus Valley line with broad gauge."—Opinion ends. Viceroy only remarks that if narrow gauge is built from Karachi to Peshawur, there will always be the rolling stock of the entire 1100 miles available for emergency on any short section, such as that above Lahore.

Lord Napier also remarked in his note of 7th July 1870, from which the above opinion was extracted, that there was immediate necessity for a line of railway to Peshawur; and as he noticed that Lord Lawrence, in his scheme for the extension of railways, had put down the Peshawur line to be completed in 1885 and the Indus Valley line in 1890, added that—

> Rather than see such a fatal delay, I should submit to any minor evil, such as a break of gauge. For instance, a narrow gauge might, I believe, be laid on the Lahore and Peshawur road to complete the communication from Jhelum in one year without turning a spadeful of earth, and would pay its value in political security and economy of transport by the time the main line, according to the programme in Sir John Lawrence's minute,

would be advanced to that point, and it might either be retained or transferred for branch lines to our hill stations.

Lord Mayo did not think that the actual state of the case was quite before Lord Napier when he recorded the above note, so he put an explanatory note on record.[1] He pointed out that no importance should be attached to the dates on the map accompanying Lord Lawrence's minute; that the Indus Valley line had been recommended to the Secretary of State as one of the first which should be made; and "that the rapidity of railway construction can only be regulated in the first instance by the financial strength of the Empire, and in the second by the power of organisation of establishment and labour" which it is possible to develop. Considering the extremely difficult nature of the country beyond Jhelum, and the resulting cost of a railway on the 4 feet 6 inches gauge, Lord Mayo also demonstrated that no line of railway ought to be made north of Jhelum which should be capable of carrying the stock of the East Indian or Delhi lines; and consequently "if a narrow gauge line is made the whole way from Karachi to Peshawur, the whole rolling stock of a line, 1100 miles in length, will always be available for working on any portion of the system; and therefore the narrow gauge, constructed as suggested, will give a much greater facility for the transport of troops and military stores from Lahore to all parts of the frontier, north or south, over that of a line which would be composed in part of light broad gauge line."

The Secretary of State again telegraphed to the Viceroy that strong opposition was being shown to the narrow gauge as applied to strategical lines of railway, but that there was a general agreement to the narrow gauge when the strategical lines had been completed. He again asked if the Government of India had fully considered how far the standard 5 feet 6 inches gauge, with a lighter rail, would be best for the

[1] Note by the Governor-General, dated 28th August 1870.

Peshawur and Indus Valley lines. In reply to this, the following telegram was sent on the 5th October 1870:—

The Punjab and Sind State Railways should in any case be laid with light rails suited to engines of moderate wheel weights, and the entire rolling stock should be capable of running from Peshawar to Karachi. The special engine stock will rule the transporting power of the line, whatever the gauge may be; and if light rails on standard gauge be adopted on northern and middle sections, we must provide new engines for whole length, otherwise efficiency of line on light sections, but particularly above Jhelum, will on an emergency be reduced by one-third compared with the line of uniform description throughout. For our views as to difficulty of country and character of line above Jhelum, see Railway Proceedings, No. 44, for August. I consider every line now contemplated north of the Nerbudda in a great degree strategical.

Meanwhile, in accordance with the desires of the Government of India, the Secretary of State had nominated a Committee of engineers to settle the actual width of narrow gauge lines which would be most suited to the wants of India. This Committee reported in September 1870, and the following summary of their proposals, and of opinions of several of the consulting engineers to the London Board of the Indian Guaranteed Railway Companies, is extracted from Mr. Danvers' Report on Indian Railways for the year 1870:—

12. A Committee, consisting of Colonel R. Strachey, R.E., C.S.I., Colonel C. H. Dickens, R.A., C.S.I., Mr. John Fowler, C.E., and Mr. A. M. Rendel, Consulting Engineer to the East Indian Railway Company, was accordingly appointed "to consider the precise gauge and general character for and average narrow gauge line of railway in India." The result of their investigations and deliberations was given in two reports—one containing the conclusions at which all the members of the Committee, except Mr. Fowler, had arrived; the other expressing

that gentleman's opinion alone. All, including Mr. Fowler, were in favour, on the ground of economy, of introducing a narrower gauge in India than the present standard of 5 feet 6 inches in districts where a break of gauge would not be productive of serious inconvenience, but they differ as to what that gauge should be. Colonel Strachey, Colonel Dickens, and Mr. Rendel recommended 2 feet 9 inches; Mr. Fowler, 3 feet 6 inches. The opinion of the former was based upon the conviction that to obtain the greatest economy in construction, and consequently the greatest possible extension of railways in India, the gauge selected should be not only narrow, but the narrowest which would combine convenience of transport for various goods and passengers with reasonable speed, and with economy and safety in working, and they were persuaded that these conditions would be fulfilled by a 2 feet 9 inches gauge. Mr. Fowler, on the other hand, was of opinion that a width of 3 feet 6 inches should be adopted, on the clear ground that it was not greater in first cost of works and rolling stock than a gauge of 2 feet 9 inches, and was greatly superior in carrying capacity, convenience, and economical working. The other members of the Committee considered that the cost of a railway was in proportion to its gauge; he did not. He felt, to secure the greatest simplicity and economy of construction and working in a locomotive, a gauge of 3 feet 6 inches was required. They thought that engines of sufficient power might be put on a 2 feet 9 inches gauge to draw at a sufficient speed the largest traffic which the lines for which a narrow gauge is suitable are likely to carry. The same differences of opinion on similar grounds are expressed in regard to the rolling stock of the respective gauges. Opinions were also given on the subject by Mr. John Hawkshaw, as Consulting Engineer to the Madras and the Eastern Bengal Railways, and by Mr. G. P. Bidder, as Consulting Engineer to the Sind, Punjab, and Delhi Railway. They are both opposed to the application of any other than the existing gauge to future lines which may be required as branches to extensions of the systems of railways with which they are connected. They attach great importance to the evils and inconveniences of a break of gauge, and contend that the very small saving, if any, which might be secured by the adoption of a narrow gauge would be more than counterbalanced by those disadvantages. Mr. Hawkshaw, however, admits in the early part of his report that if "it were a well-ascertained fact that there are districts in India where, having regard to financial reasons, a railway on a narrower gauge could be made, but where a railway on the existing gauge could not and ought not to be made, then that would be a case in which a narrow gauge might be considered as an absolute necessity." He calculates, upon certain assumptions, that the difference in the first cost of a heavy railway on the 5 feet 6 inches, and a light railway on the 3 feet 6 inches gauge would be £1810 per mile, and that saving in maintenance and renewals of permanent-way would be £50 per mile per annum, or, if capitalised at twenty years' purchase, £1000. He considers, however, that the object of economy would be best attained by constructing a lighter system of railways on the existing gauge, and calculates by this means £1250 per mile might be saved in the first cost, and £40 per annum in maintenance, or £800 capitalised. Thus, under the least favourable view of the case, a saving of about £800 per mile is admitted. The case above described in Mr. Hawkshaw's words would probably be regarded as the rule, instead of the exception, for future lines in India. If 10,000 miles are to be laid out, economy must be observed in the construction of every mile, and a saving of £800,000 in every thousand miles, or of £8,000,000 in 10,000 miles, becomes a matter of importance.

13. A much greater saving, however, is expected by the advocates of the narrow gauge. I may mention, in passing, that the estimates for the Carnatic Railway, on the broad and narrow gauge systems, made by Mr. C. Douglas Fox, the Consulting Engineer to that Company, show a saving of £1700 per mile in favour of the latter. The same capital would thus make 112 miles of the 5 feet 6 inches, or 151 miles of 3 feet 6 inches. I am informed, also, that in America 80 miles of a line which is to be 850 miles in length has been laid on a 3 feet gauge at a cost of £2500 per mile, including rolling stock, the rail being 30 lbs. to the yard, joined by fish-plates; the sleepers pine wood, 5 feet long, set 2 feet 6 inches apart.

14. The existence of another gauge in the country necessarily complicates the question of introducing a narrow one; and in some places and situations the inconveniences of a break of gauge may be so great, or the value of a line of communication for strategical purposes may be so impaired by it, as to make it worth while to pay the difference in cost; but under ordinary circumstances these kinds of difficulties may be greatly reduced by improved mechanical appliances and good traffic arrangements. The condition of things, moreover, in this country, where, within short distances, and with an immense traffic, a break of gauge has been found to be most burdensome and objectionable, is very different from that of India.

The Duke of Argyll answered the Government of India in despatch No. 72, dated 26th October 1870. Notwithstanding the very decided proposals made by the Government of India to make the Indus Valley and Peshawur lines on a narrow gauge, and the recommendations of a Committee to adopt a gauge of 2 feet 9 inches, and of one member of that Committee to adopt a gauge of 3 feet 6 inches, the Duke of Argyll would give no definite orders as to the kind of railway to be constructed over those lengths, or as to the width of the narrow gauge if such be adopted; but he confined himself to expressing his agreement with the desire of the Government of India to study rigid economy in the construction of these new railways, and eventually concluded by leaving the main questions to be decided by the Viceroy, Lord Mayo. This despatch is a very important one in the history of the gauge question.

The proceedings of the Government of India on receipt of this despatch are best summed up in the memorandum which Lord Mayo put on record,[1] stating his reasons for adhering to the previous policy of the Government of India, and deciding that the Indus Valley and Peshawur Railways should be on a narrow gauge, and that the width of that gauge should be 3 feet 3 inches. The question of adopting in India a metrical

[1] Dated 30th December 1870.

system of weights and measures was then under discussion by the Government of India, and a draft bill was actually before the Legislative Council. As the adopted gauge, 3 feet 3 inches, was so nearly the same as the proposed metrical standard, the narrow gauge for railways was changed very shortly afterwards from 3 feet 3 inches to 3 feet $3\frac{3}{8}$ inches, the length of a metre. The following is the memorandum :—

We recommended the adoption of the narrow gauge from Lahore to Peshawur, mainly on the grounds that it would be possible to construct the whole line from Lahore to Karachi on this principle; this would ultimately make available the entire ordinary rolling stock of 1100 miles of railway, which we conceive is amply sufficient for any military emergency.

The question, therefore, that we submitted to Her Majesty's Government was, whether it would be desirable to break the gauge between Mooltan and Kotri, it being assumed that, if this were decided in the negative, a narrow gauge railway northward from Lahore would not be recommended. After more than six months the whole question is now returned to us for final decision. The result will be that some considerable delay must take place in the commencement of active work on the Lahore and Jhelum line. This cannot be helped, and it is now our duty to arrive at a decision as rapidly as possible and forward it to the Secretary of State. We should endeavour then to recommend the construction of such a railway as will be amply sufficient for all the requirements of the country, and be constructed at the lowest possible cost. Our decision in this will definitely fix what the Indian narrow gauge is to be.

The history of our Indian railways does not show that a sudden outburst of traffic can reasonably be expected; and we cannot anticipate, in traversing less fertile and poorer countries than have hitherto been occupied by existing lines, the receipts we shall obtain in the first instance will increase in the same proportion as they occasionally do on American and European lines.

It is impossible to define with any degree of accuracy what the traffic on the new Indian railway is likely to be. The results of the Delhi and Lahore and Mooltan and Lahore lines are not encouraging, and I have no reason to suppose that they will suddenly improve. On the other hand, we must be certain that the railways we are about to construct will amply provide for all military wants and probable commercial requirements for a number of years.

I therefore asked the Council on our last meeting to consider whether we should adhere to our former recommendation, that a narrow gauge should be adopted between Lahore and Karachi on one side, and Lahore and Peshawur on the other. The Council having come unanimously to the conclusion that we should abide by our former recommendation, renders it unnecessary to discuss that question further. A similar conclusion was also arrived at with regard to the Rajputana and Central India lines.

It remains, therefore, only to consider what should be the dimensions of the narrow gauge line which it will be our duty now to recommend to the Secretary of State.

The great differences of opinion which exist between the high authorities who were consulted by the Secretary of State in this matter, as shown in the accompanying papers, involves us in much difficulty.

In considering unprofessionally such a subject, and in endeavouring to arrive at a sound conclusion as between the two narrow gauges recommended, viz. 3 feet 6 inches and 2 feet 9 inches, we can only be guided by experience and authority. In this view there is no doubt that we should be quite safe in adopting the 3 feet 6 inches gauge; for it has been well and effectively tried, and is admitted to be sufficient for the conveyance of a large amount of traffic.

It is also a fact worthy of notice, that those Governments and authorities who are now desirous of providing cheap narrow gauge railways, namely Russia, Canada, Queensland, and Norway, have all adopted the 3 feet 6 inches gauge.

In Norway a railway of that dimension, 120 English miles long, exists, and it is generally admitted that it has proved to be completely suited to the light traffic of that country.

No such experience is available with regard to the 2 feet 9 inches gauge. The only line of any length of such small dimensions that I know of is the Festiniog Railway. This is a short line, 2 feet gauge, with comparatively heavy rails, 49 lbs. per yard; it is worked in a hilly country under peculiar circumstances.

Therefore we have, as between a 3 feet 6 inches and a 2 feet 9 inches gauge, little or no practical experience to guide us. We know very little of the latter, but we know that the former has succeeded.

I have no means of showing very precisely the difference of cost between a 3 feet 6 inches and a 2 feet 9 inches gauge.

Mr. Fowler, in paragraph 24 of his letter, puts the difference of cost between a 3 feet 6 inches and a 2 feet 9 inches railway at £82, 10s. per mile for Scotland and £45 for Norway; for the Indus Valley he puts it at £45 a mile with iron, and £110 with wooden sleepers; but he says that in consequence of the additional length and cost of siding which a 2 feet 9 inches gauge would require, the relative cost would scarcely differ. He further states that, with regard to bridges, the dimensions for the strength and stiffness required would always include the width of a railway of a 3 feet 6 inches gauge.

The weight of rails would probably be the same. I am not an advocate of very light rails on any Indian railway, and would recommend a rail proportionately lighter than the 60 lbs. Oude and Rahilkund rail, which would be about 40 lbs. for a narrow gauge.

On the whole, therefore, according to the information at our disposal, I cannot put the difference of cost as between a 3 feet 6 inches and a 2 feet 6 inches gauge with wooden sleepers, and say a 40 lbs. rail, at a greater amount than £100 a mile. This over the distance from Mooltan to Kotri and from Lahore to Peshawur, which is about 700 miles, makes only a difference of £70,000—a sum which is hardly to be regarded if very superior advantages can be obtained.

I have no reason to suppose that the working expenses of a 3 feet 6 inches or a 2 feet 9 inches railway would differ very materially.

The size of the carriages on the different gauges proposed is a matter of the first importance.

I assume that in most railways, and especially those of narrow gauge, the width of the carriage in the clear may be equal to double the width of the gauge.

I am not aware whether on any first-class line carriages whose platforms are double the width of the gauge are actually at work; but Mr. Fowler appears to be of opinion, in paragraph 13 of his letter, that there can be no objection to a 3 feet 6 inches gauge bearing a carriage 7 feet wide. But in none of the papers placed at my disposal does the possibility of increasing the breadth of the carriage beyond this proportion appear to be contemplated.

Whether it would be safe then to put a carriage 6½ feet or 7 feet wide upon wheels 2 feet 9 inches apart, or a carriage 8 feet wide upon 3 feet 6 inches wheels, I can give no opinion which would be of value. This is a point for engineers to discuss, and one that I suspect nothing but practical experience would satisfactorily solve. I am not aware that the experiment has been tried, and certainly in ordinary conveyances steadiness could not be obtained under such conditions. I believe, therefore, that twice the width of the gauge is the limit of breadth in the construction of our carriages which we ought to recommend.

If we adhere to the principle that this limit ought not to be exceeded, it would take 6 inches off the internal width of the vehicles, and render a carriage of the 2 feet 9 inches gauge 5 feet wide; of a 3 feet gauge, 5 feet 6 inches wide; of a 3 feet 3 inches gauge, 6 feet wide; and of a 3 feet 6 inches gauge, 6 feet 6 inches wide.

I am inclined to think that from 6 feet to 6 feet 4 inches is the least width that can be conveniently given to a carriage to carry four passengers seated across. I put European and first-class passenger traffic out of the question altogether. With 6 feet 4 inches you could get 19 inches for four passengers in a row, which is one-fifth of an inch less than is now given to the new third-class carriages on the East Indian Railway, and which is not more than sufficient.

There is no advantage to be obtained either in gradients or curves as between any of the gauges. This, however, may be doubted as between a very broad gauge and a very narrow one; but certainly no increased facility in either gradients or curves is gained by a 2 feet 9 inches gauge over one of 3 feet 6 inches or 3 feet 3 inches.

A very serious further objection which is urged to the very narrow gauge is, I believe, that which is described in the 12th paragraph of Mr. Fowler's letter as regards locomotives. Mr. Fowler, who is a high authority on a practical question of this kind, states from experience that, in order to secure the greatest simplicity and economy in construction and working, a gauge of 3 feet 6 inches is required for the engine.

He says that a locomotive may be constructed for almost any gauge, but that no locomotive, simple or strong, can be made with any great chance of success to work on a gauge less than 3 feet 6 inches; and I may add, in confirmation of this opinion, that Mr. Fell told me in regard to his engines, the great mechanical difficulty with which he had to contend was the extreme narrowness of his gauge, which is 3 feet 7½ inches: this obliged the mechanism to be compressed into so small a compass that, unless workmanship and material of the very first class were used, breakages were always occurring.

The defective character of his machinery, which was made in Paris, has been the greatest difficulty with which Mr. Fell has had to contend from the commencement of his enterprise. No undue weight, however, should be attached to this opinion, because the mechanism for working the central rail complicates the ordinary construction of the locomotive, and I am told that it has lately been found desirable to use two engines on Mr. Fell's railway, one for the central and the other for the outer rails. However, it must be recollected that Mr. Fell's gauge is 10½ inches wider than that advocated by Colonel Dickens and Colonel Strachey.

With regard to the carrying capacity, it is affirmed by Mr. Fowler that a 3 feet 6 inches gauge has a carrying capacity of 63 per cent greater than the 2 feet 9 inches. I am not prepared to adopt this opinion without further proof, but still it is a statement gravely made on high authority.

It is said that even a 2 feet 9 inches gauge might be too much for the wants of the country, and that if a 3 feet 6 inches width were adopted, the stock would be little lighter than the existing stock of the East Indian Railway.

I cannot but think that the power of considerably increasing the carrying capacity of a railway is a great recommendation in its favour, because for the earlier periods of its existence it will be quite possible to build lighter and smaller vehicles than will ultimately be used.

But lightness is by no means regulated by gauge, and we can build as light a carriage on the standard gauge as on any other.

The weight of the carriage ought to be regulated, as nearly as possible, by the exact work it is expected to perform.

I think, therefore, these papers demonstrate that there is no important difference in cost between a 3 feet 6 inches and a 2 feet 9 inches gauge; that experience shows that a strong serviceable railway on the former size can be made with perfect success; that no difficulties with regard to locomotives are likely to occur; that its carrying capacity is considered much greater, and that, as far as passenger traffic is concerned, more comfort and convenience can be obtained than on the narrow line.

I cannot venture to say that the applicability of a railway to India on the 2 feet 9 inches gauge is disproved. Hereafter it may turn out that it deserves all that has been said of it. But, on the other hand, it must be admitted that weighty objections have been urged against it; whereas as regards the gauge 9 inches wider success is proved, and it is certain that it possesses requirements sufficient to provide for the locomotive wants of a country where a limited amount of traffic only can be expected, and considerable distances have to be traversed.

I confess I am unwilling to embark on anything in the shape of an experiment in a matter of such enormous importance. An error made now would be irreparable.

We must endeavour by every means to secure the most absolute certainty of success.

I have the greatest respect for the ability and judgment of the experienced engineers who have recommended the 2 feet 9 inches gauge, but the responsibility of selection now devolves upon my shoulders, and I am not prepared to recommend the adoption in India of any system which has not stood the test of experience, and is not supported by the almost unanimous opinion of skilled engineers.

I think, therefore, that the adoption of a 3 feet 6 inches gauge would be a thoroughly safe course for us to take; but if a 3 feet 3 inches one will provide for all the possible requirements of the country, I should prefer it. Some saving in cost would be gained. The small reduction in width could not affect the locomotive question, and a considerable economy of space would be obtained. This would give a carriage of 6 feet width in the interior, and would seat four third-class passengers in a row, allowing 18 inches to each seat.

This is quite as small accommodation as, in my opinion, ought to be given, and I have some doubts whether it is quite sufficient.

On the Eastern Bengal Railway, the horse-boxes are 8 feet in the clear, 7 feet in the interior, divided into three partitions, two of 2 feet 6 inches, and the middle one of 2 feet. This is, I think, too small.

The 3 feet 3 inches gauge would give, according to these proportions, a horse-box 6 feet 6 inches in the clear, and 5 feet 6 inches in the interior. This would give a space for two horses abreast of 2 feet 9 inches each (including the partition), which is precisely the space allowed on the horse-boxes of the East Indian Railway.

If, however, a great number of horses have to be moved in a short time, horse-boxes would be little used; and if a rapid transit is desired for military objects, the main portion of the troopers must always be carried in ordinary goods waggons.

Six feet in the interior of a vehicle will be sufficient to carry gun-carriages for the heaviest artillery whose wheels do not, in scarcely any case, exceed 5 feet 3½ inches.

For goods traffic, especially for the bulky goods, such as unpressed cotton, jute, etc., the additional space will be very valuable; and if a very small traffic is expected, short carriages can be used.

I incline to the opinion that the 40 lb. rail should be adopted, because it is the weight which experience shows has been most generally adopted for lines of this dimension, and bears a fair proportion to the 60 lb. rails of the Oude and Rahilkund standard gauge. But at the same time I do not wish to say more than that, with 3 tons on the engine wheel, and 2 tons on the waggon wheel, the rail should not be lighter than 36 lbs. to the yard. The final decision on this must be reserved until the precise character of engines and stock on each line is determined.

It appears that in such a country as the Indus Valley or Rajputana a railway of this kind ought to be built for less than £5250 a mile, and according to Colonel Strachey for £2645 less than the standard gauge with 60 lb. rails, or £1707 less than the standard gauge with 45 lb. rails; and it is probable that as we gain experience, the cost might be considerably lessened.

According to the best consideration I can give to this extremely difficult question, I recommend the adoption of a 3 feet 3 inches gauge.

This decision as to the width of the narrow gauge, and as to the lines that were to be made on that gauge, was duly reported to the Secretary of State.[1] These despatches stated that the Government of India generally accepted the views expressed by the Duke of Argyll in paragraphs 5 to 11 of his despatch No. 72, Railway, dated 26th October 1870, already quoted, "as to the main military and financial considerations that arise, and that we are satisfied that the economy likely to be obtained from the adoption of the narrow gauge will justify our accepting the break of gauge at Lahore with such inconveniences as it involves." The matter had been left to the decision of the Governor-General; and no sooner had Lord Mayo given his verdict in favour of the narrow gauge, than orders were issued that the Indus Valley railway, the Lahore-Rawalpindi line, the lines in Rajputana from Agra and Delhi towards Ajmere, and the line from the Great Indian Peninsula Railway to Indore in Central India should be constructed on the narrow gauge. The section between Lahore and Jhelum had already been commenced as a light railway on the 5 feet 6 inches gauge, but the work had not progressed sufficiently far to cause any considerable alterations to be required for the narrower gauge. Surveys and estimates for the other lines were then proceeded with on the basis of the gauge being a metre; and the construction of the lines on that gauge was vigorously prosecuted.

[1] Despatches Nos. 2, Railway, and 3, Railway, of 10th January 1871.

During the year 1870 the London newspapers contained many proposals for narrow gauge and light railways, and many were the arguments brought forward showing their superiority over the ordinary standard gauges. In a report on the Festiniog Railway to the Secretary of State for the Colonies by Mr. (now Sir) G. L. Molesworth, who was at that time Director of Public Works in Ceylon, the merits and demerits of these lines were discussed. His conclusions were that the arguments claimed for the 2 feet gauge of the Festiniog line were not borne out by the facts of the case, and that its superiority over the ordinary gauge of 4 feet 8½ inches under all circumstances was quite delusive. The merits of narrow gauge lines were, however, from time to time still discussed in the newspapers; and when it became known that it was decided to construct the Indus Valley and the Lahore-Rawalpindi Railways on a narrow gauge, the outcry was great. First and foremost in vehemence against the decision was Mr. Lee Smith, the engineer who had been originally sent out by the Secretary of State to construct the Lahore-Rawalpindi Railway, but who had left the Government service before much advance had been made in the prosecution of the works; and the protests were continued by many engineers of high professional standing in England. Mr. Lee Smith maintained that he could construct a light railway on the 5 feet 6 inches gauge from Kotri to Mooltan and from Lahore to Peshawur for a sum of money differing only very slightly from the accepted estimates for those lines on the metre gauge, and stated that a firm of contractors were prepared to carry out the works on the strength of his estimates. During 1872 considerable correspondence took place between Mr. Lee Smith and the Secretary of State, and this was transmitted to India for information. It was, however, not quite understood whether this correspondence was only sent for information, or whether the Secretary of State desired an expression of opinion from the Government of India (Lord Northbrook, Governor-General) as to the question of the break of gauge on the two railways. The Duke of Argyll, however, telegraphed that he had hitherto considered the question of gauge as settled, and deprecated any action which might unsettle that decision. The desultory discussion amongst the engineers in England, however, still continued; and as it was much desired to discuss the matter in a rational manner, the Secretary of State permitted the reading of a paper on the subject before the Institute of Civil Engineers. This paper, which was read on the 4th February 1873 by Mr. W. T. Thornton, C.B., the Secretary for Public Works at the India Office, stated simply and openly the reasons which led the Government of India to adopt a narrower gauge, and was followed by a lengthy, and at times acrimonious, discussion.

No direct action was taken on this discussion, but it led shortly afterwards to a discussion on the same subject in the House of Commons; and although much difference of opinion was expressed during the debate, "Mr. Gladstone intimated that the arguments on both sides would be carefully examined in the light of the discussion, and in the light of such other facts and arguments as may be considered to bear upon the policy involved." In consequence of all this opposition to the change of gauge, and in conformity with the promise made by the Prime Minister in the House of Commons, the Duke of Argyll reviewed the whole state of the case in a lengthy despatch to the Government of India.[1] In this review the Secretary of State showed that lines on the 5 feet 6 inches gauge connect the three presidency towns of India, and also are in connection with the principal centres of commerce in the Ganges valley and as far north as Lahore; that the amount of money sunk in guaranteed capital of railways was very large —nearly £94,000,000—and that the produce of the railways only returned a very small percentage on the outlay; and that as far as the commercial aspects of the districts round Lahore

[1] Despatch from Secretary of State, No. 54, Railway, of 27th March 1873.

were concerned, it appeared that, Karachi being its natural outlet, a railway on the metre gauge would amply cope with commercial demands. But as far as the military requirements of the north-west frontier are concerned, the matter might now be different; it was on this aspect of the question that doubts of the soundness of the policy pursued had been raised. With reference to these arguments, and dismissing the question of danger in India from internal disturbance, the Duke of Argyll wrote:—

29. It is evident, therefore, that whatever special importance is attached in many minds to the adoption of the standard gauge beyond Lahore is connected with the special danger of invasion from without.

30. On this important part of the subject, the facts presented by the recent war in Europe have very naturally had a powerful influence on opinion. And I have no hesitation in saying that, if the circumstances of India were the same, or had even any analogy with the circumstances of France and Germany, the argument for uniformity of gauge would be conclusive.

31. I have therefore to direct your attention to the difference, amounting to contrast, which exists between the two cases.

32. All the leading States of Europe are in close contact with other nations having armies more or less equal to their own—possessing at least the same advantages of science, of organisation, and of speedy access to their mutual frontiers. The consequence is, that in all these cases great armies with powerful artillery can be placed at very short notice in a position to invade their neighbours.

33. Since the defeat and dissolution of the army which had been trained under Runjeet Singh, and the conquest of the Punjab, no similar conditions exist on our Indian frontier. There is no nation upon that frontier, or for many hundred miles beyond it, with any military science, with any trained or regular army, or with any artillery whatever.

34. I do not place out of view the possibility—although I do place it in a distant future—of a great European power organising

offensive operations from beyond the north-west frontier. But even if such operations were possible at the present time, we may be sure of this, that no such invasion of India from that quarter could be effected without the threatened danger being known to us not only many weeks, but many months, before it could actually arise.

The conclusions arrived at by the Secretary of State were that a metre gauge railway from Karachi through Lahore to Peshawur would be amply sufficient for the trade of the country; that such a line would also suffice for all military demands in the event of a war on the frontier; and that, consequently, only weighty considerations of political necessity would induce him to reopen the question of the gauge of these frontier lines. The following are the concluding paragraphs of the despatch :—

37. In connection with such a system of narrow gauge lines, and a view to increase the amount of rolling stock available upon portions of it, it may be wise ultimately to lay down a third rail on the section of the trunk line between Lahore and Delhi, thus bringing into play the whole carriage accommodation of the projected Rajputana line. But even without this junction, the amount of rolling stock on the Indus Valley and Punjab lines alone would be sufficient, within very moderate limits of time, to afford the most important facilities for military movement.

38. It has indeed been argued, not unnaturally, that if the danger of invasion be really so slight and so distant, these frontier lines should not be made at all. But this does not follow. The time which would be ample for the working of a narrow gauge line, with even the narrowest estimate of accommodation, would not be adequate for the construction of any line whatever. Moreover, although an invasion requiring the concentration of great armies is a very remote danger, border forays and disturbances, and even incursions of a more serious character, are possible and probable enough. These, if unchecked and unpunished, are never without effect on the tranquillity of India. To meet these, the facilities which would be afforded by the narrow gauge in

moving amply sufficient bodies of men are facilities so valuable and important, that we are bound to place them in the hands of the Government of India, if we can do so at a moderate cost.

39. These are the considerations which mainly determine my assent to the construction of lines in the Punjab and down the valley of the Indus ; and I still regard them as sufficient, provided these lines can be constructed on the cheaper system now generally admitted to be suitable for subsidiary lines.

40. Your Excellency will doubtless bear in mind that the Khyber Pass is not the only, nor even perhaps the most probable, direction in which the invasion of India by a large army would be attempted. If, therefore, this danger is to determine our policy, we must be prepared to extend the more costly gauge of railways to much more distant points, and indeed to construct the whole system of lines in connection with the Indus Valley on the same scale of outlay. If the cheaper gauge be adopted throughout, there will be no break of gauge beyond our military base throughout the whole provinces of the Punjab and of Sind. But the evil of a break of gauge, whatever it may be, will at once arise unless the standard be adopted not only for the line to Peshawur, but for all other lines which may yet have to be constructed in those provinces.

41. Your Excellency will also doubtless bear in mind that although attempts have been made to show that the expense of working and of maintenance on the standard gauge need not be materially greater than on the narrow gauge, yet these attempts must be regarded as based on the same methods of reasoning which you have rejected as regards the cost of construction. The additional capital which is sunk in construction is therefore only part of the loss which will be incurred. The dead weight arising out of annual loss on traffic will be heavily increased on lines which must be of a comparatively unremunerative character, and the difficulty you experience in diminishing expenditure and in abstaining from new taxation will be increased.

42. Lastly, looking to the many other lines into and through richer provinces of India which are now competing for the favourable attention of your Government, but from which I have been obliged to withhold or to suspend my sanction until clearer

evidence be forthcoming as to their remunerative character, I am bound to say that nothing, in my opinion, short of very weighty considerations of political necessity would justify such a large increase of cost on the subsidiary lines as that which you report would be involved in a departure from the decision of Lord Mayo's Government on the gauge of those lines.

43. Should any such considerations suggest themselves to your mind, I shall deem it my duty to weigh them carefully in Council. But short of such considerations, and on any mere balance of arguments less grave in character, I should be reluctant to reverse a decision which has not only been deliberately made, but has been already, to a large extent, acted upon, and any departure from which must involve such considerable sacrifices to the revenues of India.

This despatch was received in India in April 1873, and the position of affairs at the time was as follows. Considerable progress had been made on the Punjab Northern Railway on the metre gauge, and the girders for the bridges over the Ravi, Chenab, and Jhelum rivers were made for the narrow gauge. On the Indus Valley Railway work on the metre gauge had been progressing fairly well, and a good start had been made on the bridging of the flood openings required to pass the spill waters of the Indus. Also on both lines a large outlay had been incurred in permanent-way, locomotives, and rolling stock adapted to the metre gauge, and a good deal of this material was already in the country. No arrangements had been entered into or proposals made to the Sind, Punjab, and Delhi Railway Company for the provision of a third rail along their line between Karachi and Kotri and between Mooltan and Lahore, so that, as far as was contemplated at that time, there would be a break of gauge at Kotri and another at Mooltan. Moreover, the contract with the Sind, Punjab, and Delhi Railway Company was not determinable until 1885, so that any radical alterations of their lines could only be accomplished by arrangement. In order, therefore, to have the question of gauge again thoroughly discussed from a military and political point of view, and quite independently of the commercial aspect, the opinions of the Commander-in-Chief and his military advisers were sought, as were also those of Colonel C. H. Dickens, R.A., then Secretary to Government of India in the Public Works Department, and of Mr. (now Sir) G. L. Molesworth, the Consulting Engineer to the Government of India for State Railways. All these opinions were attached to the answering despatch sent to the Secretary of State.[1] As they, and more particularly the notes by Colonel Dickens and Mr. Molesworth, formed very important features in the correspondence, and serve to indicate the change of ideas regarding these frontier lines which was at work in the Government of India, it is necessary to give in some detail the nature of the arguments and opinions therein expressed.

The Commander-in-Chief was asked if the military considerations involved in making the Indus Valley and Punjab Northern Railways on the metre gauge were of such magnitude as to justify the Government of India to revert to the old 5 feet 6 inches gauge, and to incur the large and fruitless expense that such a reversion would involve. The superiority of the broad gauge for military transport purposes was at once admitted, but the Commander-in-Chief was asked to support his opinion with statistics giving the relative value of the two gauges for military purposes, and the effect of a break of gauge in the movement of such bodies of troops as Lord Napier might think likely to require to be moved in the case of war on the north-west frontier. A practical example of concentrating 10,000 men and 36 guns was worked out by the Quarter-Master-General, and the relative capabilities of the broad and narrow gauge railways shown in an elaborate memorandum drawn up by Colonel F. Roberts, R.A., V.C., now Lord Roberts. In forwarding this to Government, Lord Napier remarked "that the arguments and statistics contained

[1] Despatch to Secretary of State, No. 140 Railway, 19th July 1873.

in the memorandum not only conclusively prove the great advantage which the broad gauge possesses over the narrow for military purposes, but he believes, moreover, that they would even now justify the Government of India in undertaking the expense of a reversion to the $5\frac{1}{2}$ feet gauge on both the Indus Valley and the Punjab Northern Railways." It had been ordered that the Punjab Northern Railway should, as far as possible, use a portion of the grand trunk road north of Lahore, and the works then being carried out occupied a portion of that road almost continuously between Lahore and Wazirabad, a distance of 60 miles. Among other deductions drawn from the Quarter-Master-General's memorandum was the one "that if the narrow gauge be determined upon, the railway will be used almost exclusively for the transport of stores, etc., and the great mass of the troops will have to march: it is, therefore, most essential that they should be able to do so with speed and regularity." Consequently the Commander-in-Chief represented the vital importance of keeping the grand trunk road free for the movements of troops by route march. Quite apart, however, from the deductions drawn from Colonel Roberts' memorandum, the Government of India had already recognised that their original orders to lay important railways on existing roads required modification, as the existence of a railway did not do away with the necessity of parallel road communication: consequently this point was readily recognised and used in the answering despatch to the Secretary of State.

The Consulting Engineer for State Railways also submitted an elaborate report on the whole question.[1] Mr. (now Sir) Guilford Molesworth commenced his report with the remark that the adoption of the narrow gauge for State railways in India had been settled before his arrival in India, and that he had been informed that the question was not to be reopened.

[1] Report on the question of the gauge for State Railways of India, dated 23rd June 1873.

In an annual report he had, however, stated his "conviction that a break of gauge was a very serious evil, and that it should, if possible, be avoided; that a break of gauge was better than no railway; and that having adopted the narrow gauge, the more it is connected and extended into one large system, the less will its evils be felt." Mr. Molesworth had before him the memorandum by the Quarter-Master-General (above referred to), and he showed the locomotives and stock designed for the metre gauge lines were little, if at all, inferior to the stock then running on English railways. Discussing the whole matter impartially, he arrived at the following conclusions :—

1. The capacity of the metre gauge stock is sufficient for all purposes of railway transport.
2. The carriages and waggons on the metre gauge railway are nearly equal in capacity to the ordinary stock of English railways.
3. The locomotives designed for *low* speed on the metre gauge are equal in tractive force to the large express engines designed for high speed on English railways.
4. The rolling stock for the metre gauge will be perfectly safe at a speed twice as great as that proposed for the State railways of India.
5. The metre gauge, in my opinion, is sufficient for all commercial and military purposes.
6. The cost of a broad gauge railway (60 lb. rails), with structures designed for the engines and other rolling stock of the guaranteed railways, will (excluding very large bridges) exceed the cost of the narrow gauge by £1650 or £2000 per mile.
7. The cost of a broad gauge railway (45 lb. rails), with structures designed only for the carriage and waggon stock of the guaranteed railways (*but not for the engines*), will exceed the cost of a narrow gauge railway by £720 or £1000 per mile.
8. The cost of a broad gauge railway (40 lb. rails), with

structures designed for the same axle loads as the narrow gauge, will exceed the cost of a narrow gauge railway by £350 or £500 per mile.

9. The last of these three would practically be as great an obstacle to the interchange of traffic as if a break of gauge existed.
10. There will be no appreciable difference between the working expenses of the broad and narrow gauge railways.
11. The break of gauge in a commercial point of view, though an evil, is not one sufficient to justify the commendation of the narrow gauge.
12. The break of gauge in a military point of view is a *very serious evil.*
13. A reserve of 1000 vehicles will suffice for any military emergency on the frontier.

Mr. Molesworth then proceeded to discuss from a military point of view the several railways in Western India with reference to strategical positions. He recommended a comprehensive system of narrow gauge lines which would include the Punjab Northern, Indus Valley, and Rajputana lines, and would necessitate the conversion to narrow gauge of the Sind, Punjab and Delhi, and the Bombay, Baroda, and Central India Railways. If such a system were adopted and a uniform policy kept in view, he considered that the adoption of the narrow gauge would be completely justified. But if, on the other hand, the Government should consider that such a comprehensive system was too remote or too difficult of attainment, and that the narrow gauge system would remain a series of railways isolated and disconnected, then he considered that the introduction of the metre gauge system was a mistake. Mr. Molesworth showed by comparative estimates what it would cost to convert the works on the Indus Valley and Punjab Northern lines into broad gauge lines; also that, with a 45 lb. rail and a light class of engine, the conversion could be effected for an increase of about 15 per cent on the estimated cost for metre gauge, and that in his opinion the maintenance of uniform gauge is worth that additional expenditure.

Colonel (now General) Dickens, the then Secretary in the Public Works Department, reviewed the whole case in a note which was attached to the answering despatch. In this he stated his concurrence in most of the arguments which Mr. Molesworth had brought forward, and supported that gentleman entirely in the sufficiency of the metre gauge even for military operations. Colonel Dickens also added that "the cases which would attach to the delay of one day, which the break of gauge at Lahore would occasion, might be left out of consideration. But there are more weighty opinions on the opposite side, and by those he thinks the Government should be guided, seeing that if they err, they err on the safe side." He thoroughly approved of the decision to make narrow gauge lines, as the Government could not afford to enter on any general extension of railways without studying the greatest economy, and selecting the lines as to ensure a quick return for the outlay. But as regards the two particular lines in question, the Indus Valley and the Punjab Northern, his—

> Own opinion was against the change from broad to narrow gauge in 1870-71, not from any doubt as to the capabilities of the narrow gauge, but from the conviction that these two lines would be generally regarded as part of the trunk system of railways in India, and as important chiefly in view to political and military objects. If any military emergency, such as to call these lines into use under severe pressure, was really to arise, the break of gauge would be a very serious matter. And if no such emergency arose, the knowledge that there was such a serious obstacle to their use would detract from the moral effect of the works. These reasons were in his opinion sufficient at least to make these lines undesirable to select as the first to be constituted on the narrow gauge. It is true that the military communication would be the better for a railway on the narrow gauge than without any railway at all. But still, the importance attached to the break of gauge,

and the dissatisfaction with which a narrow gauge in such a situation would be regarded, seemed more than to balance the financial advantage.

Colonel Dickens also stated that having been absent on leave when the decision was come to, he had not had occasion before to express this opinion officially. Another reason which guided him in thinking that the Indus Valley line should be on the broad gauge was that already 324 miles out of the 814 between Lahore and Karachi were laid and working on the broad gauge; and it was only on the conversion of these parts into narrow gauge that the line between Lahore and Peshawur was to be dependent for its extra rolling stock in cases of emergency. Regarding the adoption of the 5 feet 6 inches gauge with lighter rails, Colonel Dickens remarked:—

The adoption of the broad gauge with light rails and rolling stock would enable us to utilise much of the narrow gauge material, and would save time and money therefore. But if a change is made for military and political reasons, it should, I think, be thorough, and leave no doubt that these railways will be completely efficient and equal to all requirements of a military emergency, as much as the lines which are connected with them. In spite of all contrivances and precautions, I feel doubts of the possibility, under pressure of emergency, of keeping the heavy engines of guaranteed lines off the two lines in question; and to admit them would be to injure seriously these lines when most required to be efficient. If a change is to be made, therefore, I would adopt the 5½ feet gauge with a 60 lb. rail.

Colonel Dickens concluded his note thus:—

If any military mishap should occur after the establishment on these lines of the narrow gauge the Government would be said to have courted disaster. Nothing of the kind can be laid to their charge if they adopt the style of construction which has been in use in India heretofore to the satisfaction of the highest military authorities. Hereafter, when the metre gauge shall have been tried and gained confidence, it may be quite proper to introduce it on the Indus Valley and Lahore and Peshawur lines. But for the present I come (very unwillingly, I confess) to the conclusion that the progress of the works should be so far delayed as to allow of the introduction of the 5½ feet gauge with the 60 lb. rail.

I think also that the occupation by the railway of the Lahore and Peshawur road should be given up. But the railway should be by no means taken to such a distance from the road as to be out of reach of easy military communication throughout the route.

The extra expense of the adoption of the broad gauge in this case I would regard as a military and political expense, and not as a part of the general system for the extension of railways in India.

The extra cost of adopting the broad gauge with the 60 lb. rail instead of the narrow gauge with the 40 lb. rail is estimated by Mr. Molesworth at .	£1,536,200
To abandon the trunk road between Lahore and Jhelum, as well as between Jhelum and Peshawur, would probably cost	360,000
Total	£1,896,200

But if the railway be terminated northwards at Attock, as I think it should be, the difference will be reduced by £171,500, leaving the extra charge to be incurred in round numbers at £1,700,000.

The interest on this sum is less than the cost of maintaining one regiment of European infantry.

These opinions were all duly weighed by the Government of India, and the Duke of Argyll's despatch, dated 27th March 1873, was replied to on the 19th July 1873. The despatch was signed by all the Council, but in the opinions expressed they were not unanimous. Dissents against a new departure from the existing policy were recorded by Sir R. Temple, the finance member, and the Honourable B. H. Ellis, the member in charge of public works; and these dissents were sent home with the despatch. The despatch commences by saying that the Government of India—

> Adheres to the views originally expressed, namely, that the economy which will result from the adoption of a narrow gauge in the case of a large proportion of the contemplated railways in India overweighs the disadvantages which accompany a break of gauge; and that although it may be expedient to adopt the 5 feet 6 inches gauge on a few of those lines, new railways in India should, for economical reasons, be generally constructed with the narrow guage. Our opinion in this respect has been confirmed both by the satisfactory report which we have received of the experimental working of the State railway between Delhi and Rewari, and by the general conclusions at which Mr. Molesworth has arrived after a careful comparison of the relative advantages of the broad and narrow gauge.

But Lord Northbrook did not consider that the question now at issue extended to the general suitability of the narrow gauge for State railways, but referred solely to the propriety of continuing to build the Indus Valley and Punjab Northern Railways on the metre gauge. A glance at the map of India was sufficient to show that a line of railway from Lahore to the sea at Karachi must be considered as one of the main trunk lines of India. That distance measured 814 miles, and of this distance 324 miles in two lengths, one at either end, were already built on the broad gauge, and were in operation. It was originally proposed to convert this open length to the metre gauge, or to lay down a third rail for the passage of metre gauge vehicles, but this proposal is not dwelt on in this despatch, which only combats with the question of break of gauge. The despatch points out that some of the highest military authorities took part in the discussion on the relative merits of the 5 feet 6 inches and smaller gauges at the Institute of Civil Engineers, and that they condemned a break of gauge on military grounds. The consensus of military opinion in India was the same. Also, although the Indus Valley would doubtless be of considerable value for passenger and commercial traffic, its value for military purposes was of much more importance. The line from Lahore towards Peshawur, and which was already sanctioned as far as Rawalpindi, was designed entirely for military and political reasons; consequently the question of gauge of these lines was a matter which should be settled entirely on military grounds. On this evidence the majority of the Council agreed with the Viceroy in recommending that the 5 feet 6 inches gauge be adopted on these frontier lines, as that would settle for ever all difficulties as to a break of gauge at Lahore.

Sir Richard Temple dissented from this decision, because the evidence was quite conclusive in showing that the capabilities of the metre gauge were ample for all military requirements, and that it was very much cheaper to reduce the gauge of the open lines between Karachi and Lahore, or to lay down a third rail until those lines could be acquired from the Guaranteed Company. The dissent of the Honourable B. H. Ellis is recorded in a powerful minute, in which the whole tenor of the despatch is severely criticised. His reasons for dissent are summed up thus in his minute :—

1. The despatch of the Secretary of State, to which this despatch purports to be a reply, has anticipated all the points now urged, and has not really been answered.
2. Though Mr Molesworth and Colonel Dickens are in accord with the despatch on the particular issue, the facts stated in their notes tend to show that the narrow gauge is efficient for all purposes, and greatly more economical than the broad gauge.
3. The opinions of the military officers, quoted in the despatch, are not relevant.

4. The military objections based on the report of Colonel Roberts are overstated.
5. Substantially there will be no break of gauge seriously affecting military operations.
6. There are alternative suggestions for meeting the requirements of the military authorities in a less objectionable way than by incurring needless expense in constructing a broad gauge line, when a narrow gauge suffices for the traffic.
7. The additional cost of the broad gauge will be greater than is estimated in the despatch, and sufficient weight has not been given to the financial considerations involved.

Mr Ellis laid great stress on the financial points, and warned his colleagues of the results likely to occur if the Secretary of State sanctions a change to the 5 feet 6 inches gauge on these lines :—

In the first place, it cannot be admitted that in this discussion it is only the gauge of the two railways specially named that is being discussed. I warn my colleagues who entertain this belief that the present movement is but the thin end of the wedge ; and that if the Government give way on this occasion, the whole policy of the narrow gauge railways in India is imperilled. I know that it is even now sought to construct on the broad gauge the line from Gwalior to Agra, which forms a part of the Rajputana series of metre gauge lines connected with the narrow gauge terminus at Agra. I know also that an effort will be made to adopt the broad gauge on the line from Ajmere to Ahmedabad now under survey, this also being a part of the regular Rajputana series. Other lines will follow, and the result will be a number of isolated metre gauge lines, each of no great length ; and when these are found to be unsuccessful, it will be asserted that the whole scheme was a mistake. But such a result may fairly be attributed, not to the policy itself, but to the divergence from that policy involved in the departure from its principles in individual instances as they occur.

This despatch was not answered until November 1873, and

in the meantime, by the desire of the Secretary of State, the military aspect of the case had been reconsidered in England by General R. Strachey and Major (now Sir) E. C. S. Williams. The notes submitted by these officers were generally directed against the statements and conclusions drawn by the Quarter-Master-General in India as to the want of capacity of the metre gauge for military purposes. The question of the change of gauge was a serious one, and was discussed by the Cabinet. On the 18th November 1873 the Duke of Argyll telegraphed to Lord Northbrook—

> Cabinet consulted gauge question. Unanimously, with me, in declining to expend million and a quarter excess beyond estimate for narrow gauge; but we will not overrule you if you determine after receiving our despatch to take standard gauge with 45 lb. rail, as Molesworth suggests.

A despatch to that effect followed immediately afterwards, and reiterated the decision in the telegram. The Duke of Argyll remarks in this despatch that while—

> The Government of India and its professional advisers are satisfied of the complete sufficiency of the narrow gauge, considered in itself, for all purposes both civil and military, . . . the only objections to adhering to the decision of the Government of Lord Mayo as applied to the particular lines in question are, first, the inconvenience which may result from the occasional necessity of transferring troops and military stores from one set of conveyances to another; and, secondly, the inconvenience which may arise from a supposed limitation of rolling stock.

As regards the want of sufficient stock for the metre gauge lines, the Secretary of State remarks that he has seen no evidence to convince him that the systems as proposed by Lord Mayo would not be supplied with as much stock as could be usefully employed. He considers the inconvenience of break of gauge much exaggerated; but as the Government of India attaches so much importance to this convenience from a military standpoint, he will not over-rule that Government if it decides on the standard gauge with a 45 lb. rail, as suggested by Mr Molesworth. And in conclusion, while agreeing to the policy of removing the Lahore-Rawalpindi line from off the grand trunk road, he remarks that—

> It is not without the greatest reluctance that I shall advocate any further extension of the exceptionally broad gauge, which was adopted in India when very sanguine expectations were naturally entertained, but which experience has proved to be needlessly cumbrous and expensive for the traffic of the country. I should greatly prefer the other alternative, which is evidently regarded with favour, on its own merits, by Mr Molesworth, namely, that of making the new narrow gauge system still more extensive and still more connected.

But, notwithstanding the fact that the Sind, Punjab, and Delhi Railway Company had agreed to modify their engines so as to render practicable the Indus Valley Railway being made on the standard gauge with a 45 lb. rail, the Government of India decided not to adopt the broad gauge with a 45 lb. rail. The Government of India disclaimed that the question of gauge had been reopened at its instance; but since the Duke of Argyll had permitted its rediscussion, Lord Northbrook was now of opinion that it had been a mistaken policy to think of constructing either the Indus Valley or the Punjab Northern on the metre gauge, and that nothing short of the standard gauge with a 60 lb. rail would satisfy the exigencies of the case. The Commander-in-Chief, Lord Napier, was absent from Calcutta at the time this despatch was being discussed, and did not sign it, but his views were ascertained and embodied in the despatch. He gave his decided preference for the broad gauge with a 45 lb. rail,—not apparently on the score of economy, from which standpoint the question was being fought, but because it ensured the broad gauge winning the day, as hereafter it would be an easy matter to change the lighter rail for a 60 lb. one when required. Sir Richard Temple and Mr Ellis still retained the opinions they had recorded as dissents from the previous despatch; and it was also stated in this despatch that "Mr Hobhouse, who was unable to attend when the question was before discussed, is inclined to take the same view." The question of changing the gauge of these two lines to the standard gauge was therefore supported by Lords Northbrook and Napier of Magdala, Sir Henry Norman, and Mr E. C. Bayley.

Apart from the gauge question, the Government of India showed in this despatch that the works on the Punjab Northern Railway had proceeded so far that it was much better to allow the metre gauge line, which had been laid along the side of the grand trunk road, to be finished and used as a temporary line, pending the decision of the gauge for the eventual line which was to be made off the road. To this the Secretary of State agreed,[1] saying that "you may proceed at once with narrow gauge on Punjab Northern line. In a few days I shall tell you what I decide on the Indus Valley, if I decide at all." Mr Gladstone's Cabinet resigned a few days afterwards, and Lord Salisbury took over the India Office portfolio on the 22nd February 1874; but in the interval between sending the above telegram and the resignation, the Duke of Argyll gave his decision on the gauge question.[2] He exonerated the Government of India regarding the reopening the question of gauge, but said it was necessary in order "to test the persistent representations of those who have contended that no great excess of cost is involved in the broad gauge." The Duke remarked that no less than three members of the Viceroy's Council dissented from the views of the majority, and recorded his refusal to constructing these lines on the broad gauge in the following terms:—

[1] Telegram dated 12th February 1874.

[2] Despatch No. 20, Railway, of 16th February 1874.

9. Under these circumstances, Her Majesty's Government are of opinion that there is no sufficient reason for departing, at very considerable cost, from the careful and well-considered scheme of the late Lord Mayo's Government. That scheme will establish a cheaper system of railways commencing at Lahore, and reaching from the extreme frontier of our dominions to the sea. There it will be in unbroken communication with a separate harbour of its own on the western side of India, and as easily accessible as Bombay by the shortest route from England.

10. The system of railways will be constructed on a gauge which, as shown by your consulting engineer, can easily be made to have a carrying capacity of the English standard gauge, and one sufficient for all purposes of railway transport. On the same authority, it appears that the rate of travelling can, with perfect safety, be made double that actually proposed for the State railways of India, and that in other respects it is sufficient for all purposes, whether military or commercial.

11. I have therefore to instruct your Excellency to proceed with the scheme originally laid down by Lord Mayo's Government, and subsequently adopted under the authority conveyed by my despatch of 26th October 1870, No. 72.

12. You will consider carefully the detailed arrangements (many of which have been already suggested by Mr. Molesworth) which may secure the largest carrying capacity of carriage on the narrow gauge, and the greatest facilities in platform accommodation, etc., for transfer at the one great station, Lahore, where alone it will be required.

This was probably one of the last acts of the Duke of Argyll before leaving office, but the matter was evidently not considered as finally disposed of by that decision, for on the 21st March 1874 Lord Salisbury telegraphed to Lord Northbrook not to take the orders in the Duke of Argyll's despatch (No. 20) as final. But up to the 16th April 1874, when the Government of India forwarded to the Secretary of State a further memorandum on the question of break of gauge from a military point of view by Colonel F. Roberts, R.A., V.C.

(now Lord Roberts), no further orders had been received in India. The gauge question was, however, decided early in June of that year, as the Secretary of State telegraphed on 11th June that the standard gauge and rails were sanctioned for the Indus Valley line; but it was not until the 25th June 1874 that Lord Salisbury signed the despatch giving definite orders on the subject.

This despatch set at rest the question of gauge on these two lines; and not only have they been opened on the 5 feet 6 inches gauge, but important extensions to Peshawur, Khushalgarh, and to the foot of the Bolan Pass, are also either under construction or built on the same gauge.

During the year 1874 the question of gauge for the branch line from Agra to Gwalior was also under consideration. Mr. Ellis, the honourable member in charge of the public works, represented that this branch belonged to the Rajputana system of narrow gauge lines, that it would not be a paying line, and therefore had nothing in its favour to be considered as a trunk line. But the fact that Maharaja Sindia had promised to lend the Government of India 75 lakhs of rupees at 4 per cent if the line was made, that he had expressed a desire to have the railway on the 5 feet 6 inches gauge, and that the Commander-in-Chief's representations that such a line was a strategical one and of great importance from a military standpoint, decided the Government of India to make this branch line on the 5 feet 6 inches gauge. No further questions regarding gauge arose until the Government of India issued orders to commence the line of railway between Ahmedabad and Ajmere. For several years before it had been the desire of both the Guaranteed Railway Companies with termini in Bombay to extend their ventures northwards, and get an entrance into the Gangetic Valley. The Bombay, Baroda, and Central India Railway Company had even been permitted to make a series of surveys as far north as Agra and Delhi; and the Great Indian Peninsula Railway Company was desirous of extending its system into Malwa by means of a branch to Indore. The decision of Lord Mayo's Government to stop all further guarantees on the old system, and for Government to undertake the construction of its own railways, interfered with these proposals, as the construction of all railways through the States of Rajputana and Central India was considered a work which should be exclusively undertaken by Government. Surveys between Ahmedabad and Ajmere were commenced by the Government of India towards the end of 1872, with a view to eventually running a railway on the metre gauge through that part of Rajputana. The Government of Bombay, whose views on the subject had been invited, regretted that the line was not to be built on the standard gauge; but as a break of gauge had been determined upon, recommended that it should take place at Pahlanpur, and not at Ahmedabad, as the province of Guzerat was sufficiently fertile to demand a railway on the broad gauge. That Government also recommended that the section between Ahmedabad and Pahlanpur should be handed over to the Bombay, Baroda, and Central India Railway Company to be built under their guarantee. The London Board of Directors of this Railway Company were also pressing their claims for extension northwards and objecting to any break of gauge; but they were informed by the Secretary of State, Sir Charles Wood, that it was not intended to deviate from the policy under which it had been decided not to sanction the extension of that company's lines with guaranteed capital unless by the possible authorisation of short branches as feeders.

In July 1874, after Lord Salisbury's decision to construct the Indus Valley line on the 5 feet 6 inches gauge, the Government of Bombay again strongly urged its views, to the effect that "it is imperative that the Ahmedabad and Ajmere line should also be laid on the broad gauge, if not as far as Ajmere, at least as far as the point which is best suited for the junction of any future Sind extension." The Honourable

B. H. Ellis, before resigning his seat in Council, went over the projected line, and considered that there were no valid reasons for desiring to reopen the question of gauge for any part of this line. Consequently, in the despatch recommending the Secretary of State to give his sanction to lines from Ahmedabad to Ajmere, and from Neemuch to Nasirabad, the question of gauge was not mentioned ; the estimates were for a metre gauge line ; those estimates were sanctioned, and orders were issued to construct the lines on the metre gauge. But a feeling was growing up that the section between Ahmedabad and Pahlanpur might well stand the broad guage. Owing to the failure of the south-west monsoon in 1877, severe famine was felt in Guzerat. The Minister of the Baroda State strongly urged the immediate construction of the section between Ahmedabad and Pahlanpur on the broad gauge. This was recommended to the Secretary of State for acceptance, not only because the Baroda Railway could then work the section and so utilise its surplus rolling stock, but also because the Baroda State had contributed largely to a recent loan. The Secretary of State consented, and the earthwork and bridges on this section of the line were ordered to be made for a 5 feet 6 inches gauge. It was considered that this part of the line would probably form part of any line going towards Hyderabad in Sind ; and the surplus engineers set free by the completion of the Indus Valley Railway were employed during the cold season of 1877-78 in running trial lines between Deesa and Sind. Sir Andrew Clarke, member of Council for Public Works, considered that such a connecting link was absolutely essential for strategic purposes, and that it would soon have to be undertaken.

It was, however, presently discovered that the Bombay, Baroda, and Central India Railway Company had no powers to work any other line except their own ; and that even if they obtained the requisite Parliamentary power, which they were anxious to get, they would want a large increase of stock to work the extension. Consequently, in May 1878, the Secretary of State asked by telegram if the Government of India was still of "opinion that the portion of the railway between Ahmedabad and Pahlanpur should be constructed on the broad gauge." This was not officially replied to until January 1879, when the Government of India reported[1] that the orders regarding the construction of portion of the line between Ahmedabad and Pahlanpur on the broad gauge had been rescinded, and that now the whole line between Ahmedabad and Ajmere would be on the metre gauge. Difficulty had been experienced on the southern part of the line in brick-burning; and although the earthwork on the section to Pahlanpur was completed for a broad gauge line, little or no bridgework had been commenced; the additional expense due to the orders in 1877, when famine-relief operations were needed, was consequently trifling. The following extract from the despatch gives the argument of the Government of India:—

Our reasons for accepting the alteration from the broad to the metre gauge suggested by your Lordship, between Ahmedabad and Pahlanpur, are, first, that the change will effect an immediate saving of some 12 lakhs of rupees; secondly, that it is better to have a break of gauge at a military station like Ahmedabad than at an outpost like Pahlanpur; thirdly, that the prospect of an extension towards Sind is remote, and that, even when the extension is taken up, it is probable it will be built on the same gauge as the Rajputana system, instead of on the broad gauge of the Baroda Railway; and, fourthly, that, as far as can be judged at present, there are no reasonable grounds for apprehending that the metre gauge will not suffice to carry the traffic between Pahlanpur and Ahmedabad.

2. We are aware that the conclusion we have arrived at will be distasteful to the mercantile community of Bombay and also to the Baroda Railway Company. But the aim of the former is to

---

[1] In despatch No. 24, Railway, 24th January 1879, to Secretary of State.

convert the whole line from Ahmedabad to Delhi and Agra into a broad gauge undertaking, a result which could not be achieved without an expenditure of two or three millions sterling; while the object of the latter is to secure the control of the traffic working of the State railway. Both parties are earnest in their conviction that the interest of Bombay, as a seaport in competition with Calcutta, is injured by a break in the direct road to the North-Western Provinces, and that the existence of two gauges, with double proprietorship and management, will increase charges for transport, diminish conveniences for travelling, and cause delays in transmission of goods. We believe there is some exaggeration in these apprehensions, and that it would be unjustifiable for us, even if it were feasible under the financial existing circumstances of the Empire, to expend in their removal two or three millions sterling.

To this despatch Sir Andrew Clarke recorded a dissent, as he believed that the economy could only amount to 6 lakhs, which was not commensurate with the advantages to be gained. He also pointed out that, in his belief, the traffic along the Rajputana Railway would be so great soon after its opening right through as to compel its conversion into the broader gauge at no very distant date. In this view he had been supported both by the press and by sundry representations made from time to time in the shape of memorials and resolutions at public meetings. The Government of India, however, stood firm, and was supported by the Secretary of State, Lord Cranbrook. The question of the gauge on the Rajputana-Malwa system of railways was supposed to be finally set at rest. The anticipations of Sir A. Clarke have, nevertheless, been proved to have been based on sound judgment. The traffic on this system has already become too heavy for the gauge, and the question of converting it to the broad gauge, or of increasing its carrying power in other ways, has been before the Government for some years past.

It having been determined to adopt a second gauge in

India for secondary lines, a constant and fruitful source of discussion arose on the question of gauge for each new project that came forward. It was not, however, until the revival of projects by companies, on the basis of "private enterprise" in railways, that any serious difficulty arose, ending in practically resuscitating the old gauge controversy. The subject was formally reopened in 1883-84, by the Government of India, asking for the opinions of experts as to the relative cost of transport on each gauge, having arrived, though somewhat incorrectly, at the conclusion that the figures would be in favour of the broad or standard gauge. It was admitted, however, that in first cost the narrow gauge showed a material saving. In April 1884 the Government of India considered it advisable to refer the whole question to the Secretary of State, and in their despatch (No. 48, Railway), they said that they understood that the policy accepted for some years past by both themselves and the Secretary of State was in effect that the metre gauge was to be invariably adopted for local and provincial railways, "specially designed for a slow goods traffic," and that a network of subsidiary lines of this nature, and at the lowest possible cost, should be promoted as far as possible. The standard gauge was, on the other hand, to be regarded as suited to "supplementary through lines of communication," or those which are designed for military or strategic purposes. In applying those broad principles to the selection of gauge for each project, the Government of India thought that certain further points must be borne in mind.

First, as the evil of break of gauge and cost of working a railway are intensified in proportion to the shortness of the lead, short connections of a different gauge from the railways connected should be avoided as far as possible; and, in the case of through communications, should be deemed absolutely inadmissible. *Second*, in estimating probable traffic, full allowance must be made for development under the stimulus of the line itself, and of the general progress of the Empire, and also for special circumstances (such as a famine in the case of a "protective" railway), which may throw on the line an abnormally heavy traffic at particular periods in a year or a cycle. Earlier estimates appear to have been too often below the mark in this respect. The advance in doubling the East Indian and Great Indian Peninsula Railways indicates that a vast country like India will at no very distant date need the double broad gauge for all its arterial communications. *Third*, that it is not indispensable that all branches should be on the same gauge as the trunk line they feed. "Provincial and local" branches situated where the metre gauge is apparently ample to satisfy "local needs and local means" may be on that gauge, though the trunk line be broad gauge. The evil of break of gauge is the penalty, so to speak, which the locality must pay for the poverty of its resources.

The Select Committee of the House of Commons, which sat in 1884, substantially adopted these views, as the following passage from their report will show:—"With regard to the question of gauge, your Committee are of opinion that all the leading trunk lines, with their principal feeders, should be on the broad gauge, the metre gauge being as a rule confined to tracts of country where that system is already in successful operation, and to local lines where the traffic is likely to be so light, that cheapness of construction more than counterbalances the undoubted disadvantage of break of gauge." This decision was of service in dealing with questions of gauge then pending, but was clearly too vague, and perhaps intentionally so, to afford permanent guidance to the Government of India for the future. As a fact the question again arose in dealing in 1887 with the subject of the gauge for the Bengal-Nagpore Railway. This was settled in favour of the broad gauge. But the need, or at least the desire, on the part of some of the authorities in India for a more definite policy on the subject, caused in a great measure by proposals for the conversion of an important line from the metre to the broad gauge, led to a further reconsideration of the subject in 1889-90. Before the end of 1888 a total length of 800 miles of metre gauge had been converted to the standard gauge, and nearly 200 miles of the latter to the metre gauge, involving an expenditure to the State of not far short of four millions sterling, while proposals for further conversions were being brought forward. It was not, therefore, too soon that at the end of 1889, the Director-General of Railways, then Colonel L. Conway-Gordon, R.E., submitted a note to the Government of India, in which he vigorously urged the necessity for a declaration of policy on the gauge question, and concluded by offering two alternatives for consideration. The first was to follow the English precedent, and make it illegal, without the special sanction of Government, to make any line of railway in India on any other than the standard gauge of 5 feet 6 inches; or, secondly, to localise the gauges to certain areas, and to make it illegal without special sanction to construct any line of railway, within the specified areas, of any other gauge than that approved for that area. He added that the first alternative would, in his opinion, be in the end the more economical to the nation; while the second, as a political measure, would be the most feasible.

Colonel Gordon's note was accompanied by the opinions of twenty-two railway officers, engineers, and traffic experts, the majority of whom were in favour of a definite policy, and of the adoption of geographical limits for each gauge; but on other points they were not in entire accord with Colonel Gordon's views, notably on the proposal for broad gauge lines of a light character. The subject was most carefully considered by the Government of India, and in June 1890 a despatch was sent to the Secretary of State, in which the evils of break of gauge were again dwelt upon, and definite proposals formulated, which were to the following effect:—That it was not desirable to legislate with the view of enforcing decision on the gauge question; that certain areas now occupied by the metre gauge should be as a rule reserved for that gauge;

but that, exclusive of these areas, it was proposed to lay it down as an absolute rule that no new main line should be constructed except on the standard (broad) gauge. It was, moreover, proposed to allow no material expansion of existing metre gauge systems, and to rule that the areas now in possession of that gauge should not be held to be unconditionally surrendered to it, but that if held advisable broad gauge lines of a light character might be laid through such areas.

In replying to this despatch in August of the same year, the Secretary of State for India (Viscount Cross) agreed with the Government of India that legislation was not needed, and that the power should be retained of deciding the gauge to be adopted on any projected railway. He held that, as reported by the Committee of the House of Commons, "it should be accepted as a rule that the main lines should be on the broad gauge, and the metre gauge lines confined to tracts of country where that system is in successful operation," and as regards questions relating to branches and feeder lines, he considered that each case should be decided as it occurs, and that there appeared to be no necessity for laying down any more positive rule. A suggestion in the Government of India's despatch, to the effect that it might ultimately be found necessary to convert a great part of its railway mileage in order to obtain uniformity, was met by the Secretary of State with but small encouragement. He held that the financial considerations in such an idea would be very serious, and that the money required for such purpose would be "better employed, and the object in view equally well secured, by making new lines of a uniform gauge with those connected through districts unprovided with railway accommodation." He concluded by saying that the decision as to the gauge for branch lines should be left with the Government of India, and that any scheme for conversion must be reserved for special consideration.

In submitting this question to the Home Government, the Government of India made no reference in their despatch to the fact that gauges narrower than the metre—viz. of 2 feet and 2½ feet—had been already introduced on some small lines, although permitted in their origin, as being nothing more than steam tramways on existing roads. Since the date of the Secretary of State's reply, and owing, perhaps, to the evident intention of the Home Government that the gauge question should be left open, there has been an inclination to recognise and allow the 2½ feet gauge for short feeder lines, on either independent substructure or on the side of existing roads. For lines of the latter class, which can be made and stocked for from 15,000 to 17,000 rupees per mile (£950 to £1100), there is certainly a large field in India, and it seems probable that this small gauge may before many years show a large mileage. The 2 feet gauge has at present a very small mileage, and is not likely to extend. It was laid down as a tramway originally on the east road between the plains and Darjeeling, a hill station on the Himalayas, but this line has since become practically a railway in nearly every condition.

How the gauge question will be determined in India, or whether indeed it will ever be settled, is very difficult to foresee. The development of late years of competitive lines, the steady growth of traffic, and a healthy spirit of rivalry, has led to a marked increase in train loads, and consequently in the weight of engines and in the weights on axles. This has been recognised by the Government, and revised standard dimensions and wheel loads have recently been sanctioned for each gauge, which, it may be hoped, will be held to be final. If this is done, and if the traffic on Indian railways expands in the future in anything like the same ratio as has been shown in the last ten years, it may be expected that fresh proposals will arise for the conversion of the narrow gauges into broader, and that considerable pressure may be brought to bear on the Government of India to assent either to this or to a further revision of the standards. The conversion from the metre to the standard gauge has so far shown that the cost, exclusive of rolling stock, will be from £3000 to £3500 per mile, allowing for the sale, in a very limited and steadily decreasing market, of the metre gauge material. The operation is consequently one that cannot be lightly entertained. The original scope of metre gauge lines has certainly been largely extended. In lieu of being the field for mere branch or subsidiary lines, it can now show large systems of arterial communication, embracing many hundreds of miles of line, and carrying a traffic which would in some cases perhaps be more conveniently and more cheaply dealt with on the standard gauge. But these developments were difficult if not impossible to foresee. The surprising effects of the opening of the Suez Canal on the export trade of India was not realised by the projectors of the metre gauge, nor were the effects of the railways themselves in stimulating production, even in very unhopeful districts, in any sufficient degree anticipated.

But the saving to the country by the introduction of the metre gauge is undoubted. In capital cost alone, the difference between the metre and the standard gauge has been found on careful estimates, over the same ground, to be on the average in the ratio of about 6½ to 8, which represents about £1100 per mile of line, and thus on the present mileage of the metre gauge the saving is considerably over seven millions sterling. For the same traffic, under similar conditions as to grades, cost of fuel, and establishments, there is practically no difference worth notice in the cost of working as compared with the standard gauge, and the inconveniences of break of gauge have certainly not been recognised by traders, nor as yet in military emergencies. Had the standard broad gauge been insisted on throughout the country, excluding from consideration the broken reed of a "light" broad gauge, many a district now prospering under railway communication would for many a year have had to see its produce still carried by bullock carts over cross country tracks, or have given up the attempt to compete with more favoured localities.

CHAPTER V

RATES AND FARES

Passenger Fares

The original contracts with the guaranteed companies afford the first indication of the views of the Government of India on the subject of rates and fares. In these it is stipulated that the companies shall allow the use of the railways to the public "on such terms as shall be approved by the East India Company," and shall not charge higher tolls without approval; it being further required that when the net receipts of the lines shall afford a dividend on the capital outlay in excess of 10 per cent, the fares and tolls are to be reduced, with the view of limiting the net receipts so that they shall not produce a return beyond that figure. The determination of suitable rates was necessarily at the outset, and indeed for some years, a source of perplexity to both the officials of the Government and of the companies, neither of which were in a position to do more than theorise on the subject, and thus the rates first adopted were admittedly tentative. It was, in fact, agreed on both sides that rates should not be held to be fixed, or approved finally by the Government, until the lines had been fairly open for some time, and the tendencies and character of the traffic sufficiently established. On one point there was at the first a very general agreement, viz., that but little was to be expected in the shape of passenger traffic, and that the receipts would be mainly derived from goods.

The first report on Indian railways to the Secretary of State for India, in 1859, said that experiments had been tried with varied success, that the incomplete state of the lines made it difficult to ascertain the precise rates which were most suitable and remunerative; but that there was no longer any doubt as to passenger traffic, and that the people of India had shown that they were as eager as those of any European country to avail themselves of this mode of travelling. This report went on to urge what is not now generally accepted, viz. that low rates and remunerative rates were not always synonymous, that increase of numbers necessarily produced an increase in working expenses, and that it was doubtful whether it was possible to carry passengers with profit, and in proper vehicles, at a lower rate than one-fifth of a penny per mile, which was then the lowest fare for this traffic on one of the Indian railways. At the end of 1861 there were nine railways in progress in different parts of the country, on which there was an aggregate open mileage of 1600 miles. Taking the exchange value of the rupee as being then at two shillings, the rate and fares, highest and lowest, in force for goods and passengers are shown in the following table :—

	Passenger Fares.			Goods Rates.				
	1st Class.	2nd Class.	3rd Class.	1st Class.	2nd Class.	3rd Class.	4th Class.	5th Class.
	P. mile	P. mile	P. mile	Per ton per mile	Per ton per mile	Per ton per mile	Per ton per mile	Per ton per mile
	d.	*d.*	*d.*	*d.*	*d.*	*d.*	*d.*	*d.*
Highest .	$2\frac{1}{4}$	$1\frac{1}{8}$	$\frac{3}{8}$	$1\frac{1}{8}$	$1\frac{11}{16}$	$2\frac{1}{4}$	$3\frac{3}{4}$	$6\frac{3}{4}$
Lowest .	1	$\frac{1}{2}$	$\frac{1}{5}$	1	$1\frac{1}{4}$	$1\frac{5}{8}$	$1\frac{5}{8}$	$3\frac{3}{4}$

The general charge for the lowest class of passenger traffic at this time was three pies per mile, which at an exchange of two shillings per rupee represented $\frac{3}{8}$d. The lowest, or first-class goods rate, was generally one-third of a pie per maund (82 lbs.) per mile, equal to about $1\frac{1}{8}$d. per ton mile. The action of Government as regards rates and fares already tended towards what has since been accepted as the most politic and rational course, viz. that of fixing maximum rates for goods and passengers within which the companies were free to alter at their own discretion. The question of the minimum had not yet arisen, and did not come forward until competition between rival lines forced on the Government the necessity of protecting its interests as regards the guarantee, and to make a stand against what appeared to be unremunerative rates. The natural desire of both the Government and the companies was to make the railways as profitable as possible; but the latter, fully alive to their advantages as monopolists, were not inclined to regard the increase of numbers or tonnage as of so much importance as the increase of receipts; while, on the other hand, the Government had to elect between the claims of the public at large to early relief from the burden of the guarantee, and the clamour of the travelling and trading classes for low fares and rates. The tendency in the earlier years was to increase rather than reduce rates, although this appears to have been due in some measure to a scarcity of rolling stock; but the Indian traffic manager was already in the toils of the "cost of conveyance" heresy; he had not yet realised that this is a variable, and, in the absence of serious competition, sought to base his rates and the volume of his business on what appeared to be finality in the cost of transit.

The earliest rates in force for passenger traffic are given on page 195, and these were continued for some years. It was soon found, however, that this traffic, especially of the third or lowest class, which afforded over 90 per cent of the coaching receipts, was likely to become a very important source of income. In a report to the Secretary of State on Indian railways in 1860, it is observed that "it is worthy of note how greatly the traffic of the third class preponderates. The proportion of the first and second class put together is to the third class as 1 to 16½. This shows conclusively how strong has become the desire of the population at large to move about when the means of doing so has been provided. If railways have produced this result with a people usually regarded as inactive and stationary, it may reasonably be expected that an impulse will be given to the already expanding trade of India the advantages of which will be equally felt in this country." The cost of travelling by rail in India is compared in a subsequent report (in 1864) with that in England at the time, and it is shown that for a journey of 100 miles, by third class, the fare averaged on seven railways about 3s. 2d. (exchange being at about 2s.); while in the United Kingdom the charge for the same distance, in the same class, by "parliamentary" train, was 8s. 4d. Thus the native earning, or on a wage of say 10s. a month, was being charged 38 per cent of what was levied on an English artisan, whose income may be put at £5 a month. At this period the open lines carried a length in the aggregate of 2687 miles, and the third-class traffic showed a yearly total of numbers conveyed of about 8¾ millions, or no more than 3260 per mile open.[1] It was not then seen that it was to this third-class traffic that the subsequent success of the Indian railways would be so largely indebted, nor was it seen that they were charging almost prohibitive fares, and stifling a most valuable source of income. The third class affords, in fact, in India the backbone, if not nearly the whole body, of the coaching receipts; the other classes might, as far as profit is concerned, be abolished; indeed, on most lines their removal would be a positive gain, and it is not many years ago that a leading railway manager in India stated it would pay him to give every first-class passenger twenty rupees to stay away. Thus in dealing with this subject it is only proposed to refer to fares in the third class, and to

[1] At the present time (1892) the last returns show an open mileage of 18,042, a total of all classes conveyed yearly of 127,456,913, and the number per mile open 7064.

disregard the other classes as having no practical effect on the revenues of Indian railways.

The obstacles in the way of reduction of fares were to be found in two leading principles, which appear to have been then considered the foundation of all policy. The first was that the lines must be made promptly profitable; and, secondly, that "the cost of conveyance" was merely a fixed figure. Thus in 1866 we find it said, in a report to the Secretary of State, that "there has been a tendency during the past year to increase rates and fares. . . . It is not yet possible to judge what the established rates for passengers should be," but that "lower rates *may* be found more profitable than higher. If, however, the traffic goes on increasing in the same ratio as it has done during the last two years, the rates will in some cases have to be raised higher than they are now, in order to realise the profits which the railways could command. Considering the question in the abstract, the first point to be ascertained, before fixing charges of this kind, is the *cost* of *conveyance*, and then the charge which, in addition to what is required to cover the cost, will produce the greatest aggregate return; for it should be borne in mind that it is not the high profit upon the unit, but the small profits upon large numbers or quantity which should be sought for." It is not necessary at the present day to comment on this peculiar mixture of views, but it took many years before the dictum conveyed in the last sentence was acted upon in India. The tendency to charge high fares and rates appears, at any rate, not to have been shown by the Government, but by the railway companies, the former having been charged indeed with allowing them to be too low, and thus neglecting the interests of the general taxpayer, who had to find the interest guaranteed on the capital outlay of the companies. This consideration had necessarily considerable weight in influencing the action of the Government. It recognised the broad, general benefit which railway communication conferred on the country, both directly and indirectly, but it was bound to recognise that it endowed the trading and travelling classes with special advantages, and that the burden of the guarantee must not be allowed to lie too heavily on the public at large. The firm intention of the Government not to relinquish or loosen their control over the passenger fares levied on the companies' lines is well illustrated in a despatch to the Secretary of State in 1867.[1] This was in reply to one in which a minimum of interference was suggested, unless on the ground of the fares being more or less likely to be profitable to the company concerned. They said, referring to the views of the Secretary of State, that—

> 2. No recognition appears therein to be made of any duty on the part of the Government to protect the interests of the people. This duty is recognised in England in the institution of parliamentary trains. In India, where the Government gives a guarantee of interest, in addition to other privileges allowed to railway companies, we are of opinion that it has a still stronger right, and is bound by a more imperative duty, to look to the interests of the people in this matter. Further, our belief is that a railway best serves its own interests as well as those of the Government by accommodating itself to the wants of the public.
>
> 3. While freely admitting that the control of the Government should not be so exercised as to compel the railway company to carry passengers without a profit, we should suggest that in any arrangement for the re-adjustment of fares of the lower classes, the accommodation of the public should be considered, so far as it is not manifestly incompatible with the interests of the company, or the means at their disposal for providing such accommodation. The cases which we have more particularly in view are those in which there is doubt, and in such cases we think the companies should try first the proposals most favourable to the public.
>
> 4. We beg that the principle we have now advanced may be considered as the rule in dealing with questions of railway fares.

In a circular issued in the Public Works Department in

[1] No. 26, dated 8th February 1867.

October 1867,[1] the Government of India decided that, as regards the guaranteed lines, the fares then in force and sanctioned should be held to be the maxima, and that in the case of lines to be opened in the future, the maximum would be fixed for the lowest class at the rate of 2 pies per mile, the accommodation to be provided being "in covered carriages without seats." This latter condition was, however, never carried out, notwithstanding that the habits of the natives would have made it quite acceptable; but the main reason against it was the difficulty of providing against overcrowding, and of giving each passenger adequate space. On receipt of a copy of this circular by the Secretary of State, he objected to the intention declared therein, that the Government of India should fix such maxima or withdraw powers of this nature from the local Governments, in whose hands should be left "the settlement of the maximum scale of rates and fares for every description of traffic on railways within their Presidencies."[2] He held that it was as much the interest of the companies as of the Government "to give the maximum number of passengers with the maximum of profit." In replying to this, the Government of India felt obliged to protest against the decision, and before carrying out these instructions, said—

. . . . We beg to submit the following observations for your consideration, referring to the opinion that the railway companies have, in common with the Government, as much interest in regulating fares so as to "give the maximum number of passengers with the maximum profit," and that there is every reason to expect that they will exercise their powers judiciously in this respect. He would observe that it does not appear to us to be the interest of the railway companies to carry the maximum of passengers with the maximum of profit, but on the contrary, to get the maximum of profit with the minimum of passengers; thus it would

[1] No 10, Railway, dated 16th October 1867.

[2] Despatch No. 17, of 29th February 1868, from Secretary of State.

be preferable to them to carry two million passengers in a half-year at 3 pies (per mile), instead of three million passengers at 2 pies. Now the interest of the Government, acting in behalf of the people, is directly opposed to this. At the same time, we do not desire that the companies should lower their fares so as to lose the maximum profits, nor indeed are we of opinion that the companies would wish to raise their fares so as to cause the number of passengers to fall below what would give the maximum of profit. But between these two extremes the interests of the Government and the people are opposed to the interests of the railway companies and their officers.

Later on, in 1869, we find the Government of India so intent on promoting the movement of the lower class, as to be prepared to incur the risk of losing dividend to meet the outlay on guaranteed interest. In a despatch to the Home Government in 1869,[1] they say that it is of the last importance to fix the third-class fare on Indian railways "at the lowest possible amount," in the interests of the companies and of the vast masses of the native population; that they will prefer to travel on foot or in carts, regardless of personal inconvenience or loss of time, so long as they can make a saving by such methods over that of travelling by rail; that it is to this class that returns must be looked for from passenger traffic in India, and that therefore fares should be pitched so as to secure the greatest possible number. In a letter written previously to the Government of Madras (in August 1869), this view is put even more plainly with reference to reduction of fares on the Madras Railway. "His Excellency in Council is accordingly strongly of opinion, that it will be to the ultimate benefit of the company to look more at present to an increase of numbers, by the adoption of a lower fare for the third class, than to any immediate important addition to the receipts. . . . It can neither be to the financial interest of the company nor to the well-being and prosperity of the country, that the fares should

[1] No. 115, Railway, 24th November 1869.

be pitched so high that the millions may not be induced to travel."

In 1869-70 the Government of India commenced the construction and working of a system of State railways, by the direct agency of its own officers, with the avowed intention of endeavouring to reduce and simplify rates and fares. As soon as the first sections of these lines approached completion, the Government addressed the Secretary of State on the subject.[1] They said that they proposed to adopt, with some minor alterations, the rules and regulations as regards working which were then in force on the guaranteed railways, and to simplify the classification and rates for goods; while for this and for passenger traffic they intended to have four classes, as follows, based as regards charge on a station-to-station rate, the unit for goods being on a weight of a "maund," viz. 82 lbs.

Goods.		Passenger.	
	Pies.		Annas.
Special	2	1st class	8
1st class	4	2nd ,,	4
2nd ,,	6	3rd ,,	2
3rd ,,	8	4th ,,	1

The lowest passenger fare of one anna between stations worked out then at from 1 to 1½ pie per mile, which was equal to about half a farthing. It was considerably lower than that on any other Indian railway at the time, the lowest fares being on the Great Indian Peninsula and Madras Railways, on which there were fares of 2½ and 2 pies per mile; but the service for these rates was worked with so many vexatious restrictions, that it gave but little hope of becoming successful. An attempt had, it is true, been made on two other lines, in 1861, to give what were called "coolie" trains, with a fare of 1½ pie per mile; but for the same reason, and

[1] In Despatch No. 26, Railway, of the 29th January 1873.

because the people had not then become accustomed to railway travelling, this was abandoned as unremunerative. The rates above quoted for State railways were duly put in force, although on lines which passed through comparatively poorly populated areas. On one of them three classes only were in use, and on the other four classes, and when these two lines were about to be connected and amalgamated under one management, it became necessary to have the same classes on both. In advising the Government on this point, the Director of State Railways (then Colonel E. C. S. Williams, R.E.) said that he was satisfied, from a study of the traffic by classes on the older lines generally, and particularly on the open lines of State railways, that the attraction of the lowest class, "whether it be 1 or 1½ annas per station, is so great, that practically no large section of the masses will pay even half an anna extra per station distance for mere segregation." The passenger mileage on the lowest rate was then, in fact, more than double that which obtained on the next higher, and, as Colonel Williams truly said, "the mass will always go for the lowest class, and the lower its fare the greater will be the tendency to two classes only;" and again, "It is solely to the lowest class of passenger traffic that we can look for profit in coaching, if such profits be a *sine quâ non*,[1] and the really important question, and to which we shall shortly come, is, What shall be the fare in the lowest class henceforth?" The report recommended for adoption on State lines the three classes above mentioned, which then worked out for the lowest class at from 2½ to 1¼ pies per mile, according to the distances between stations. These recommendations were accepted by the Government of India, and in the letter in which this was intimated there is a sentence worth quoting as a typical illustration of paternal solicitude for the native passenger. The Director was instructed, that "without allowing any caste distinctions, the Government of India are of opinion that general instructions

[1] To the State.

should be issued to station-masters and guards not to force very dirty people into carriages with decently-dressed passengers, so long as there are vacant seats elsewhere." To this was added the further instruction, that accommodation was to be reserved on every train for women in the third class. In reporting their decision in this matter to the Secretary of State, the Government stated that, while the determination of the fares in the first and second classes was comparatively unimportant, that of the lowest class was quite otherwise, as this was the one that paid, and that in accepting an average of about 2 pies per mile, they thought that this was the lowest that could safely be adopted for the present.

With the aim, kept steadily and constantly in view, of attaining simplification, and as far as possible reduction in rates, the Government issued a circular letter in May 1876, putting forward statements showing the existing classification of goods, the average goods rates, and average passenger fares on all the Indian railways, and invited the agents and managers to endeavour to arrive at uniformity; and later on, in September of the same year, proposed a conference of railway officials for the discussion of sundry disputed matters, among which was that of the reduction of passenger fares. These then stood as follows in each class :—

[AVERAGE

AVERAGE PASSENGER FARES ON INDIAN RAILWAYS IN 1876.

	Average Fare per Mile.			
	1st Class.	2nd Class.	Intermediate Class.	Lowest Class.
	Pies.	Pies.	Pies.	Pies.[1]
Madras	15	6.5	3.5	2
South Indian	12	5	...	2
Great Indian Peninsula	18	9	4	2.5
Bombay, Baroda, and C. India	15	7	...	3
East Indian	18	9	4.5	3
Eastern Bengal	12	6	4.5	3
Oude and Rahilkund	...	9	...	2
Punjab and Delhi	17.78	8.94	4.47	2.77
Sind	13.52	4.8	...	2.84
Calcutta and S. Eastern	...	9	...	2.55
Nalhati	28.13	14.07	7.06	4.62
[2]Rajputana	10.38	4.61	...	2.03
[2]Holkar	11.79	4.42	...	2.21
Khamgaon	18	9	4	2.5
Amraoti	18	9	...	4
Wardha Valley	18	9	4	2.5
Nizam's	18	9	4	2.5
[2]Tirhoot	12.09	4.36	...	2.18
[2]Punjab Northern	9.43	4.71	...	1.87

The Government subsequently issued a resolution on the effect of low fares, recommending the adoption of a maximum for the lowest class of 2½ pies per mile (about a farthing), and in this they urged that low fares had been adopted on the State lines, and that in guaranteeing interest on the company's lines, they would in effect be liable for any loss which the adoption of a similar course might cause on these railways. The resolution went no further, but on the East Indian Railway, where under a new contract the Government had powers to reduce fares in the lowest class to 2 pies per mile, a firmer position was assumed, and the agent of the line was required, while thoroughly opposing it, to reduce his rate of 3 pies to 2½ pies. The agent (Mr., now Sir Bradford Leslie) objected, on the ground

[1] The value of a pie might be taken then at a little over half a farthing.

[2] State Railways.

that he was satisfied that the existing fare did not exclude "a single *bonâ fide* traveller, whether on business or on pleasure," and that the 2½ pie rate would not only result in increasing the passenger mileage, by the amount requisite to yield the same net receipts, but would not even give the same gross receipts. Fortunately, however, the Government, under strong and able advice, stood firm, enforced the lower rate, and said that if it was as they anticipated successful, they would require it to be lowered still further, viz. to 2 pies per mile. It is worth while to notice how fully the result justified the action of the Government. In 1880, when the 3 pie per mile rate was in force, the number of third-class passengers conveyed was 7,792,724, and the numbers and receipts per mile open 5181, and Rs.5748. In 1892, the lowered rate of 2½ pies having been in action since 1881 over the whole system, the total numbers carried of the same class was 11,769,923, and the numbers and receipts per mile open were respectively 8841, and Rs.7310. But, in fact, from the very first the beneficial effect of the reduced fare was clearly seen, not only in the increase of numbers and in the slow but steady increase in receipts, but in the manifest advantage which it gave to trade and to goods traffic in facilitating the movement of the smaller traders.

Again, in the same year 1880, in reviewing the accounts of the South Indian Railway Company (a guaranteed line), the Government of India, in a letter to the Government of Madras, urged that a fair local train service should be maintained on the lines in that province for the benefit of the poorer classes at a rate of not more than 2 pies per mile, and that the company referred to should be informed that, as there was no immediate prospect of their being able to earn surplus profits over and above the figure of guaranteed interest, they should be "liberal in their dealings with native travellers," and that "any loss that may arise from such liberality will not fall on the shareholders, but on the Government; while if there is a development of trade and of passenger traffic, the shareholders will get the advantage hereafter when surplus profits begin to be realised." Early in 1881 [1] the Government of India issued a pamphlet giving the opinions of provincial Governments and of leading railway officials on the subject of low passenger fares. The general feeling was strongly in favour of the principle, but there was a marked divergence of view as to what a low fare implied. The publication was however distinctly useful, not only in the dissemination of opinion on the general aspects of the question, but in offering facts and figures which required to be more widely known to railway men. The manager of one of the State lines [2] put the case in a way which is still applicable, and is worth reproducing. He said that "if we look at what railways have done, in view of the conditions they have had to face, we shall find that they have adopted, in competition with carts and boats, comparatively low goods rates, but that they have never thought of lowering their passenger fares sufficiently to enable an ordinary coolie to travel more cheaply by rail than he can travel on foot, though this can undoubtedly be done. . . . It is not, therefore, to be wondered at that railways have altogether failed to attract the masses, and have only succeeded in getting the well-to-do classes. . . . To attract the masses railways will have to lower their fares until a journey can be done as cheaply on the railway as on foot. To do this, the fare must not exceed $1\frac{1}{2}$ annas for twenty miles, or say 1 pie per mile, and perhaps in the poorer districts it may have to be reduced to $\frac{3}{4}$ of a pie." In issuing this pamphlet, the Government observed that third-class fares had been reduced by order to $2\frac{1}{2}$ pies per mile on the East Indian Railway (as above noticed), and that the effects of this reduction would be watched "with care and interest," with the view of proceeding further in the direction of a

[1] Circular No. VII., Railway Government of India—Public Works Department—21st January 1881.

[2] Major (now Colonel) Sedgwick, R.E.

general reduction of fares, and it was added that this opportunity was taken of impressing on all railway administrations that increases of fares were deprecated, and should not be permitted except on the clearest and strongest grounds.

To those who are conversant with the habits and character of the Oriental, it will be readily understood that no difficulty has at any time arisen on the question of the speed or accommodation in trains in dealing with native passenger traffic. To the vast majority of native travellers, a distance of 200 miles in the 24 hours is fully as much as they expect, and they prefer, for many reasons (among others the absence, owing to sundry objections, of the provision of conveniences in the carriages), to find long halts every few hours, where they can "spread themselves out," buy and eat such food as they allow themselves on such journeys (which is found for sale on the platforms), discuss the incidents of travel, the prospects of crops, or the chances of some everlasting law-suit. The discomfort, which to a European would be intolerable, in such a climate, of cramped accommodation, hard boards to sit on, the crush at booking-offices, and the many worries incidental to the discipline of railway arrangements, are accepted by them with a patience, and even good-humour, which is really surprising, and which is, or at least should be, standing evidence of the possibilities of development of this traffic. In the direction of improving the comfort of the lower class very little has been done, or indeed has been possible. Stringent rules have been issued from time to time against overcrowding in carriages, for the provision of reserved compartments and conveniences for native women, and for giving ample water supply at all stations, especially in the hot season; while the introduction of an "intermediate" class, at a slightly increased fare, affords for long journeys, to those who can afford it, some possibility of sleeping at length on a rather hard bench, instead of sitting in one posture for hours or days on an equally hard seat. But nothing would, in fact, be gained even in competition by the provision of such luxuries as the cushions and lavatories which are now considered indispensable in the third class on the leading English railways. All that the lower classes require in railway travelling is the means of transit at less cost than that of doing it on foot. Temporary discomfort or inconvenience, or the loss of a few hours at stations, are wholly disregarded as compared with money cost, and it is with this factor and this only that we have to reckon in fixing our fares for the bulk of our native passengers.

It is not necessary to notice in detail the successive phases of the efforts made by the Government for the reduction of the fare in the lowest class. On the State railways, and on those of the "assisted" companies, under whose contracts the Government had full control over rates and fares, the issue of an order was sufficient to ensure its being carried out promptly and loyally; but in other directions, as for instance on lines controlled by native States, or on lines on which there were good prospects of surplus profits over and above the guaranteed interest, and the terms of whose contracts prevented any extreme measures of interference, the Government was constrained to act with caution, and to be content with offering advice and the example of the State lines. On these, moreover, while it could be shown that the low rates induced a most noticeable increase in numbers, it could not be as clearly proved that they were directly, or at least promptly, profitable. The gross receipts improved, but, on the other hand, working expenses, including train mileage, increased, and allowance had to be made for interest on the capital outlay for additions to rolling stock. To the State, the evidence of net profits was not so material as the fact of the increased movement of the people, and the consequent indirect advantages which this implied in so many ways. Up to the year 1890, the minimum fare aimed at by the Government was $1\frac{3}{4}$ pies per mile,[1] but was

[1] Public Works Department, No. 1446, Railway Traffic, of 12th December 1887.

not acted on, the lowest fare on State lines being 2 pies per mile. In July 1891[1] this minimum was further reduced to 1½ pie per mile, a decision for which the author may claim to have contributed by a communication on the subject in October 1890. As yet one line only, the Madras Railway, has had the sense to adopt this fare, and with results that are so far very encouraging; while another, the Bengal and North-Western Railway, closely follows with a station-to-station rate, which is equivalent to about 1¾ pies per mile, and with entirely satisfactory effect. What is needed is that the Government should have the courage of its opinions, and show the lead by giving this low rate a full and fair trial on some large State line. There is good reason for the hope that this course will be shortly taken; but until this is done, it will continue to be held, by those well qualified to hold the opinion, that we have not yet reached, and that by a long way, the limits of our passenger traffic on Indian railways, and to this it will be impossible to offer any adequate refutation. At the same time, it is conceded that a rate of 1½ pie per mile is not properly applicable over the whole Empire, but is only suited for adoption over areas in which the population is at once dense and poor, and where low wages, and the general struggle for existence, renders them unable to contemplate journeys by rail on more onerous terms. The statistics of the railways which serve such districts point to the certainty that with large numbers, low speeds, and properly-fitted vehicles, passengers of the lowest class could be carried at a fare of 1 pie per mile, and leave a profit of from 20 to 30 per cent; but the cost of carriage is a quantity varying with the volume of traffic, and it may be found that an even lower rate is possible. If, however, we can profitably carry at 1 pie a mile—a rate which implies that a man can travel 24 miles for the lowest daily wage now paid in India—we may rest satisfied that we have placed railway travel within the means of the poorest classes, and may

[1] See Appendix.

be content to wait for the results. The following table shows the average fares in the three periods 1872 to 1892 on the principal Indian railways:—

Railway.	Fares, Lowest Class.			
	1872.	1882.	1892.	Remarks.
East Indian	3	3	2.5	State Line.
Great Indian Peninsula	2.5	2.5	2.5	Guaranteed Line.
Madras	2	2	1.5	Do. do.
Bombay, Baroda	3	2.5	2.25	Do. do.
Sind-Punjab	3	2.5	2	Now North-Western Railway.
Great Southern	2	2.5	2	Now South Indian Railway.
Eastern Bengal	3	3	2.5	State Line.
Oude and Rahilkund	2	2.5	2.5	Do.
Rajputana	...	2	2	Do., leased to Company.
Tirhoot	...	2.5	1.75	Do. do.
Nizam's	...	2	2	Company's line.
Indian Midland	...	...	3 to 2	According to distance.
Bengal-Nagpore	...	...	2	

Schedule of Maxima and Minima Rates and Fares in Coaching Traffic, given in Appendix A to P. W. D. Resolution No. 1446, R.T., dated 12th December 1887, and at present in force.

	Maximum. Pies per mile.[1]	Minimum. Pies per mile.
Passenger Fares—		
1st class	18	12
2nd class	9	6
Intermediate class	$4\frac{1}{2}$	3
3rd class	3	$1\frac{3}{4}$
	Maximum. Pies per maund per mile.	Minimum. Pies per maund per mile.
Luggage	2	1
	Maximum. Pies per mile.	Minimum. Pies per mile.
Carriages[2]—		
Single carriages	42	30

[1] One pie may be taken as one-twelfth of a penny.

[2] Subject to a minimum *charge* of Rs. 5.

	Maximum. Pies per truck.	Minimum. Pies per truck.
Two or more carriages on one truck	54	42

	Maximum. Pies per mile.	Minimum. Pies per mile.
Horses [1]—		
Single horse . . .	24	18

	Maximum. Pies per fifty miles or portion thereof.	Minimum. Pies per fifty miles or portion thereof.
Dogs—		
Each . . .	96	48

Parcels—

The rates passed at the Railway Traffic Conference of 1884, as under:—

	First 100 miles. Annas.	Every additional 100 miles. Annas.
Not exceeding 5 seers or 1 cubic foot [2]	3	1
,, 10 ,, 2 cubic feet	6	3
,, 20 ,, 4 ,,	10	5
,, 30 ,, 6 ,,	13	6½
,, 40 ,, 8 ,,	16	8
For every additional 10 seers or 2 cubic feet, or portion of 10 seers or 2 cubic feet . . .	4	2

Parcels exceeding 40 seers in weight, or 8 cubic feet in measurement may be booked if accommodation will allow.

Goods Rates.

It must be stated at the outset, in dealing with this subject, that the object of this work is to indicate the policy of the Government of India, and that only incidental notice will be taken of the minor or comparatively unimportant action or dealings of local governments and officials. Nevertheless, it was from this source that in the earlier years of Indian railways

[1] Subject to a minimum *charge* of Rs.5.

[2] Subject to a maximum *charge* of one rupee for a parcel not exceeding 5 seers, irrespective of distance.

the interpretation and working of the contracts with the guaranteed railways was sought and obtained, and it was not until the year 1867 that the Supreme Government felt it necessary to determine on a definite course as regards the extent of their control over rates and fares generally. In that year the Government of India addressed a despatch on the subject to the Secretary of State for India,[1] and in replying on the 16th May of the same year they were informed by the Secretary of State that the conclusion he had arrived at, "after careful examination of all the circumstances of the case," was that the companies should be left free, within the maximum to be fixed by Government, to make such alterations in their scale of rates and fares as they might at any time think desirable. On this the Government of India issued a circular from the Public Works Department,[2] addressed to all "local Governments and Administrations," which propounded certain principles for their guidance in controlling rates, and indicated the part which the Supreme Government should take in this respect. It held that the Government of India should only so far interfere as might be necessary to fix a general policy, and "to regulate matters by which a railway company working within the territories of one local Government may affect a company working within the territories of another Government." Beyond this the Government of India desired to leave the subject of maximum rates and fares entirely to the local officials concerned. They further declared that the only policy of the Supreme Government, as regards the fixing of the rates and fares on railways, should be to make them as generally useful to the mass of the people as was consistent with due profits to the companies; that the powers of the Government under the contracts were limited to the approval of increases of fares after they had been once fixed, and to the fixing of fares on the first opening of a railway. It was clear,

[1] No. 26, of 8th February 1867.
[2] No. 10, Railway, of 16th October 1867.

it was said, "that it can never be proper to insist on any fare or rate that shall not afford a reasonable profit with ordinarily filled trains, and that there are only a few cases in which the Government should interfere with the freedom of the companies to act according to their judgment on the ordinary system of trial of the relations of supply and demand." The matters which it was held should be retained in the hands of the Government of India were the fares for the lowest class of passengers, the rates for food grain, and for the carriage of coal. As regards the two last, the circular said that the rates already in force and sanctioned were to be considered as the maximum on lines already opened, and that on future lines the maximum rate was to be $\frac{1}{4}$ of a pie[1] per mile, or (at the then rate of exchange) $\frac{27}{32}$ of a penny per ton mile. The then maximum rates on four of the principal Indian railways at the time was as follows in each class, to which terminal charges were added:—

Classes of Goods.	Rates per Ton Mile Pies.			
	East Indian Railway.	Great Indian Peninsula Railway.	Bombay, Baroda, and Central India Railway.	Madras Railway.
1st	9	8	8	14
2nd. . . .	13½	10	10	18
3rd	18	16	16	24
4th . . .	27	20	20	36
5th	54	30	30	54

The interference of the Government had not taken place too soon, for the railway companies had already begun to experience the pressure of traffic, and to recognise that in the absence of competition they had the game in their own hands. The want of rolling stock further increased both the need and the possibility of charging higher rates, especially in the busy

[1] A pie is one-twelfth of an anna, and 16 annas = 1 rupee.

season, while the agents of the two companies on the Bombay side had represented the enormous difference between the rates they were allowed to charge and the rates for carriage by cart, which was seven times greater than those by rail. It is curious to note, however, that thus early in this discussion the companies offered to accept minima if they could be allowed to increase their maxima. There being then no competition, this did not then seem to be a matter of importance to the Government, and, unfortunately, as it proved eventually, it passed unnoticed in the circular above referred to.

The action taken by the Government of India did, however, meet with the approval of the Home Government.[1] The Secretary of State agreed in the view that the Government of India should only interfere so far as to fix a general policy, but held that in keeping in their hands the fares for the lowest class of passengers, and the rates for food-grains and coal, the suggested limit had been passed, and that the settlement of the maximum for every description of traffic should be left in the hands of the local authorities. He said that in directing the establishment of maximum rates and fares he had intended that such bounds should be fixed as would leave it to the discretion of the companies to vary the rates in force, and that in some of the rates mentioned in a recent circular no such discretion was left. He held that the companies were not advocates of high rates, as it was as much their interest as that of the Government that their charges should be so regulated as "to give the maximum of passengers with the maximum of profit." The despatch thus made pointed reference mainly to passenger traffic, and the reply of the Government of India[2] dealt only with this phase of the question, laying stress on the importance, or rather the necessity, for control in this respect, and insisting that the interests of the Government and the

[1] See despatch No. 17, of 29th February 1868, from Secretary of State for India.

[2] No. 76, Railway, of 25th April 1868.

companies could not be considered to be identical. This protest, nevertheless, appears to have had but little effect in moving the Secretary of State from his original position. In replying in June of the same year[1] he regretted that he was unable to agree with the views of the Government. He was quite sensible, he said, of the advantage of low rates to the travelling and trading public, and that they would most probably in the long-run be remunerative, but he thought that, as regards passenger traffic, the interests of the lower class of travellers would be sufficiently protected by the maxima to be fixed by local Governments; and that as regards rates generally, the right policy was to leave to the companies the duty of fixing them within such limits. He concluded by stating that it was his wish "that maximum rates should be fixed by local Governments, that the actual rates within such maximum should be regulated by the railway companies, and that the maximum rates fixed by local Governments should leave a reasonable margin for exercise of discretion by a company in varying working rates as circumstances may, in their opinion, require."

Views, or rather orders, thus plainly stated, left the Government of India no option but that of compliance, and in October a fresh resolution was issued[2] giving effect to them in practically similar terms. In forwarding a copy of this resolution to the Home Government on the same date, the Government of India did not attempt to conceal their objections. They admitted that the local Governments were as well able to protect the interests of the people as they were; but that, apart from the obvious difficulty of getting various distinct and distant authorities to adopt the same means to attain the desired end, there was the financial objection, insomuch that the different means adopted were so many experiments made at the risk of the Government of India, which was responsible

[1] Despatch No. 48, dated 25th June 1868, from Secretary of State.

[2] Nos. 1174-80, Railway, of 6th October 1868.

for the finance of the Empire. They further urged that one central authority was the most suitable in order to carry out an approved policy with consistency and success. No difficulties of any moment arose in carrying out this policy so long as the main lines were free from competition, and no further references appear to have been made until then to the Secretary of State. Each line had a definite territory of ample dimensions, and within the maxima rates fixed by the local authorities it was free to adopt such rates as the traffic would bear. No attempt had been made by the Government to secure any uniformity in the scales of rates or in classification. The divergences in the rates may perhaps be accounted for, in some measure at least, on the ground that in India, and indeed elsewhere, the traffic managers were apparently bound by the assumption that the cost of carriage was some definite figure, within narrow limits, on each railway, and influenced to only a small extent, by the volume or character of the traffic dealt with. But powerful agencies were ere long to come into action, and to disturb the peaceful career of the guaranteed lines. The opening of the Suez Canal, and the consequent introduction of Indian produce into the European markets on favourable terms, led to a keen rivalry between lines leading to the sea-board; a series of severe famines in different parts of the country had similar results, and traffic officers began at length to realise that the volume of tonnage was an important factor in determining the cost of transport by rail, and that rates, which at one time would have seemed to spell ruin, proved to be the principal source of profit. Later on the era of State and competitive railways arrived, with the inevitable effect of a war of rates, and appeals for the interference of the Supreme Government.

The first indications of the storm which was to set in later, came in the shape of a memorial from Calcutta traders in 1881, pointing out that the rates for produce between Upper India and Bombay were injuring the trade of Calcutta, and praying that relief might be afforded them, by requiring either that higher rates should be enforced on the Bombay route or lower on the Calcutta route. This plaint was supported by the Bengal Chamber of Commerce, and as a part of one of the routes to Bombay was over a State line, the Government of India felt it necessary to take action. This took the form of instructions to the manager of the State line that the charges to Bombay should not be lower than what was charged on similar goods to Calcutta. It should be observed, that at this time the route to Calcutta was, as regards rates, wholly under the control of the Government, as the East Indian Railway had become the property of the State in 1879. The course thus taken by the Government of India was promptly objected to by the lines leading to Bombay and the Bombay Chamber of Commerce, and supported by that Government. Both the Bombay lines were guaranteed, and were thus free from anxiety on the score of low, or even unremunerative rates, more especially as there was then but little prospect of their yielding returns in excess of the guaranteed rate of interest, or, in other words, of affording surplus profits over and above that figure to the shareholders. The views of the Government of India as conveyed, at the end of 1881, to the Government of Bombay [1] were, that while they did not intend that there should be an absolute equalisation of rates from Upper India to Calcutta and Bombay, under all circumstances, based only on mileage, they thought that this principle should be adopted if "tempered with the proper commercial principle of an even return on the capital expended." They stated that from the point of view of the general welfare of the country, it was immaterial to what party its surplus produce was directed so long as the course of trade was unfettered by artificial obstacles. "The lines of railway which the State has become instrumental in providing have been constructed for the purpose of carrying goods and passengers at the lowest rates consistent with

[1] Letter to Bombay Government, No. 1192, of 19th October 1881.

yielding a fair and reasonable return on the capital laid out. As trade increases these rates will decrease; but the ultimate limit of legitimate competition between the various lines must be regulated by their capabilities of making an equally fair profit from the traffic they carry." They were quite willing to admit the advantages of competition in stimulating traffic, but held that the disastrous results of this, when recklessly followed, as on the English and American railways, had taught the world a lesson which could not be ignored.

These views were strongly objected to by the Government of Bombay. It was urged that it was quite impossible to adjust rates on theoretical principles, which should be absolutely fair to the railways concerned; that the practical, simple, and intelligible principle was that of equal mileage rates; while to attempt to fix rates with the object of insuring an equal return on the capital invested, would assuredly lead to endless dispute, and would fail to give satisfaction to traders. This remonstrance from Bombay had been strengthened by the receipt of a dispatch from the Secretary of State,[1] in which he held a similar opinion, and indeed considered the position taken up by the Government of India to be altogether unsound. He held that it was impolitic to interfere with any idea of adjudicating on the rivalry between the two lines affected, and "that the advantages due either to geographical position, or other circumstances, should furnish no reason for imposing on either artificial restrictions in the shape of enhanced rates, in order to produce an equal return of net profits on the capital of both." This warning note failed in its effect, for in May of the same year, we find the Government of India addressing the Government of Bombay on the same subject, and stating that the conclusion arrived at, "after careful consideration of all the arguments adduced on this somewhat complicated question," was that in fixing the charges for the carriage of the same commodity on different railways, the cost

[1] No. 41, Railway, 9th March 1882, to Government of India.

of carriage could not be neglected, nor could this "important element" be omitted in the division of through rates between lines working in connection. They pointed out the effects of steep gradients in enhancing cost of working; that it was "perfectly clear" that a line under such conditions could not carry at the same mileage rate as one under more favourable conditions, and on the latter it would be manifestly unfair to require its rates to be raised so as to produce equality. A copy of this letter was communicated to the Secretary of State in reply to his dispatch above referred to, stating that it was the desire of the Government, in the interest of the country generally, that all rates should be reduced to the lowest limit which will give a fair profit, and that "this cannot be obtained by the adoption of uniform mileage rates on all lines."

The reply of the Secretary of State[1] was very decidedly opposed to these views. He admitted that the cost of fuel and the character of the gradients on a line must be considerable factors in determining the lowest rates at which goods can be carried with a "fair margin of profit," but that elements still more important were the capital cost and volume of traffic, and that if the two Western lines were the property of private companies, "they would certainly not raise their mileage rates above those of the Eastern line, because their fuel was dearer and gradients steeper." He held that it was impracticable to attempt to proportion the rates on competing lines on the basis of the supposed aggregates of the factors of cost of transport on each; that it would not be desirable, if it were practicable, and that managers should be left to fix rates as they may deem most advantageous for their respective lines, subject to the interposition of Government in extreme cases. The concluding paragraphs of the despatch are worth quoting in full:—

12. In the present condition of the Indian railway traffic, I am

[1] Despatch No. 132, Railway, of 19th October 1882.

not apprehensive of evil results from the course now indicated; I am rather disposed to think that the interests, both of the railways and of trade generally, will be better served by accepting the legitimate consequences of competition, regulated, as it necessarily will be, by the desire to apply skill and economy to the work of management, and stimulating as it must do, the introduction of improvements in the harbour arrangements at the ports of shipment to which competing lines lead.

13. As regards the division of receipts among the different lines over which the traffic passes, it seems to me that the practical difficulties in the way of establishing any agreement based upon calculations of the cost of working would be insuperable, and that the principle of a mileage division, which is applied under the Clearing-House arrangements in this country, may fairly be applied to Indian lines, whatever their original cost of construction or their present cost of working may be. . . .

This solution of the difficulty, as offered by the Secretary of State, was clearly the only practical one. It was not, however, until the following March (1883) that the Government of India felt able to take action, and in a letter[1] to the Government of Bombay, enunciated its views on the principles on which rates and fares should in future be regulated. Starting with the axiom that the fundamental aim in the management of a railway was to attract the maximum quantity of traffic the line can carry at the best rates obtainable, it might be considered that, in one sense, all rates would be special, though capable of classification into groups, and that each rate would depend on what the article would bear, what quantity of it is obtainable, and what is the approximate cost of hauling it; that the cost of carriage would be one of the limits within which rates may vary, the tax which the trade will bear being the other. But in the determination of a rate, it was necessary to consider the whole circumstances of the traffic dealt with as regards empty running, the intermittent nature of it, and the effect of competition by

[1] No. 162, R.T. (Railway Traffic), of the 2nd March 1883.

other routes. The theory of equal mileage rates was held to have been condemned by competent authorities in England; while "telescopic" rates, or rates varying inversely as the distance, were recognised as legitimate in all cases where the favoured traffic would be lost without such rates, and as being financially possible owing to the lower proportionate cost of the longer lead. In a case where a railway had the practical monopoly of the traffic, the fixing of rates was a simple matter, in which the State need only interpose for the purpose of fixing maxima in the interests of the public; but that when competition arose, the basis for the calculation of rates would be materially changed. While bearing in mind such factors as capital cost, gradients, cost of fuel, and carrying power, rates had to be eventually governed by the necessity of attracting traffic, and "not by any arbitrary standard of profit to which it is thought fair to attain." A railway which was disadvantageously affected as to cost, gradients, fuel, etc., must expect "to go to the wall" in rivalry with another more favoured naturally; and from this it followed, that when traffic passed over more than one railway, and the division of receipts could be agreed upon on no other method, it would be necessary to apportion them according to mileage run.

The next point considered was whether, in the case of competition, those principles could be held to be affected by the fact of the State being either the proprietor of or holding a certain interest in and control over, one or more of the conflicting railways. It was held that they were not; that the State ought not, and often could not, interfere so as to put all on a theoretically fair and equal footing; that it could not legitimately make a common purse among its railways, in order to support one at the expense of another, or still less to drive an independent competitor from the field. Rival routes must be left alone, to get the highest traffic they can. The net result would be "the greatest aggregate of traffic upon all combined, which is consistent with a profit, the maximum of accommodation to traders and the public, of gain to both producers and consumers, and the highest possible development of the resources of the country." There was one contingency, however, in which the State would be justified in exerting such influence as in any case it might possess, namely, when from either "ignorance, recklessness, or idle rivalry" on the one hand, or on the other from the indifference derived from the security of a Government guarantee, rates were unreasonably or unnecessarily lowered. In concluding the letter, the Government of India stated that, subject to interposition on such grounds, the agents and managers of railways might be left free to fix rates on the principles laid down, but that they should carefully examine their existing rates, both for goods and coaching, especially in the latter, the third-class fares, to see how far they were capable of modification or reduction. Copies of this letter were sent to the Secretary of State, and it was published in the Government Gazettes and newspapers, as indicating the general policy of the State on the subject.

It was not expected that this declaration on the part of the Government would suffice to relieve it from further interference in the competition which the rapidly expanding export trade was giving rise to in all directions. Indeed, no sooner was the difficulty between Bombay and Calcutta disposed of or quieted down for a time, than a fresh crop of troubles arose, from the rivalry of the lines serving the North-West Provinces, with Calcutta as a base. Over the administration of the State lines the Government had obviously ample powers, but its position with regard to the guaranteed and assisted companies was very different, and it seemed certain that complications would become more frequent and embarrassing with every extension of the railway system. The prominent difficulty lay in the adjustment of the goods rates of competing trunk lines, in order that no undue advantage should be afforded to one line over that of another—more especially with respect to those in which the State had a definite interest. The Government of

India seemed at length to see a refuge from their troubles in the establishment of a Clearing-House, which should be independent of the Government, have powers not merely to allocate the distribution of the receipts from through traffic, but to settle disputes as to routes for traffic, charges by rival routes, and the simplifying of goods classification. This idea had been already submitted to a Traffic Conference of the principal railways, but had not been favourably received. The Government decided, however, to refer the proposal to the Secretary of State for India, which was done in August 1885,[1] requesting that the opinion of Boards of the different railway companies in England should be invited. The reply to this was sent in February 1886,[2] the Secretary of State then being Lord Kimberley. The views of the railway companies generally were decidedly opposed to the proposition. They held that it was both premature and unnecessary, and that, moreover, the scope of the functions of the proposed Clearing-House Committee would go far beyond that of the institution under this title at home. The Secretary of State considered that more evidence of its necessity was required before he could press the matter further, but that if its main object was to settle the rates on lines competing for traffic to the sea-board, he thought it was beyond the proper duties of Government to interfere in such matters, otherwise than by the influence it possessed, either under existing contracts or as owners of the State lines.

The course thus generally indicated by the Secretary of State was one which the Government of India would have willingly adopted, but the exercise of mere "influence" was clearly inadequate for the purpose of determining disputes in which the guaranteed railways were involved, nor had the Government as yet arrived at any general principles under which they could recognise the rights of managers to fix such

[1] Despatch 120, Railway, of 7th August 1885.
[2] No. 16, Railway, of 25th February 1886.

rates and fares as would seem to them to be best suited to the traffic to be dealt with. The necessity for definite action in this direction was brought to the notice of the Government in August 1887, in the form of an able and exhaustive note by Colonel L. Conway-Gordon, R.E., then Director-General of Railways. In this he laid down certain principles for acceptance, based upon practice in England and elsewhere, with regard to railway rates and fares, reviewing at the same time the position of the Government as to its power of control over the guaranteed and "assisted" railways and those under Native States in this respect. The recommendations made in this note were generally accepted by the Government, and were embodied in a resolution in December 1887;[1] but owing to the terms of the contracts with the guaranteed lines, it was not considered possible to make the orders wholly applicable to other than State railways, or to other lines only so far as was consistent with existing contracts or agreements. In the remarks preceding the resolution, the Government of India stated that they endorsed, without reservation, the general principles "that managers of railways should be left to fix their own rates and fares; that the interest of railways and trade generally would be better served by accepting the legitimate consequences of competition; and that the interposition of Government would be justified only in cases where companies under the security of a guarantee might fix rates below what would cover the cost of transport with a margin of profit." The terms of the resolution were as follows:—

(*a*) That the schedule of maxima and minima rates and fares, forming Appendix A to this resolution, shall be adopted on all railways worked directly by the State, and by all other railway administrations, whether their lines be already opened or not, so far as this schedule is not inconsistent with any contracts or agreements previously

[1] No. 1446, Railway Traffic, dated 12th December 1887.

entered into; and that it shall not be departed from without due cause being shown.

(*b*) That in order that the public may have complete information as to the maxima rates and fares which every railway is authorised to charge, the maxima and minima rates and fares fixed for each railway shall be published in their goods and coaching tariffs, under the signature of a consulting engineer if a private company, and of the Secretary to Government in the case of a State line.

(*c*) That unless sufficient reasons can be brought forward against the adoption of this course, the general goods classification now in force on the East Indian Railway shall be accepted for all railways worked directly by the State, and by all other railway administrations, with the same proviso as to interference with existing contracts as under (*a*) above.

(*d*) That there shall be no undue preference, either as between two railway companies or between a railway company and a particular person or class of individuals, by making preferential bargains, or by granting to one particular company or person more favourable conditions for the carriage of goods than to the rest of the public at large.

(*e*) That the Director-General of Railways be instructed to place himself in communication with the several railway companies, with a view to establishing a Standing Committee of Railway Managers.

As regards the first clause (*a*) the Government considered that the principle of fixing maxima rates and fares had been recognised in every English Railway Act, and in legislation in Europe and in America. In India, however, it was not only necessary to follow this course, but on account of the guarantee of interest to certain railways, it was also necessary to fix minima rates. It was held that this guarantee would enable a railway to work at a loss to Government without affecting the pecuniary interests of the shareholders in any way, and at the expense of the taxpayer, *i.e.* when such guaranteed line was not paying the guaranteed interest, and had no near prospect of so doing. Thus a company, under such circumstances, might in competitive traffic lower rates below a point which would yield profit, and, consequently, it was necessary that the Government should have the power to enforce a minimum "when circumstances have shown them to be necessary" in the financial interests of the State. The restriction of the minimum was, moreover, a salutary check on the action of managers of State railways in competition with each other or with a guaranteed line. On the question of terminal charges, the Government admitted that it was impossible to prescribe any maximum or minimum which would meet all cases, and that they must remain content with reserving power, in case any cause should be shown for interference, of fixing what may appear a fair and reasonable charge. Having fixed the maxima and minima in each class, and established a standard for the classification of goods for State lines, the Government conceded that railway administrations should be allowed to alter rates within these limits, and that while abstaining from making preferential bargains or allowing "undue preference," the various railways should give reasonable facilities for through traffic, and should aim at serving the country "as if they were under one management," and that a trader should not be forced to base his calculations on as many different scales of rates as there may be railways between the starting-point and destination. The protection of the public in this sense was subsequently effectually carried out in the revision of the Indian Railway Act, to which reference is made in another chapter. On the question whether the charging of a lower or equal rate for a longer than a shorter distance constituted "undue preference," the Government of India held that it appeared to be as yet unsettled in England, although the weight of legal authority was much opposed to the practice, and that it might be held to be *primâ facie* evidence at least of such preference.

The managers of State railways were required to accept this view, and it was to be urged on the officers of the guaranteed lines by the local officials.

The Schedule which accompanied the resolution above referred to fixed a maximum and minimum rate for goods for each class, but this was illusory, as they were one and the same, or in other words, no latitude was given as to charges within any class, and the only way left to a railway manager was to alter his classification in any case in which he desired to raise or lower his rates. To have permitted this would have been to abandon the policy which, up till then, had been firmly pursued, viz. of endeavouring to bring all the railways into line with a uniform classification. It was eventually admitted that the terms of the Schedule should be altered, that a separate maximum and minimum should be fixed for each class of goods, and that within these limits managers should have power to vary charges without reference to Government, while alteration of classification, when once fixed, should not be made without formal sanction. A revised Schedule was appended to a resolution on the subject,[1] which was as follows:—

	Maximum. Pies[2] per maund per mile.	Minimum. Pies per maund per mile.
Goods Rates—		
5th class	1	$\frac{1}{6}$ (5th to 1st class)
4th "	$\frac{5}{6}$	
3rd "	$\frac{2}{3}$	
2nd "	$\frac{1}{2}$	
1st "	$\frac{1}{3}$	
Coal, edible grain, and other low-priced staples carried at special rates	$\frac{1}{3}$	$\frac{1}{10}$

This Schedule was to apply to railways on the standard or metre gauge administered or controlled by the Government, and was applicable to both local and through booking. A standard classification to be adopted on these lines was laid

[1] No. 563, Railway Traffic, of 16th July 1891.

[2] One pie may be taken as equal to $\frac{1}{12}$ of a penny.

down, and the guaranteed and other lines invited to accept it, which was done by nearly all. The question of terminal charges remained to be settled, but so far (1893) the only action taken by the Government has been to declare that it could not recognise the right of any railway administration to levy special charges, in addition to the prescribed maxima, on traffic passing through junctions, and that statements showing all terminal charges on every railway were to be periodically submitted for consideration. Previously to this the Indian Railway Act of 1890 had been passed, and this point had been briefly dealt with in sections 45 and 46. The former merely said that "a railway administration may charge reasonable terminals," and in the latter, the determination of what was reasonable was to be referred to the Commissioners—the wording or intent of this section being adopted from the English "Railway and Canal Traffic Act" of 1888.

The effect of this action of the Government has been to relieve it almost entirely of the burden of settling disputes between the different administrations, and in great measure to reduce the number of cases in which dispute arises. All lines which have accepted the minimum are bound by it in competition, and it is only when this is infringed that a reference is or can be made by opposing lines. The result that may be expected from the practically unrestricted rivalry for through traffic which is now allowed, is that rates that are now thought impossibly low will be found on the contrary to be not only possible, but distinctly remunerative under certain conditions, and that ere long the present minimum in the special classes may be reduced still lower. On three of the principal State railways it has been ascertained that the actual cost of carrying a maund one mile on the whole traffic has averaged no more than $\frac{1}{11}$ of a pie, while the average sum received has been $\frac{1}{5}$ of a pie, thus indicating a profit of over 100 per cent.

The introduction of through booking by rail and sea, on the American system, between India and England, has been effected as yet on one line only, viz. the North-Western Railway, having its terminus at Karachi. The first proposals on the subject were made, in 1884, by Sir W. P. Andrew, then chairman of the Sind, Punjab, and Delhi Railway Company. Nothing was done, however, until after this line became the property of the State, and was merged in the system of the North-Western Railway. In 1886 negotiations were entered into by the manager of this line with the Hall line of steamers, on the basis of giving them through booking from any station on the railway of passengers, parcels, and goods to Europe, and as a set off to purchase from them a certain tonnage of English coal monthly. Difficulties arose mainly on the grounds of the legality and responsibility of the railway in granting through bills of lading; but these, after considerable delay, were got over, and an agreement was entered into for five years dating from the 1st January 1890. So far there has been no similar movement at other ports, nor does it seem likely, under the existing conditions of Indian business, and the essentially conservative character of the trading classes, that any initiative will be taken on that side. There are, moreover, substantial differences between India and America, in both the methods of conducting such operations and in the class of men who would be engaged in them. In India there are but few places where at present firms can be found who could be safely entrusted to ship to Europe to order on a sample or mark, and the crowd of large and small agents at the ports, who are at present a necessary part of the machinery of both the export and import trade, would certainly be likely to oppose an innovation which would probably deprive them of a large share of their present profits. At the same time, it must be allowed that it is these profits of the agent or middleman that represent a considerable factor in Indian prices, and that they would be reduced on a system of through booking. The success of the arrangement on the North-Western Railway has not been so far encouraging as regards goods traffic, and at the present time (1893) is practically confined to the occasional transactions of one firm.

The table given at the end of this chapter affords information that may be of interest as regards the third or lowest class of passenger traffic on Indian railways, and shows that while the charge per mile is generally 2½ pies, the average cost of haulage, including all charges, on both the standard and the metre gauge is less than one pie per mile.

[TABLE

Table relating to the Lowest Class Passenger Traffic on Indian Railways, 1892-93.

Railway.	Average length of lowest class journey.	Lowest class fares.	Average number of lowest class passengers in a train.	Average number of vehicles in a train.	Average number of passengers in a vehicle.	Cost of hauling a passenger vehicle one mile	Cost of hauling a lowest class passenger one mile.
Standard Gauge Lines.	Miles.	Pies per mile.			Full load = 60.	Pies.[1]	Pies.[1]
East Indian . .	60.00	2.5	235.45	10.77	21.86	10.43	0.48
Bengal-Nágpur . .	41.80	2.5	227.46	11.90	19.11	21.19	1.11
Indian Midland . .	69.88	2.5	126.96	6.26	20.28	21.89	1.08
North-Western (State).	42.03	2.5	192.40	8.97	21.45	21.29	0.99
Oudh and Rahilkund (State) . . .	47.62	2.5	230.35	10.18	22.63	13.81	0.61
Eastern Bengal (State) and Bengal Central .	23.04	2.5	165.08	8.08	20.43	15.45	0.75
Great Indian Peninsula	36.87	2.4	132.20	6.34	20.85	22.10	1.06
Bombay, Baroda, and Central India . .	17.75	2.3	178.12	6.84	26.04	23.31	0.89
Madras . . .	27.30	1.5	260.36	10.41	25.01	21.28	0.85
The Nizam's Guaranteed (State) . .	54.72	2.0	194.54	10.75	18.10	21.22	1.17
Average. .	42.1	...	...	...	21.58	19.20	0.90
Metre Gauge Lines.					Full load = 32.		
Bengal and North-Western and Tirhoot	37.78	1.7	290.06	19.21	15.10	7.33	0.48
Rajputana-Malwa .	48.70	2.0	235.08	13.26	17.72	10.15	0.57
Southern Mahratta .	41.81	2.3	171.91	9.30	18.48	22.55	1.22
South Indian . .	33.60	2.0	246.19	13.71	17.96	15.28	0.85
Eastern Bengal (State)	24.81	2.5	157.10	11.15	14.09	12.82	0.91
Burma (State) . .	35.84	3.0	235.71	16.94	13.91	14.29	1.03
Bhávnagar-Gondal-Junágarh-Porbandar .	39.09	2.7	187.31	11.97	15.65	23.48	1.50
Average. .	37.38	...	...	...	16.13	15.13	0.93

[1] One pie at present rate of exchange may be said to be equal to one-twelfth of a penny.

CHAPTER VI

INDIAN RAILWAY LEGISLATION

It is intended in this chapter to give a brief account of the legislation that has been carried out from time to time in India for the control of railways, and for defining the responsibilities of railway servants and the public generally. The first enactment was applicable to railways in British territory only, and to those only "under Government control," viz. Act xviii. of 1854. This practically did little more than give legal effect to regulations such as were then in force on English railways, as for instance the prepayment of fares, tickets, smoking, fraud, and the liability of companies as to luggage and valuable property. The usual clauses as to carriage of goods, trespass, and obstruction were also included, and every railway was required to erect and maintain good and sufficient fences on each side of the line, and failing therein, to be liable to a fine of fifty rupees for every offence, the procedure for the recovery of fines and other penalties being laid down at length. The Act gave no list of "definitions," nor was any procedure laid down as to the inspection of railways, or as regards inquiry into accidents. On the latter point, all that a railway company was required to do was to report the occurrence of accidents to the local Governments, and to submit a return of the same in such form as the Government might deem necessary. The last clause required that a copy of the Act, of the general regulations, the time-tables, and tariff of charges, should be published and exhibited in English and the vernacular of the district at all stations.

The first difficulty of any importance in the working of this Act is disclosed in a circular letter [1] from the Government of India to local Governments, in which it is shown that there was a defect in the Act as to the recovery of fines from a railway company, and that an amendment of the Act on this point was necessary. The opinion of local Governments was invited with regard to this, and to any other defects that may have appeared in the working of the Act, and a proposed draft for the amendment of the same accompanied this circular letter. Many suggestions were submitted in reply to this, the substance of the principal of which were referred to in a resolution of Government of India in the Public Works Department in August 1865.[2] The main points which seemed to need attention in a new Act were as follows :—That it should be applicable to all railways of every description, including tramways worked by steam; that it should apply to railways in foreign as well as British territory. That whereas the old Act made companies liable for loss or injury only when such had been "caused by the gross negligence or misconduct" of their servants, it should be laid down that loss or injury was held sufficient proof of negligence somewhere, and that the companies should be liable in all such cases. More stringency was suggested also as to dealing with accidents, and for procedure in preventing the opening of a railway for traffic before it had been declared fit for such purpose. There was also a strong feeling shown in the correspondence as to the need for more severe measures in dealing with cattle trespass, and the provision of a sufficient number of level crossings. In a brief Act passed in 1871 (Act xxv. of 1871), this question of cattle trespass was dealt with among some other minor matters;

[1] No. 836-9 of the 3rd March 1862, from Government of India Public Works Department.

[2] Resolution 704-14, Railway, of 19th August 1865.

and previously to this, in 1870, another short Act was passed giving certain requisite definitions for the Act of 1854. An important clause was inserted in the first of these Acts (1871), in which "the officers for the time being intrusted with the control of a railway" (meaning the principal officer or agent of a company), should make "general rules and regulations for the use, working, and general administration" of a railway, and might vary these from time to time; but that all such rules, etc., should be submitted for the sanction of the Governor-General in Council, and when sanctioned, published for general information. Breach of such rules rendered persons liable to a fine not exceeding fifty rupees, or in default, to imprisonment which might extend to two months.

Another resolution of Government on the same subject had been issued in November 1866,[1] but meanwhile a draft Bill for a new Act had been sent home for opinion to the Secretary of State (then Lord Cranborne), viz. in March of the same year, who replied commenting on it in December.[2] He fully agreed in the necessity for a fresh enactment, and in having "one comprehensive digest to refer to, instead of numerous and fragmentary enactments." He held that one essential consideration had been originally overlooked, which was that all the existing railway companies had very extensive rights and privileges secured to them under their contracts, and that legislative interference with such contract rights might, independently of any question of justice, not improbably subject the Home Government to serious legal liability. One way of meeting this, he suggested, was the insertion of a clause saving existing contracts, but that this would impair the efficiency of the Bill, and afford a large scope for litigation; yet that it was not easy to suggest any other course, unless the companies would engage to be consenting parties. Another important

[1] No. 1096, Railway, of 3rd November 1866.

[2] No. 44, of December 1866, from Secretary of State to Government of India.

point was that as the new Act was to apply to all Indian railways, whether already sanctioned or hereafter to be constructed, it might be well to reserve the right to Government of determining the gauge of a line, of having troops and mails conveyed at convenient times, of reducing rates and fares, and of "insisting on specially cheap trains for poor passengers." He also thought it might be possible to adopt such clauses of the English Act regulating the Clearing-House system as would be suitable for India. This despatch was accompanied by the opinions of the Home Boards of the different Indian railway companies on the proposed Bill. The Government of India replied in January 1868,[1] sent a fresh draft of the proposed Bill, and explained the grounds for the principal alterations. The new Bill as modified proposed a far more complete and inclusive enactment than that of 1854. There were clauses for the acquisition of land, for mines under railways, for the provision of sufficient crossings, the inspection and opening of new lines, the carriage of troops and of mails, and revision of the procedure for the recovery of fines. The amended Bill was published in India for opinion generally, and in October 1869[2] the Government of India suggested to the Home Government, that as there was likely to be delay in passing the Bill, certain parts of it might be dealt with separately, as being more or less urgently required. No action was, however, taken in this direction, and correspondence continued mainly on the question of the competency of the Government to traverse the rights of the companies in any new legislation.

In the meantime the Government of India had resolved on a new and important departure in the direction of the construction and working of State railways, and this materially altered the position of affairs. The result was the issue of a Government resolution in 1871,[3] in which this point was

[1] No. 1, Railway, of 3rd January 1868, to Secretary of State for India.

[2] No. 109, Railway, dated 12th October 1869, to Secretary of State.

[3] No. 407, Railway, of 12th March 1871.

particularly referred to. It stated that it was evident that "the law of the land relating to railways should be the same to whomsoever such railways may belong, and that the law which governs the companies' lines must also govern the railways of the State." Thus, such points as to the general liability of railway administration as distinguished from that of their servants, the imposition of fines, and other matters, which were manifestly inapplicable to the State as the Bill then stood, rendered it necessary to reconsider, and indeed to reconstruct the greater portion of it. The resolution contemplated what was termed "partial legislation" to begin with, in the revision of the old Act, and indicated that this could probably be carried out without difficulty, if it did not injuriously affect the position of the companies under their contracts. It was subsequently arranged that the desired Bill should be drawn in England, in communication with the companies, but it was stated by the Government of India later on,[1] that there did not appear to be any pressing need for further legislation, considering that urgent points had been met by the short Acts of 1870 and 1871, and that it might be as well to wait for further experience in the working of State railways before further consideration of the new Railway Act. It seemed also desirable that, as a matter of policy, any change in railway law should not be promoted by the State just at the time its own railways were about to be opened; while it still stood as the controlling authority over the guaranteed lines. The subject was consequently allowed to remain in abeyance for some time.

In 1875 an incident occurred on one of the guaranteed lines (the Oude and Rahilkund Railway) which appears to have led to a reopening of the question of further legislation, more especially as the point involved was important. It appears that a village near the railway was set on fire by, it was

[1] Despatch No. 22, Railway, of 27th January 1873, to Secretary of State for India.

alleged, the sparks from a locomotive engine, and the company was sued for compensation by one of the sufferers. Damages were decreed against the company, on the ground that it had no statutable powers to use locomotives on the line, and that, without such powers, it was liable for injury caused by engines in setting fire to adjoining property, or otherwise. The judgment was upheld on appeal in India, and the directors of the company contemplated a further appeal to the Privy Council. This was, however, deprecated by the Secretary of State, who said that the point would be dealt with in the new Railway Act.

In 1876 a new Bill was introduced in the Viceroy's Council by Sir Andrew Clarke, then member in the Council for Public Works, and on this further comments and suggestions were received in due course; but it was not until the 13th March 1879 that the Bill became law.[1] Its provisions extended to the whole of British India, and to the subjects of the Queen in Native States. It came into force on the 1st July 1879, the Acts of 1854, 1867, 1870, and 1871 being repealed, and it was laid down that nothing in the Carriers' Act of 1865 should apply to carriers by railway. The term "railway" was, under certain clauses, to cover the case of lines under construction, and a "railway administration" was to cover the case of the managers of State lines, lines worked by Native States or by companies. The difficulty above referred to as to the powers to run locomotives, was dealt with in a short clause, making it lawful to use "locomotive engines, or other motive power," with the previous sanction of the Governor-General in Council. Under Clause 5 no railway was to be opened for the public carriage of passengers (not of goods) until the railway administration gave notice of intention to open, until the line had been duly inspected by an officer appointed for the purpose, and until he had reported that the opening could be allowed without danger to the public.

[1] As Act No. iv. of 1879.

Rules were also laid down for reporting accidents, and defining the classes into which they should be divided. The power of a railway administration to frame general rules for working a line was repeated from the old Act of 1854, the sanction of the Governor-General in Council being still required. Under the head of "offences and procedure" the provisions were considerably amplified, and amongst these was a clause providing for the punishment of hackney carriage and omnibus drivers at railway stations, in case of obstruction or misbehaviour. The Act gave power to the Governor-General in Council to extend it, or any portion of it, to "any tramway worked by steam."

The above Act was defective as regards the inspection of railways, both before and after opening, and it was found necessary to pass a short Act amending it in this respect in 1883;[1] but as the provisions of this Act were subsequently modified and enlarged in the Act of 1890[2] (now in force) detailed notice of them may be deferred until later. The principal object of the Act was to empower the Governor-General in Council to take action for the protection of the public against dangers arising from the inefficient maintenance of a railway, and to appoint officers for the purpose of making periodical inspections with this object. The absence of powers of this nature in other countries, and especially in the United Kingdom, has yet to be recognised by the travelling public. The provisions of Sections 5 and 5B of this Act enabled definite rules to be issued for the first time under legal authority in a resolution of Government,[3] for the inspection of all railways instead of for State lines only prior to their being opened for passenger traffic. One month's notice was to be given, the inspecting officer was to be supplied at the same time with full information regarding the manner of

[1] Act iv. of 1883. [2] Act ix. of 1890.
[3] Circular No. 19, Railway, of 30th August 1883.

construction of the line, and certificates as follows were required to be given at the time of inspection :—

1. That no infringement in structures had been made of the standard dimensions prescribed for the gauge of the line by the Government.
2. That no engine or vehicle exceeded the maximum moving dimensions prescribed.
3. That no infringement of such dimensions would be made in future without due sanction.
4. That no more than two engines would ever be allowed at one time on any one track of a bridge.
5. That no alterations in the loads of rolling stock which would involve line loads on bridges in excess of those which might from time to time be prescribed for the gauge by the Government would be permitted.

The resolution concluded by prescribing the nature of the tests on girder bridges.

The above sketch leads up to the period more closely antecedent to the Act of 1890, which, being now in force, deserves to be noticed at some length. The need for further legislation in the shape of a general railway law had been recognised before the passing of the Act of 1883, mainly owing to the questions which arose in the interchange of traffic, and in the settlement of the differences which arose on this account. So much had this been felt that some of the leading railways had pressed for a special enactment for arbitration. A draft Bill was eventually prepared, and sent home for approval and criticism to the Secretary of State in November 1884, the draft being at the same time freely circulated in India for opinion.[1] The principal feature in this first draft was the introduction of clauses allowing for the settlement of disputes between railways by means of arbitration, but besides this, the Bill of 1879 was more or less modified in nearly every clause. The collection of opinion, criticism, and

[1] Circular No. 1036, Railway Traffic, of 5th November 1884.

suggestion forms some bulky volumes extending over the years 1885 to 1890. The passing of the "Railway and Canal Traffic Act" of 1888 for the United Kingdom, or rather the discussions and debates on the measure before it had become law, led to a substitution of the machinery of a Commission for that of arbitration in the draft Bill, and to the renewal of discussion on this important alteration. In discussing the draft as it stood in July 1890,[1] the Secretary of State appears to have had misgivings as to the applicability of this method under the peculiar conditions of the Indian railway system, and in consideration of this fact that the Government had large powers of control over all the lines, while being the absolute owners of many of them, which would give exceptional scope for dealing with the action of the companies. On this, and on other grounds, the Secretary of State gave a somewhat partial sanction to the proposal. The Home Boards of the guaranteed lines viewed it from the point of its infringing their rights under their contracts, and that from the fact that the Bill provided for a temporary and not a standing tribunal, composed possibly to some extent of Government officials, it was to be feared that questions in dispute might not always be treated in the impartial and judicial way which characterised the proceedings of the English Railway Commission.

The objections on the above grounds, together with the multifarious proposals and modifications suggested from all sides, were disposed of ultimately by a Select Committee appointed for the purpose by the Government of India, and on the 21st March 1890 the Bill was passed as Act ix. of 1890, and was to come into force on 1st May of that year. The Act as it stands represents so largely the policy of the Indian Government as regards railways, that it has been considered advisable to give it *in extenso* in the appendices. Some comment may be offered also on its leading features. The first

[1] See Secretary of State's despatch, No. 75, Railway, 4th July 1889.

chapter merely consists of the usual and any necessary definitions. The second chapter, on the Inspection of Railways, differs but little from the provisions of the Act of 1879. It will be observed that Sub-section E (a) gives powers to make periodical inspections of any railway; while Sections 23 and 24 of the fourth chapter gives power to close a railway for traffic if it is held to be unsafe, and to forbid the use of rolling stock on similar grounds. The third chapter is practically new. It establishes the powers and responsibilities of railway administrations as regards the construction and maintenance of the lines and the provision of accommodation works. The want of enactment on this latter point was much felt by both the railways and the public, more especially as regards road crossings of a railway, either on the level or by over or under bridges. The fourth chapter, relating to the opening of railways for traffic, will be observed to refer only to passenger traffic. For goods traffic a railway administration may open a line on its own responsibility. Section 22 has been amplified by detailed rules for inspections, and for the procedure with regard to them. Sections 23 and 24, which are extremely important for the public safety, have been referred to above.

The fifth chapter is wholly new. It establishes railway commissions for the settlement of disputes or claims between companies, or between them and the public, and provides for what are known as "traffic facilities." The provisions in this chapter are largely copied from "The Railway and Canal Traffic Act" of 1888 of the United Kingdom, the prominent difference being that the Indian Commissions are to be merely temporary tribunals, as already mentioned, which are to be appointed as occasion may require, and only if the Governor-General in Council may think fit. The contrast between this and the standing Railway Commission in England is very marked, and is, moreover, characterised by the anomaly that in the Indian Act the decisions as to the necessity for appointing a Commission, as also the selection of its members, is left in the hands of the Executive. As the owner of most of the lines, and copartner in others, the Government in India could hardly be regarded, from a legal point of view, as able to exercise strictly impartial judgment in these important initiatory steps, more particularly if, as might well happen, the case to be dealt with was one in which the interests of the State were involved. But although this view might be advanced theoretically, it is not likely that there would be the slightest ground for apprehension on this score, should it be found necessary to put in force this portion of the Act.

The sections of the sixth chapter deal with the working of railways, and confer powers on a railway administration to make general rules with this object, which rules must be sanctioned by the Governor-General in Council. The sections on this head are practically similar to those in the Act of 1879, but new sections have been added, giving powers to the State to determine arrangements or disputes regarding a common terminus or junction, and the proportion of the cost of the same to be borne by each line. The chapter also provides for the making of working agreements between railways, for the establishment of ferries, for providing roadways for cart traffic on bridges, and even for the construction of approach roads to railway stations, and for charging tolls on these works. A very important section provides that every railway shall submit returns in prescribed forms regarding its capital and revenue transactions, and its traffic. The remaining sections in this chapter refer to the carriage of goods and passengers. Under the former head some of the provisions, such as Section 61, are copied or modified from the English Act of 1888.

Chapter VII. defines the responsibilities of railways as carriers, and it is to be noticed that Section 82 exempts a railway from responsibility for loss or damage in case of contracting to carry by sea, under the conditions of the ordinary bill of lading. The eighth chapter prescribes the duties of a railway administration in the case of accidents, and under Section 84 detailed rules have been laid down defining the duties of all concerned and the classes of accidents which are to be recognised. Chapter IX. deals with penalties and offences of railway companies, railway servants, and travellers or traders, and it is to be noticed that in Sections 87 to 98 the penalties refer to railway companies only, and thus exclude the officials of State lines, whose misdemeanours are, it is to be presumed, to be dealt with by the Government. Chapter X. contains supplementary provisions, in which is to be noticed specially Sections 137 and 138. On the whole the Act appears to be a thoroughly workable and carefully-considered piece of legislation, and so far no material defects or omissions have been noticed.

The effect of the Act upon the position of the guaranteed companies, in respect to their contracts with the Secretary of State, had been duly considered by the Select Committee which was appointed by the Government of India to advise on the new provisions. They had arrived at the conclusion that any saving clause regarding these contracts should not be inserted in the Bill. They held that such a clause might bring each company under a different law, and would certainly cause grave inconvenience. "Each company might claim to interpret the Act according to its view of its rights under the contract, and the attempt to do this, even if not successful, might very seriously impair the operation of those parts of the proposed Act which deals with the creation of traffic facilities and the prevention of undue preference." As soon, however, as the Bill became law, four of the companies, three of them being the only remaining of the old guaranteed companies, lodged protests with the Secretary of State against the infringements of their rights, and declared (under legal advice) that the passing of the Act, as regards the guaranteed companies, was *ultra vires* on the part of the Governor-General in Council. Their principal objection was to Chapter V. of the Act, which dealt with the subject of traffic facilities, undue preference, and the institution of a Railway Commission for the settlement of claims or disputes arising from these subjects; while one company[1] held that the Act was incompatible with the relations between the Secretary of State and the railway companies, and was "an ill-advised attempt to transplant into India legislation not adapted to its conditions." It was held, on the other hand, that the "Railway and Canal Traffic Act" of the United Kingdom was compatible with the conditions under which British railway companies existed, as they were merely statutory commercial concerns, "with which the Government have neither privity nor contract." These representations of the companies were forwarded to the Government of India by the Secretary of State,[2] together with opinions on the same by the legal adviser to the India Office. In replying to this in 1891,[3] the Government of India took a firm position. They traversed the view that the Act was *ultra vires*, and considered that unless it could be shown that very unreasonable interference with the companies' contracts had been enacted, the companies had no reason to complain, and that they were satisfied that no such interference could be shown, or would be likely to occur. They deprecated the suggestion that a further reference on the subject should be made to the law officers of the Crown, and believed that the companies would soon be led to the conclusion that the provisions of the Act were no less beneficial to them than to the public. Up to the present (1893) no further action on the general question has been taken on either side.

The application of the Act to railways belonging to or passing through Native States was a matter of more difficulty and delicacy. In the case of a railway wholly isolated in one

[1] The Madras Railway Company.

[2] No. 95, Railway, of 28th August 1890, from Secretary of State for India.

[3] Despatch 36, Railway, 29th April 1891, from Government of India.

State, the Government of India had no direct concern, other than as the paramount power, with what was in fact administration within foreign territory. But when, as in many cases, such lines formed part of through routes, it became evident that civil and criminal jurisdiction for damage, or offences under the Act, must lie with the Government of India, and more particularly when a line passed through several contiguous States. After considerable negotiation, conducted on the part of nearly every Native State in the most friendly and loyal spirit, this end has now been attained.

The general tenor and perhaps intention of railway legislation in India has been to follow more or less closely the example of the United Kingdom in this respect, and there are but few indications, either in the enactments or in the proceedings of the Government, of any desire to go beyond this, or to regard the circumstances and habits of the people as requiring any special treatment, whether of restraint or protection in their dealings with railway administrations. If we bear in mind the position of the Government of India as the owner or potential owner of the whole of the Indian railways, and remember that it holds far closer and more defined relations with the people than is the case with any European Government, while possessing the complete initiative in legislation, we may be surprised that it has not been tempted to venture on exceptional measures. This abstention is to be accounted for, however, in great degree by the fact that the Government is possessed of ample executive power in the control of its railways, and that thus many matters which elsewhere might need to be supported by legal sanction, are dealt with promptly and easily by a circular or resolution of the Supreme Government. The only direction in which special legislation is noticeable, and that not wholly with reference to railways, is to be found in the Act relating to the acquisition of land for this and other public purposes,[1] but in this—a

[1] The Land Acquisition Act, 1870.

measure of the greatest benefit to both buyer and seller—the Government is the principal party in the transactions covered by the enactment, and indeed may be regarded in most cases as selling itself in one department and buying in another, the only point to be dealt with being the equitable compensation of the tenants.

CHAPTER VII

CONCLUSION

It will have been gathered from the foregoing chapters that railway policy in India has passed through some important changes, and that it is even yet far from having reached finality. To some extent the various phases of policy have been due to the influence of changes in the *personnel* of the Government, but the main cause is to be found in the serious financial difficulties resulting from a silver standard, which have made it necessary to have recourse to one expedient after another in order to avoid any serious curtailment of operations. The charge of weakness and vacillation which from time to time has been laid at the door of Government is, when all the circumstances have been duly weighed, not only unreasonable, but unjust, and it would be much nearer the truth to credit it with unusual courage and persistence in having pushed on railway communication in the face of embarrassments which might well have daunted others in a similar position. The whole story, and more especially the result so far, afford a striking testimony to the ability, and above all the honesty of purpose of our Anglo-Indian statesmen. The motive throughout has been to obtain the much-needed railway extension on terms the least burdensome to the revenues of the Empire, and in avoiding as far as possible the undue relief of the present taxpayer at the expense of his successors.

Beginning in 1849, under Lord Dalhousie, with a system of broad gauge lines under guaranteed companies, no material change was made until the end of Lord Lawrence's tenure of office in 1869-70, and when the trunk lines were virtually completed. Then at length, and somewhat tardily, we find that the burden of the contracts with the companies is clearly recognised, and for the next ten years there is an era in which the extension of the railway system is carried out entirely and directly by State agency, and the metre gauge introduced. From 1880, again, and up to the present time, the policy of the Government has been forced by circumstances to be constantly changing, and in the financing of railways, in the agencies for construction or working, and on the question of gauge and other matters, there has been no evidence of settled aim. The complication which now exists in the methods of constructing and working Indian railways is not, as already noticed, entirely owing to financial reasons. It is almost as largely referable to the frequent divergence of opinion as to the relative advantages of direct State agency compared with that of companies, coupled with a distinct tendency, both in India and at home, to abandon the former and relieve the Government as far as possible of the commercial part of its administration of the railways, while reserving full powers of general supervision and control.

The various alterations in railway policy are well exemplified in the list given in the Appendix C, which shows the different agencies that are now employed both for construction and management in the Indian railway system. They may be classed as follows :—

1. State lines worked by the State.
2. State lines worked by companies.
3. Lines constructed and worked by guaranteed companies.
4. Lines constructed and worked by assisted companies.
5. Lines owned by Native States and worked by companies.

6. Lines owned by Native States and worked by the Government of India.
7. Lines owned and worked by Native States.
8. Foreign lines.

These comprise mileage under four different gauges, viz. the standard gauge of 5½ feet, the metre gauge, the 2½ feet gauge, and the 2 feet gauge—the two latter being characterised as "special gauges"; but the 2½ feet gauge is now regularly recognised, and standard dimensions for it will be found in the appendices. The total mileage open for traffic at the end of 1892 on each gauge was as follows:—

	Miles.
Standard gauge	10,346
Metre gauge	7,451
Special gauge	245
Total . . .	18,042

And in addition to this there was a small mileage, 53½ miles only, of steam tramways outside municipal limits. The total sum expended on Indian railways up to the end of 1892 was 23,408 lakhs of rupees.[1] The average cost per mile of the lines on each gauge is given in rupees in the table in the appendices, together with other data relating to them.

Had it not been for the serious loss by exchange, the Government of India might claim that the Indian railway system is an unparalleled instance of successful national investment, for the average return on the capital expenditure on all the railways in 1892 was 5.43 per cent, but unfortunately, partly owing to the cause above mentioned, this is only the statistical result of working, the net loss to the State in the financial years 1892-93 being about 135½ lakhs of rupees, which, however, includes interest on lines under construction. Had silver remained at par, the Indian railways would have afforded a magnificent source of revenue to the Government,

[1] A "lakh" of rupees is 100,000, equivalent at 2s. to the rupee to £10,000.

as the loss on exchange alone is estimated in that year to be on 153½ lakhs. The principal cause of loss at present is in the payment of interest at figures varying from 5 to 3 per cent in sterling, on the guarantees, the older guaranteed lines being entitled to payment at an exchange of 1s. 10d., while it has steadily fallen since 1872, and in 1892 the average rate has been but little over 1s. 4d. The sterling interest charges now payable on Indian railways by the Government, which have to be remitted to England, are equivalent to a payment of interest of over 7.6 per cent on the total capital raised, if converted into rupees at par. The load of the guarantee will, however, be greatly lightened within the next twelve years by the expiry of the contracts of two of the most important of the older guaranteed lines, and in 1907 the last of them, the Madras railway, will fall into the hands of the State. Further relief is to hoped for from the recent currency legislation, and if the exchange value of the rupee can be got to 1s. 6d. the outlook will be good indeed.

Were, however, the direct loss to the Government far larger than it is now, it could not be held to be serious for so vast a country, and especially for a railway system which has shown steady and even rapid growth in its traffic and its receipts. But it is not sufficient to estimate the value of Indian railways to the State by their direct results. We must attach an equal if not greater importance to their indirect benefits. Those which are obvious to every one are the increased facilities they afford in the general administration of the country, in the greater mobility they give to our military forces, the firmer grasp they allow to our tenure of the country as a whole, and, lastly, in the protection they insure against famine; but they do more than this, they are sweeping away the mental cobwebs of centuries, they are binding together in unity, in sympathy, and in trade, what scarcely more than 100 years ago were isolated kingdoms in constant strife and enmity with each other, and slowly but surely spreading peace and prosperity over the land. The value of such results may be soberly said to be incalculable. It must be observed, however, that the considerable figure on the wrong side on the account which the working of the Indian railways as a whole now shows, would have been largely reduced had it not been for large mileage of unproductive lines which it has been necessary to make for military and famine protective reasons, and would have been still further reduced were it not that so large a proportion of the railways has been made over to working companies which share in the net profits.

In all the contracts and engagements between the Government and the working companies, the share of the State in surplus profits is carefully guarded, and is always considerable, varying between one-half and four-fifths; but, nevertheless, the annual sum paid or surrendered to the companies is in the aggregate very large. In the year 1891-92 this amounted, together with contributions to provident funds, to nearly 122 lakhs of rupees. It would not, however, be right to view this as being an absolute loss to the State; indeed, it might be held to be a part only of the additional earnings of the lines due to the zeal and capacity of the officers of the working agencies, to their development of the traffic, and by the exercise of due economy in administration. In this light it may be regarded as a measure, or as some proportion of the measure, of the advantages to be derived from the operation of such lines on more rigorously commercial conditions than could be expected at the hands of State officials. This can clearly be no more than an assumption, which could only be tested in the most crude way; but judging from such data as bear on the question, it might safely be asserted that if the surrender of profits to the companies rested solely on this ground it could not be fully justified. The really weighty reason in support of this policy must be found in the desire on the part of the Government to free itself from the details and commercial phases of railway working and administration, and more remotely, perhaps, in the recognition of the political advantage of attracting the investments and interests of English capitalists in this direction.

The share of the State in the net profits of the lines worked by companies, and the whole of the profits from lines belonging to and directly worked by the Government, are absorbed in the general revenues of the country. Doubts have been expressed from time to time as to the propriety or equity of this procedure, and it has been urged that the profits from the best paying lines are thus devoted, and at the expense of the trading classes in their vicinity, to the assistance of lines in less favoured localities. The present exigencies of Indian finance would forbid the serious consideration of this question, and the time seems as yet far distant when it can be held to be within the sphere of practical politics; but were it otherwise, and if it was not necessary to husband and absorb every possible source of income to meet the cost of the general administration of the country, it would not be difficult to establish a strong *prima facie* case against the present policy. There are instances, such as that of the East Indian and other railways, which are exceptionally profitable concerns, and are paying a large revenue to the State. The trading and travelling public from whom this revenue is derived might contend, and not without reason, that the surplus profits of such railways should not be considered as revenue for general purposes, or to be devoted as it might be to the support of railways elsewhere, but should be held apart for the promotion of railway extension within the sphere of the lines concerned, or regarded as indicating that rates and fares should be reduced. The first of these courses would be supported by the shareholders in the working companies, but they would not so readily agree to the latter, being equally interested with the Government in obtaining as large profits as possible from the lines they are operating, or, in other words, to take "all that the trade will bear," so long as the rates are within the maxima agreed upon.

This question cannot, however, be viewed in India from the same standpoint as that which would be allowable in a country where the railway system has been but little indebted to the State for its existence or support. In India, on the contrary, the railways have been financed almost entirely by the assumption by the State of responsibility from their results as investments; and thus while the risk is an Imperial one, the disposal of their surplus revenues must be considered, not in the light of local interests, but in that of the Empire as a whole, and as, moreover, a set off against the losses incurred by the State in the early days of such railways. The whole country paid its share for many a year of the interest on the capital of the guaranteed lines, and with only the most remote benefits from them, while the public who then used and profited by them were indebted to the country at large. It would thus seem fair enough that in the days of their prosperity they should contribute towards helping in other directions. The commercial classes and the shareholders must, consequently, be content with the facilities and possibilities which the Indian railways afford them under existing conditions, and bear steadily in mind that without them their investments in the country would either have been impossible or at least far less profitable.

But whatever may be the views taken of the policy of the Government in this respect, no intention could in any way be imputed to it of having encouraged or approved the adoption of high rates as means of increasing profits and obtaining revenue from this source, even upon lines which have had a complete monopoly of the traffic. On the contrary, as has been shown in the preceding chapters, persistent endeavours are evident from the very beginning towards inducing the railway administrations to find their account in the carriage of large quantities or numbers at low rates, rather than in small quantities at high rates; and in recommending or enforcing this policy, the Government has been prepared to forego their own share of profits, in the hope that the indirect benefits to trade and to the people would justify the temporary loss. A steady adherence to this policy has resulted in the attainment of rates, apparently profitable, for the carriage of food-grains, minerals, and the lowest class of passengers, which, it is believed, are lower than in any other country. This, it must be borne in mind, has been effected, not on railways of a temporary character, but carried out, as must necessarily be done in a tropical climate, in the most solid and permanent manner, and maintained at the instance of the State, both as to works and rolling stock, with a more rigorous attention to a proper standard of efficiency, and to the safety of the public, than is the case on many of the railways in the United Kingdom. At the same time, it is by no means to be assumed that rates and fares on Indian railways have yet reached their lowest remunerative level; indeed, there is good reason for the belief, that in the class of goods above mentioned and in the third or lowest class of passenger fares, further reductions are certainly to be expected in the near future, and on sufficiently profitable conditions. The movement in this direction must be necessarily slow, however, and in the case of those railways which have been made over to working companies, their copartnership with the Government and the responsibility of their agents for showing adequate returns render it necessary to proceed with great caution.

Upon the question of gauge the action of the Government will have been noticed to have shown less stability of policy than in other directions. This may be accounted for, as in other matters, from the frequent changes in the *personnel* of the higher officials, and to a less degree from changes in the Home Government. What is fully and apparently finally discussed in one decade, is rediscussed, remodelled, or even wholly altered in the next. This inevitable condition of things in Indian affairs has both its advantages and disadvantages. New men bring new ideas, and change must be always expected in the light of experience; while India, linked as her fortunes are to the changing phases of a representative Government, has no reason to expect immunity from such influences. As a whole the fluctuations in policy on the gauge question have been distinctly beneficial to the country, and although the alterations of view which were exhibited during the period of the introduction of the metre gauge led to some waste of money, it was in one sense justifiable waste, and in any case was no great penalty for India to pay for a decision of such importance. If, for instance, the standard 5½ feet gauge, which was first adopted on Indian railways by Lord Dalhousie in 1849, had been persistently adhered to throughout the Empire for all further extension, we must have had, for financial reasons, either a very much smaller system than at present, or, with our existing mileage, have found our railways a crushing burden on the revenues of the State. The introduction of the metre gauge by Lord Mayo in 1870 was undoubtedly a move in the right direction, the only doubt that has been expressed being, whether it would not have been wise to have made a still greater reduction from the broad gauge, and to have fixed the narrow gauge at say 2 feet 9 inches or 2 feet 6 inches, the latter being now recognised as one for purely feeder lines. The narrow gauge would then have been so clearly suited only for lines of limited traffic, that mistakes might have been avoided of laying them down in areas where there was good reason for expecting an ultimate development of traffic that would require the standard gauge. However, the metre gauge was a distinct boon to the country. It afforded a sufficient and much needed means of communication to poorly populated and backward districts, it was made more cheaply mile for mile than the broad gauge, and it swept away the bugbear of the evils of break of gauge which threatened to inflict on India a permanent source of embarrassment.

In admitting the metre gauge as a secondary standard for feeder and subsidiary railways, it was not supposed that the growth of traffic on them would have been so pronounced, nor perhaps was it foreseen that they would, as has been the case, be formed up into large systems, as important competing and through routes. That this has happened, however, does not afford fair ground for the condemnation of the principle they represent, nor can it be rightly asserted, except perhaps in one instance, that these lines have as yet been unable to accommodate the business which has been drawn to them. To have insisted on a uniform gauge of 5 feet 6 inches for the whole Indian railway system would have been a very serious mistake, and the advantages it would have offered were more theoretical than practical. The great bulk of the traffic on railways in India can be amply well accommodated by moving it at slow speeds, while breaks of gauge, especially at comparatively long intervals, whether for goods or for passengers, is in no respect considered as an inconvenience by the mass of the people, so long as it implies cheapness. This gauge question is the only point on which railway policy in India has been seriously attacked, and no little ability has been exhibited and wasted in the advocacy of uniformity. The character of the earlier discussions was, though often evidently biassed by surroundings, merely academic and certainly disinterested, but some recent revivals of the controversy bear indications of being prompted, or at least coloured, by the aims of competing railways, and the arguments put forward have been duly discounted in India on this ground. But in England the opposition to break of gauge is always sure of an appreciative audience, and there it may be readily conceded it would be an evil incontestably serious; but there also, unfortunately, the tendency is to test every measure by an insular standard, and to imagine that what is admirably suited to the conditions of the United Kingdom must be equally applicable over the whole Empire. Those who insist on the necessity of a uniform gauge are perhaps inclined to overlook the fact, that the English railway system offers (and only recently) one of the few exceptions in this respect, and that in applying their arguments to India they either ignore or do not realise its enormous extent, the striking differences of conditions between its provinces, and still greater contrast in the habits and aims of the people compared with those of advanced European countries. Their principles may be sound as applied to the circumstances of a small, rich, and populous country, where the value of time and the meaning of comfort and convenience are fully understood, but they are unsound and misleading if sought to be extended to widely different surroundings. Fortunately for India and for Indian finance, this is the view that has been taken by her statesmen.

In claiming that the Government of India can show a good account of its stewardship in the matter of railway communication, it is not intended that their work in this respect should be considered as approaching completion, on the contrary, the task is still far from being fulfilled, and many thousands of miles, on the three gauges, have yet to be made. The estimate of the Famine Commission of 1880 was that India needed 20,000 miles of railway in order to effectually protect the country against famine. This figure has not even yet been reached, and the province of Orissa, where over one million lives were lost in the famine of 1865-66, is still unprovided with a single mile of railway. During this terrible time ships laden with grain lay off the coast unable to land their cargoes, while the people were dying of starvation, and no sufficient help could reach them from the interior. Progress has, in fact, been slow, but the Government has been forced to pursue a cautious policy, and to keep steadily before them the necessity that investment in this direction should not reach such limits as might endanger the credit of the country, or even disturb the financial equilibrium from year to year. Taking the period from 1850 to 1892, it will be found that the yearly average of new lines opened for traffic is no more than 430 miles; while the average annual expenditure on railways from all sources during this period, has been about 557 lakhs of rupees, representing at a mean exchange of say 12 rupees to the pound sterling a little over 4½ millions. With a population, which may be taken to have averaged 260 millions, this would mean no more than an addition of one mile yearly for every 430,000 persons, and if the present open mileage be taken, of all gauges, we have still only one mile of railway for every 16,000 persons. The estimate of the Famine Commission referred only to the needs of the country in the event of the failure of crops in any large area, and represented no more than the framework of the structure. The rest has yet to be filled in. On a moderate computation there are at least 3000 miles of trunk lines on the broad gauge which have still to be made, without counting branch lines, and an almost indefinite extension seems possible on the metre and 2½ feet gauges. In the North-West Provinces, in Bengal, and in Burma, from four to five millions sterling could be laid out in each on narrow gauge lines, which would with almost absolute certainty show an early return of at least 4 per cent. In fact, if India can only obtain some stability in her currency, and a more certain figure of exchange, the field for the investment of English capital in railways in that country would be second to none in the world. All that would then be needed is that projects should be taken up on sound advice, and carried out with strict economy in the first instance, leaving them to be improved in character and capacity as the traffic increased. It may, moreover, be safely assumed that the policy of the Government will be directed in the future towards definite and hearty encouragement of *bona-fide* private enterprise in Indian railways, and that no schemes will be countenanced that do not show reasonable prospect of being remunerative.

There is one particular and almost unique feature in the relations of the Government with the railways in India. They are, fortunately, free from the evil influences of political or party jobbery; even favouritism or bias from this source is entirely absent, and the machinery of "wire-pulling" and "log-rolling," which seems destined to accompany the adoption of any important measure under representative governments, have no existence. The fate of a policy or a project is decided on no other ground than that of the best interests of the State at large, and the history of Indian railways is thus happily free from any trace of the imputations of bad faith or official dishonesty which in some countries have disgraced and embittered the connection between the Government and private enterprise. The reins have been held, whether in high or in low places, by men who could justly lay claim to a high standard of ability and rectitude, and who, both in spirit and in action, have deserved, if they have not earned, the respect of the English investor. The charges not unfrequently made against the Government of dilatoriness and vacillation in the disposal of the proposals of promoters have doubtless had some foundation, but it should be borne in mind that this defect is largely and yet inevitably traceable to the system of dual control by the Home and Indian Governments, and also to the fact that the only motive which actuates official discussions is the anxious and honourable desire to arrive at decisions based on a complete investigation of the claims of all concerned. The alleged, and perhaps in some cases the real, evils of the State-ownership of railways, of which such highly coloured pictures have been drawn, have happily as yet not been exhibited in India, nor does it seem in any way likely that they will be in the future. It has there been fully established that under certain conditions this system can be adopted without involving elements which are either undesirable or impolitic, and so as to offer equal benefits both to the State and to the investor.

The one serious defect of direct State action, whether in the construction or the working of railways, lies in the almost inevitable tendency to over-centralisation—a defect indeed which, more or less, is to be observed in every form of

Government administration. It depresses the zeal of local officers, weakens their sense of responsibility and the habit of prompt decision, and involves inordinate and often serious delay in the despatch of public business. But tolerable as this may be in the ordinary work of civil government, its effects are far more injurious in the conduct of such essentially commercial undertakings as railways. At the outset of State railway operations in India this evil was certainly very pronounced, and it was some time before it was recognised that the State official should be endowed with no less powers than those who were conducting the companies' lines. To the public the effects of centralisation on State lines were equally objectionable, and it would not be far wrong to refer the reversion from purely State agency to the combination of this with the agency of companies to this cause. Of late years a great deal has been done to remove this objection to State railway administration, and at present, indeed, the Government railway manager is probably under less restrictions than the agent of a railway company. There is, nevertheless, a lingering suspicion among the commercial classes that the State lines are worked with less sympathy for the trader than is the case on the railways worked by companies—that there is less desire to stimulate traffic, or to meet business competition half-way. Placed as the Government officer is on the safe pedestal of permanent service, and secure of this and of a pension whatever may be the financial results of the line he is operating, there may be some sort of ground for comparing him unfavourably with his *confrère* in the service of a company, but on the whole the difference must be more theoretical than practical, and could scarcely amount to any sensible effect on individual profits.

One point of importance must be noted before concluding this chapter. The Government of India has been urged for many years past to extend the construction of railways with the main object of finding fresh markets for the English manufacturer. This must be held to imply that the Indian tax-payer is to incur all the risk, and that the manufacturer is to reap all the profit. It may also mean that the progress of manufactures in India, which is now steadily increasing, will be more or less retarded by the introduction of cheap European products. But it cannot be expected that the Government of India should be prepared to further railway extension on such grounds. As the custodian of the finances of India, and of the interests of its people, it is bound rather to look for new outlets for Indian produce than for new markets for English manufactures. Their duty is to administer the resources of the country for its benefit, and to regard the advantages to other countries as of strictly secondary importance. In short, if the expansion of English trade is to be dependent on a more rapid or reckless extension of the Indian railway system, the money should be found by those who expect to profit by it. If we are to allow our Indian Empire to become a happy hunting-ground for the iron and cotton manufacturers of England, we must abandon the aims and principles which have guided us hitherto in governing that great possession, and be prepared to admit that we are no longer worthy to hold the great trust that has been bequeathed to us by our predecessors.

APPENDIX A

STANDARD DIMENSIONS TO BE OBSERVED ON RAILWAYS IN INDIA

5 *feet* 6 *inches Gauge*

NOTE.—The maximum, minimum, and fixed dimensions and loads given in this schedule may not be infringed under any circumstances without the special sanction of the Government of India. Where it is proposed to execute any work or to procure bridge girders, station machinery, rolling stock, or other railway material which will infringe these dimensions or loads, the sanction of the Government of India is to be obtained before such work is commenced or order given.

I. FORMATION

		FT.	IN.
SINGLE LINE—			
	Minimum width of formation—		
(1)	In embankment	20	0
(2)	In cutting (*excluding side drains*) .	18	0
DOUBLE LINE—			
	Minimum width of formation—		
(3)	In embankment	34	0
(4)	In cutting (*excluding side drains*) .	32	0
(5)	Standard distance centre to centre of tracks (out of stations)	14	0

CURVES—

Maximum angle of curvature—

(6)	In ordinary country	3° 0′ (rad. = 1910 ft.)
(7)	In difficult country	6° 0′ (rad. = 955 ft.)

N.B.—The angle of curvature is taken as the angle at the centre subtended by an arc of one hundred feet in length. Thus the radius for a one degree curve is 5729·578 feet.

The maximum angle of curvature should *only be worked to in special cases* where the adoption of an easier curve would be impracticable or involve considerable extra expense. Under very exceptional circumstances, where it may appear necessary that this rule should be relaxed, the matter should be referred to the Government of India for orders.

The maximum angles of curvature given above do not apply to curves in station yards.

II. BALLAST AND PERMANENT WAY

BALLAST—

		Ft.	In.
(8)	Minimum width of ballast at rail level .	11	0
(9)	Minimum depth of ballast below sleepers .	0	8

N.B.—These minimum dimensions may be relaxed in the case of a line being opened to traffic before the banks have settled.

SLEEPERS—

Minimum dimensions for timber cross sleepers—

(10)	Length	9	6
(11)	Breadth	0	9
(12)	Depth	0	5
		Sq. in.	
(13)	Minimum area in cross sections . .	50	
		No.	
(14)	Minimum number of cross sleepers per mile	1760	

N.B.—On bridges where the cross sleepers rest directly on longitudinal girders, the sleepers are to be spaced not more than 2 feet 6 inches apart, centre to centre, and are to be not less than 6 inches deep exclusive of any notching which may be required on the under side to allow for the cover plates, camber, etc.

RAILS—	FT.	IN.
(15) Maximum clearance of guard rail for points and crossings	0	$1\frac{7}{8}$
(16) Minimum clearance of guard rail for points and crossings	0	$1\frac{3}{4}$
(17) Minimum clearance of guard rail for curves and level crossings . . .	0	2

N.B.—The *maximum* clearance for curves and level crossings will vary according to the radius of curve.

(18) Minimum depth of space for wheel flange, from rail level	0	$1\frac{1}{2}$

III. FIXED STRUCTURES—IN STATIONS

(*See also Diagram No.* 1)

PLATFORMS—

(19) Standard horizontal distance from centre of track to face of platform wall or nosing (if any)	5	6

N.B.—The upper edge of the nosing or coping to platform wall is to be finished to form an arris without any rounding or chamfer.

If the platform be on a curve, the horizontal distance from centre of adjacent track is to be increased as follows :—

For a curve of 8 degrees (*716 ft. rad.*) allow $5\frac{1}{4}$ in. extra
,, 6 ,, (*955 ft. rad.*) ,, 4 in. ,,
,, 4 ,, (*1432 ft. rad.*) ,, $2\frac{1}{2}$ in. ,,
,, 2 ,, (*2865 ft. rad.*) ,, $1\frac{1}{4}$ in. ,,
and for other curves in proportion.

(20) Standard height above rail level for passenger platforms	3	0
(21) Alternative height above rail level for passenger platforms at minor stations .	1	0

N.B.—Where passenger platforms are provided their height above rail level must be either 3 feet 0 inches or 1 foot 0 inches as specified above, no other height being permissible. At places where passengers are intended to get into or out from trains, but at which no platform is provided, a piece of ground for a length of not less than 800 feet, and for a width of not less than 20 feet from outer rail, is to be brought to a smooth even surface at rail level, and properly finished with gravel or similar material.

5 ft. 6 in. GAUGE.

STANDARD DIMENSIONS.

STANDARD DIMENSIONS IN STATIONS.

DIAGRAM No. 1.

CARRIAGE FOOT-BOARDS. — Every carriage is to be provided with two continuous foot-boards on each side, to the following dimensions:—

	Height above rails.	Width across outsides.
Upper foot-board	3 ft. 6 in.	9 ft. 6 in.
Lower foot-board	1 ft. 6 in.	10 ft. 6 in.

The height above rails is to be taken to the upper surface of board with buffer centres at the maximum height of 3 ft. 7½ in. above rail level.

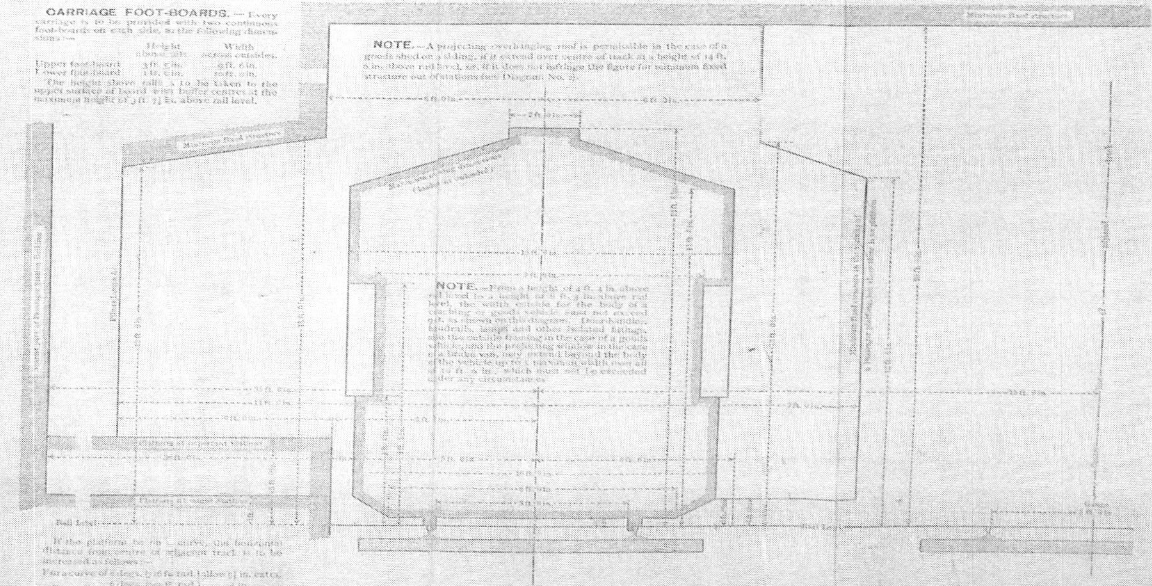

If the platform be on a curve, the horizontal distance from centre of adjacent track is to be increased as follows:—

For a curve of 8 degs. (716 ft. rad.) allow 5½ in. extra.
" " 6 degs. (955 ft. rad.) " 4 in. "
" " 4 degs. (1,432 ft. rad.) " 2½ in. "
" " 2 degs. (2,865 ft. rad.) " 1¼ in. "

Scale ⅛ Inch to 1 Foot.

To face page 258.

	Ft.	In.
(22) Standard height above rail level for goods, carriage, and horse landing platforms .	3	6

N.B.—The ends of *all* platforms must be ramped, the slope being not steeper than 1 in 6.

BUILDINGS—

(23) Minimum horizontal distance of any building from the edge of a *passenger* platform	30	0

N.B.—For an island platform, where it would be undesirable to allow the full width here specified, a plan showing the arrangements proposed is to be submitted to the Government of India for special sanction.

(24) Minimum horizontal distance from centre of track to any structure in the vicinity of a *passenger* platform (but not *on* a platform), within a height of 12 feet from rail level	9	0

N.B.—This rule does not apply to point levers between tracks, to water cranes, or to loading gauges. (*See items Nos.* 38, 45, *and* 77.)

For extra allowance on sharp curves, see item No. 19.

(25) Minimum horizontal distance from centre of track to any structure not in the vicinity of a *passenger* platform, from platform level, if any, or from 1 foot above rail level if there be no platform, to a height of 11 feet 6 inches above rail level .	7	0

N.B.—Under the last entry, coal or any material stacked by the side of any track is to be considered a structure in the sense in which the word is here used.

A projecting overhanging roof is permissible in the case of a goods shed on a siding, if such roof extends over the centre of a track at a height of not less than 14 feet 6 inches above rail level; or if it does not infringe the outline of the figure for minimum fixed structure out of stations. (*See Diagram No.* 2.)

For extra allowance on sharp curves, see item No. 19.

PILLARS, LAMPS, ETC.—

(26) Minimum horizontal distance from edge of platform to pillars, columns, lamps, or

	FT.	IN.
similar isolated structures within a height of 12 feet from rail level . . .	6	0

ROOFS, OVER-BRIDGES, ETC.—

	FT.	IN.
(27) Minimum height above rail level, at centre of track, of tie-rods or underside of any continuous roof or covering in *passenger* stations	20	0
(28) Minimum height above rail level at centre of track for passenger foot-bridges crossing the line in stations . . .	18	6
(29) Minimum height above rail level for telegraph wires crossing the line, or above surface of road where carried over roads within the boundary of a station . .	20	0

IV. FIXED STRUCTURES—OUT OF STATIONS

(*See also Diagram No.* 2)

BUILDINGS, ETC.—

	FT.	IN.
(30) Minimum horizontal distance from centre of track to any structure, out of stations, from 1 foot above rail level to a height of 11 feet 6 inches above rail level. (*See Diagram No.* 2) . . .	7	0

N.B.—Under this entry any material stacked by the side of the line is to be considered a structure in the sense in which the word is here used.

Where the line is on a curve the horizontal distance of a fixed structure from the centre of adjacent track is to be increased as follows :—

For a curve of 8 degrees (*716ft. rad.*) allow 5½ in. extra
,, 6 ,, (*955ft. rad.*) ,, 4 in. ,,
,, 4 ,, (*1432ft. rad.*) ,, 2½ in. ,,
,, 2 ,, (*2865ft. rad.*) ,, 1¼ in. ,,
and for other curves in proportion.

OVER-BRIDGES, ETC.—

	FT.	IN.
(31) Minimum height above rail level at centre of track for over-bridges out of stations .	14	6

5 FT. 6 IN. GAUGE.

STANDARD DIMENSIONS

DIAGRAM No. 2.

STANDARD DIMENSIONS OUT OF STATIONS.

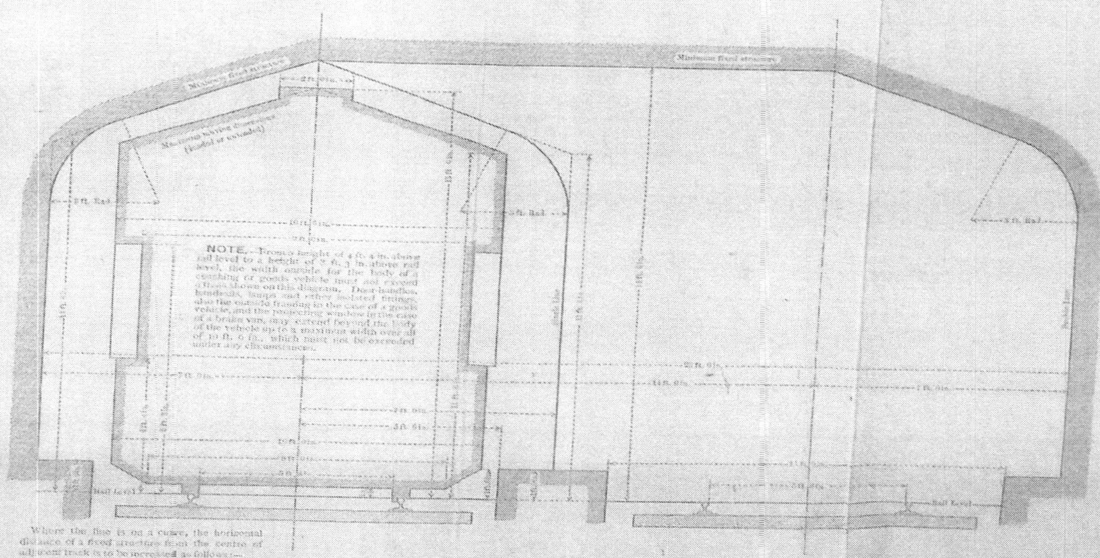

Where the line is on a curve, the horizontal distance of a fixed structure from the centre of adjacent track is to be increased as follows:—

Scale ½ Inch to 1 Foot.

To face page 260.

	Ft.	In.
(32) Minimum height above rail level for telegraph wires crossing the line, or above surface of road where carried over roads at level crossings . . .	20	0

N.B.—The minimum horizontal distance, from the centre line of nearest track, at which a telegraph post may be erected, is the total height of the post plus 7 feet. Also, where the line is in cutting, a telegraph post erected on the berm must be at a distance from the edge of the cutting of not less than the total height of the post.

TUNNELS—

(33) For minimum dimensions, see Diagram No. 3.

V. STATION YARDS

SPACING OF TRACK—

	Ft.	In.
(34) Minimum distance centre to centre of tracks	15	6

POINTS AND CROSSINGS—

The following (items Nos. 35, 36, and 37) are recommended for general use, and are to be adopted on all State railways :—

	Ft.	In.
(35) *Minimum radius of curve* . .	800	0
(36) *Standard crossings* .	1 in 6 1 in 8½ 1 in 12	
(37) *Standard lengths for tongue rails* .	12 15	0 0
(38) Minimum horizontal distance from centre of track to point handle, indicator, or any part of point apparatus above rail level .	7	0

N.B.—A point handle may not, in any position, be within 7 feet of the centre line of nearest track ; a clear distance of 7 feet is also to be preserved from centre of nearest track to any part of the point apparatus, fixed or movable, above rail level. An arrangement involving the placing of a point handle between tracks should be avoided as far as practicable ; but where this arrangement is adopted, the point handle must work parallel with the rails, not at right angles thereto.

ACCOMMODATION—

	Ft.	In.
(39) Minimum length for passenger platform (if provided)	600	0

		Ft.	In.
(40)	Minimum clear available length of through siding at any roadside station which may be used as a crossing station . .	1600	0

N.B.—The "available length" of siding (whether the line be curved or straight) terminates where the distance between the centre line of the siding and the centre line of an adjacent track begins to be less than 14 feet.

On any section of a railway having a ruling gradient heavier than 1 in 100, the length of platform and sidings may (with the sanction of the Government of India) be reduced to such an extent as may appear advisable. But for each such special case the sanction of Government is to be obtained to the proposals *before* work is commenced.

VI. STATION MACHINERY

Water Tanks—

	Minimum height for bottom of tank above rail level *at water column* :—		
(41)	For watering engines . . .	20	0
(42)	For washing out engines . .	30	0
(43)	Minimum distance from centre of track to face of tank house when adjacent to a passenger platform . . .	30	0
		C. ft.	
(44)	Minimum capacity of tank at any station .	1000	0

Water Cranes—

		Ft.	In.
(45)	Minimum distance in the clear from centre of track to nearest part of water column from 1 foot above rail level . .	7	0
(46)	Standard height above rail level for discharge orifice of water crane jib . .	12	0
(47)	Standard internal diameter for piping from tank to water crane . . .	0	8

N.B.—This diameter should be increased where the same pipe serves two or more water columns likely to be used at the same time.

Ash-pits, etc.—

(48)	Minimum clear length at bottom for ash-pits in station yards . . .	60	0

	Ft.	In.
(49) Standard average depth for ash-pits in station yards	3	0
(50) Standard depth for examining pits for carriages and waggons . . .	2	6
Engine Running Sheds—		
Minimum width for running sheds inside in the clear :—		
(51) For two lines of rail . . .	45	0
(52) For one line of rail . . .	28	0
(53) Minimum distance centre to centre of tracks in running sheds . . .	17	0
Running shed doorways :—		
(54) Minimum width . . .	15	0
(55) Minimum height, if flat at top .	14	6
(56) Minimum height to crown of arch, if with semicircular arch . .	16	0
(57) Standard average depth for wash-out pits in running sheds	2	6
(58) Standard average depth for repairing pits in running sheds	2	0
Turntables—		
(59) Minimum diameter for engine turntables .	50	0
(60) Minimum diameter for carriage or waggon turntables	18	0
Traversers—		
(61) Minimum length for carriage or waggon traversers	18	0
Weigh-bridges—		
(62) Minimum length for weigh-bridges for ordinary stock . . .	18	0

	Tons.
(63) Minimum weighing power, for weigh-bridges for ordinary stock . . .	24

VII. LOCGOMOTIVE ENGINES.

Maximum moving Dimensions—

(64) The maximum moving dimensions laid down for carriages and waggons apply also to locomotive engines.

	Tons.
Weight on a Pair of Wheels—	
(65) Maximum under any circumstances	15
(66) Maximum per foot of diameter	3.75
Weight per Foot run of Wheel base—	
(67) Maximum for either engine or tender separately, in the case of tender engines	3.0
(68) Maximum for tank engines	4.0
Weight per Foot run over Buffers—	
(69) Maximum for engine and tender together, in the case of tender engines	1.625
(70) Maximum for tank engines	1.875
Total gross Weight—	
(71) Maximum for engine and tender together in the case of tender engines	86
(72) Maximum for tank engines	60

N.B.—The weights given above are the maximum permissible under any circumstances, with engine in working order and full load of fuel and water.

In exceptional cases, engines of weights in excess of the specification given above may be used under the special sanction of the Government of India. Such special sanction must be obtained *before* the engines are ordered, and the application for sanction must be accompanied by a diagram of the proposed engine, giving full particulars, and by a certificate by the Government Inspector that the bridges on the section over which the engines are intended to work are of sufficient strength.

VIII. CARRIAGES AND WAGGONS.

Maximum moving Dimensions. (*See also Diagram No.* 1)—

Maximum width :—

		Ft.	In.
(73)	From rail level to a height of 4 feet 4 inches above rail level	10	0
(74)	From a height of 4 feet 4 inches above rail level to a height of 11 feet 6 inches above rail level	10	6

N.B.—These heights are to be taken with the vehicle unloaded and buffer centres at the maximum height of 3 feet 7½ inches from rail level. For further details see Diagram No. 1.

		Ft.	In.
	Maximum height from rail level :—		
(75)	For unloaded vehicle at centre .	13	6
(76)	For unloaded vehicle at sides . .	11	6
	Loading gauge for goods :—		
(77)	Maximum width . . .	10	8
(78)	Maximum height from rail level at centre	13	7
(79)	Maximum height from rail level at sides	11	7

MAXIMUM GROSS WEIGHT—

		Tons.
(80)	On any pair of wheels . . .	12
(81)	Per foot run over buffers . . .	1.2

N.B.—The weights given above are the maximum permissible under any circumstances, with the vehicle fully loaded. The weight on a pair of wheels includes the weight of the wheels, axles, axle-boxes, and springs.

WHEEL BASE—

		Ft.	In.
(82)	Maximum rigid wheel base for passenger vehicles	16	0
(83)	Maximum rigid wheel base for goods vehicles	12	0

BUFFERS AND COUPLINGS—

(84)	Standard distance apart for centres of buffers	6	5
(85)	Maximum height above rail level for centres of buffers for unloaded vehicles . .	3	7½
(86)	Minimum height above rail level for centres of buffers for fully loaded vehicles .	3	4½

HEIGHT FOR FLOORS—

(87)	Maximum height above rail level for floor of any vehicle unloaded . . .	4	4
(88)	Minimum height above rail level for floor of passenger vehicle fully loaded .	4	1
(89)	Minimum height above rail level for floor of goods vehicle fully loaded . .	3	8½

WHEELS AND AXLES—

(90)	Standard wheel gauge, or distance apart for all wheel flanges . . .	5	3

	Ft.	In.
(91) Standard diameter on the tread for new wheels	3	7
(92) Maximum projection for flange of worn tyre below rail level	0	$1\frac{3}{8}$
(93) Minimum thickness on tread for tyres for passenger stock when worn . .	0	$1\frac{1}{4}$
(94) Minimum thickness on tread for tyres for goods stock when worn . . .	0	1
Roof Lamps—		
(95) Standard diameter inside in the clear for rings of carriage roof lamps . .	0	$8\frac{1}{4}$
(96) Standard diameter for carriage roof lamps at level of ring	0	8

STANDARD DIMENSIONS
TO BE OBSERVED ON RAILWAYS IN INDIA

Metre Gauge

Note.—The maximum, minimum, and fixed dimensions and loads given in this schedule may not be infringed under any circumstances without the special sanction of the Government of India. Where it is proposed to execute any work or to procure bridge girders, station machinery, rolling stock, or other railway material which will infringe these dimensions or loads, the sanction of the Government of India is to be obtained before such work is commenced or order given.

I. FORMATION

	Ft.	In.
Single Line—		
Minimum width of formation—		
(1) In embankment	16	0
(2) In cutting (*excluding side drains*) .	14	0
Double Line—		
Minimum width of formation—		
(3) In embankment	28	0

		Ft.	In.
(4)	In cutting (*excluding side drains*) .	26	0
(5)	Standard distance centre to centre of tracks (out of stations) . . .	12	0

CURVES—

Maximum angle of curvature—

(6)	In ordinary country . . .	5° 0′ (rad. = 1146 ft.)
(7)	In difficult country . . .	10° 0′ (rad. = 573 ft.)

N.B.—The angle of curvature is taken as the angle at the centre subtended by an arc of 100 feet in length. Thus the radius for a one degree curve is 5729.578 feet.

The maximum angle of curvature should *only be worked to in special cases* where the adoption of an easier curve would be impracticable or involve considerable extra expense. Under very exceptional circumstances, where it may appear necessary that this rule should be relaxed, the matter should be referred to the Government of India for orders.

The maximum angles of curvature given above do not apply to curves in station yards.

II. BALLAST AND PERMANENT WAY.

BALLAST—

		Ft.	In.
(8)	Minimum width of ballast at rail level .	7	6
(9)	Minimum depth of ballast below sleepers	0	6

N.B.—These minimum dimensions may be relaxed in the case of a line being opened to traffic before the banks have settled.

SLEEPERS—

Minimum dimensions for timber cross sleepers—

(10)	Length	6	0
(11)	Breadth	0	7
(12)	Depth	0	4½

		Sq. in.
(13)	Minimum area in cross section . .	36
		No.
(14)	Minimum number of cross sleepers per mile	1936

N.B.—On bridges where the cross sleepers rest directly on longitudinal girders, the sleepers are to be spaced not more than 1 ft. 6 in. apart, centre to centre, and are to be not less than 5 inches deep exclusive of any notching which may be required on the underside to allow for the cover plates, camber, etc.

RAILS—	FT.	IN.
(15) Maximum clearance of guard rail for points and crossings	0	$1\frac{3}{4}$
(16) Minimum clearance of guard rail for points and crossings	0	$1\frac{5}{8}$
(17) Minimum clearance of guard rail for curves and level crossings	0	2

N.B.—The *maximum* clearance for curves and level crossings will vary according to the radius of curve.

(18) Minimum depth of space for wheel flange, from rail level	0	$1\frac{3}{8}$

III. FIXED STRUCTURES—IN STATIONS

(*See also Diagram No.* 1.)

PLATFORMS—

(19) Standard horizontal distance from centre of track to face of platform wall or nosing (if any)	4	5

N.B.—The upper edge of the nosing or coping to platform wall is to be finished to form an arris, without any rounding or chamfer.

If the platform be on a curve, the horizontal distance from centre of adjacent track is to be increased as follows :—

For a curve of 8 degrees (*716 ft. rad.*) allow $5\frac{1}{4}$ in. extra
,, ,, 6 ,, (*955 ft. rad.*) ,, 4 in. ,,
,, ,, 4 ,, (*1432 ft. rad.*) ,, $2\frac{1}{2}$ in. ,,
,, ,, 2 ,, (*2865 ft. rad.*) ,, $1\frac{1}{4}$ in. ,,
and for other curves in proportion.

(20) Standard height above rail level for passenger platforms	2	0
(21) Alternative height above rail level for passenger platforms at minor stations	1	0

N.B.—Where passenger platforms are provided their height above rail level must be either 2 ft. 0 in. or 1 ft. 0 in. as specified above, no other height being permissible. At places where passengers are intended to get into or out from trains, but at which a platform is not provided, a piece of ground for a length of not less than 800 feet and for a width of not less than 20 feet from outer rail, is to be brought to a smooth even surface at rail level, and properly finished with gravel or similar material.

DIAGRAM No. 1.

STANDARD DIMENSIONS IN STATIONS.

CARRIAGE FOOT-BOARDS.—Every carriage is to be provided with one continuous foot-board on each side, at a height of 1 ft. 5 in. above rail level, the width across outsides of foot-boards being 8 ft. 2 in. The height above rails is to be taken to the upper surface of board with buffer centres at the maximum height of 2 ft. 11 in. above rail level.

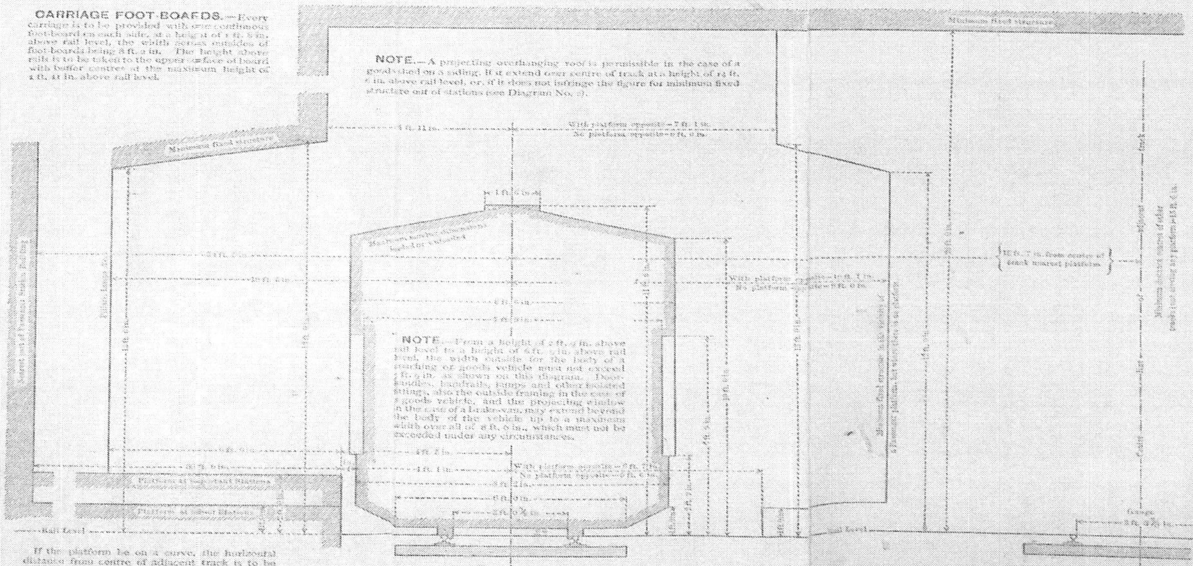

NOTE.—A projecting overhanging roof is permissible in the case of a goods-shed on a siding, if it extend over centre of track at a height of 14 ft. 6 in. above rail level, or, if it does not infringe the figure for minimum fixed structure out of stations (see Diagram No. 2).

NOTE.—From a height of 2 ft. 9 in. above rail level to a height of 6 ft. 3 in. above rail level, the width outside for the body of a coaching or goods vehicle must not exceed 7 ft. 9 in. as shown on this diagram. Door-handles, handrails, lamps and other isolated fittings, also the outside framing in the case of a goods vehicle, and the projecting window in the case of a brake-van, may extend beyond the body of the vehicle up to a maximum width over all of 8 ft. 6 in., which must not be exceeded under any circumstances.

If the platform be on a curve, the horizontal distance from centre of adjacent track is to be increased as follows:—

For a curve of 8 degs. (716 ft. rad.) allow 5½ in. extra.
" " 6 degs. (955 ft. rad.) " 4 in. "
" " 4 degs. (1,432 ft. rad.) " 2¾ in. "
" " 2 degs. (2,865 ft. rad.) " 1⅜ in. "

Scale ⅜ Inch to 1 Foot.

To face page 268.

	Ft.	In.
(22) Standard height above rail level for goods, carriage, and horse landing platforms .	2	3
N.B.—The ends of *all* platforms must be ramped, the slope being not steeper than 1 in 6.		
BUILDINGS—		
(23) Minimum horizontal distance of any building from the edge of a *passenger* platform .	30	0
N.B.—For an island platform, where it would be undesirable to allow the full width here specified, a plan showing the arrangements proposed to be submitted to the Government of India for special sanction.		
(24) Minimum horizontal distance from centre of track to any structure in the vicinity of a *passenger* platform (but not *on* a platform), within a height of 12 feet from rail level. (*See Diagram No.* 1) . .	10	0
N.B.—This rule does not apply to point levers between tracks, to water cranes, or to loading gauges. (*See items Nos.* 38, 45, *and* 77.) For extra allowance on sharp curves, see item No. 19.		
(25) Minimum horizontal distance from centre of track to any structure not in the vicinity of a *passenger* platform, from platform level, if any, or from 1 foot above rail level if there be no platform, to a height of 11 ft. 6 in. above rail level	7	0
N.B.—Under the last entry, coal or any material stacked by the side of any track is to be considered a structure in the sense in which the word is here used. A projecting overhanging roof is permissible in the case of a goods shed on a siding, if such roof extends over the centre of the track at a height of not less than 14 ft. 6 in. above rail level; or if it does not infringe the outline of the figure for minimum fixed structure out of stations. (*See Diagram No.* 2.) For extra allowance on sharp curves, see item No. 19.		
PILLARS, LAMPS, ETC.—		
(26) Minimum horizontal distance from edge of		

	Ft.	In.
platform to pillars, columns, lamps, or similar isolated structures within a height of 12 feet from rail level . . .	6	0
ROOFS, OVER-BRIDGES, ETC.—		
(27) Minimum height above rail level, at centre of track, of tie-rods or underside of any continuous roof or covering in *passenger* stations	20	0
(28) Minimum height above rail level at centre of track for passenger foot-bridges crossing the line in stations . . .	18	6
(29) Minimum height above rail level for telegraph wires crossing the line, or above surface of road where carried over roads within the boundary of a station .	20	0

IV. FIXED STRUCTURES—OUT OF STATIONS

(*See also Diagram No.* 2.)

	Ft.	In.
BUILDINGS, ETC.—		
(30) Minimum horizontal distance from centre of track to any structure, except a girder carrying the track, and not designed for 5 ft. 6 in. gauge loads, out of stations, from 1 foot above rail level to a height of 11 ft. 6 in. above rail level. (*See Diagram No.* 2.)	7	0
(30 A) Minimum horizontal distance from centre of track from 1 foot above rail level, to 10 ft. 6 in. above rail level, to any part of a girder carrying the track, and not designed for 5 ft. 6 in. gauge loads . .	6	6
Minimum horizontal distance from centre of track from rail level to 1 foot above rail level	4	5

N.B.—Under this entry any material stacked by the side of the line is to be considered a structure in the sense in which the word is here used.

METRE GAUGE.

STANDARD DIMENSIONS.

DIAGRAM No. 2.

STANDARD DIMENSIONS OUT OF STATIONS.

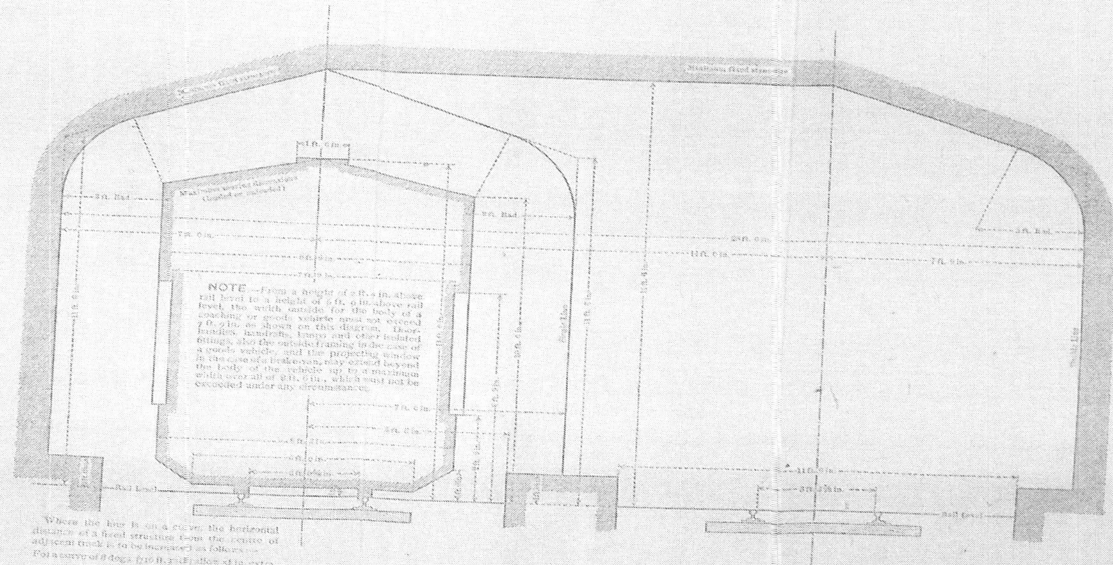

Where the line is on a curve, the horizontal distance of a fixed structure from the centre of adjacent track is to be increased as follows:—

For a curve of 8 degs. (716 ft. rad.) allow 5½ in. extra.
" " 6 degs. (955 ft. rad.) " 4 in. "
" " 4 degs. (1,433 ft. rad.) " 2¾ in. "
" " 2 degs. (2,865 ft. rad.) " 1¼ in. "

Scale ½ Inch to 1 Foot.

To face page 270.

Where the line is on a curve the horizontal distance of a fixed structure from the centre of adjacent track is to be increased as follows :—

For a curve of 8 degrees (*716 ft. rad.*) allow $5\frac{1}{4}$ in. extra
,, ,, 6 ,, (*955 ft. rad.*) ,, 4 in. ,,
,, ,, 4 ,, (*1432 ft. rad.*) ,, $2\frac{1}{2}$ in. ,,
,, ,, 2 ,, (*2865 ft. rad.*) ,, $1\frac{1}{4}$ in. ,,
and for other curves in proportion.

OVER-BRIDGES, ETC.—	FT.	IN.
(31) Minimum height above rail level a centre of track for over-bridges out of stations .	14	6
(31 A) Minimum height above rail level at centre of track for overhead bracing of girders carrying the track, and not designed for 5 ft. 6 in. gauge loads . . .	12	6
(32) Minimum height above rail level for telegraph wires crossing the line, or above surface of road where carried over roads at level crossings . . .	20	0

N.B.—The minimum horizontal distance, from the centre line of nearest track, at which a telegraph post may be erected, is the total height of the post, plus seven feet. Also, where the line is in cutting, a telegraph post erected on the berm must be at a distance from the edge of the cutting of not less than the total height of the post.

TUNNELS—

(33) For minimum dimensions. (*See Diagram No.* 3.)

V. STATION YARDS

SPACING OF TRACKS [1]—

(34) Minimum distance of tracks centre to centre—

	FT.	IN.
Track nearest platform to next track .	16	7
All other tracks in station yards .	15	6

---

[1] When platforms are built on opposite sides of the line their distance apart face to face must be :—

26 ft. 6 in. if there are *two* tracks between,
42 ft. 0 in. if there are *three* tracks between,
57 ft. 6 in. if there are *four* tracks between,

and so on, adding 15 ft. 6 in. for each additional track.

POINTS AND CROSSINGS—

The following (items Nos. 35, 36, *and* 37) *are recommended for general use, and are to be adopted on all State railways :—*

		Ft.	In.
(35)	*Minimum radius of curve* . .	478	0
(36)	*Standard crossings* . { 1 in 6; 1 in 8½; 1 in 12 }		
(37)	*Standard lengths for tongue rails* .	9 12	0 0
(38)	Minimum horizontal distance from centre of track to point handle, indicator, or any part of point apparatus above rail level .	7	0

N.B.—A point handle may not, in any position, be within 7 feet of the centre line of nearest track ; a clear distance of 7 feet is also to be preserved from centre of nearest track to any part of the point apparatus, fixed or movable, above rail level. An arrangement involving the placing of a point handle between tracks should be avoided as far as practicable ; but where this arrangement is adopted, the point handle must work parallel with the rails, not at right angles thereto.

ACCOMMODATION—

		Ft.	In.
(39)	Minimum length for passenger platform (if provided)	600	0
(40)	Minimum clear available length of through siding at any roadside station which may be used as a crossing station . .	1600	0

N.B.—The "available length" of siding (whether the line be curved or straight) terminates where the distance between the centre line of the siding and the centre line of an adjacent track begins to be less than 14 feet.

On any section of a railway having a ruling gradient heavier than 1 in 100, the length of platform and sidings may (with the sanction of the Government of India) be reduced to such an extent as may appear advisable. But for each such special case the sanction of Government is to be obtained to the proposals *before* work is commenced.

VI. STATION MACHINERY

		Ft.	In.
Water Tanks—			
	Minimum height for bottom of tank above rail level *at water column*:—		
(41)	For watering engines . . .	20	0
(42)	For washing out engines . .	30	0
(43)	Minimum distance from centre of track to face of tankhouse when adjacent to a passenger platform	30	0
		C. ft.	
(44)	Minimum capacity of tank at any station .	1000	
Water Cranes—			
		Ft.	In.
(45)	Minimum distance in the clear from centre of track to nearest part of water column from 1 foot above rail level . .	7	0
(46)	Standard height above rail level for discharge orifice of water crane jib . .	12	0
(47)	Standard internal diameter for piping from tank to water crane . . .	0	6
	N.B.—This diameter should be increased where the same pipe serves two or more water columns likely to be used at the same time.		
Ash-pits, etc.—			
(48)	Minimum clear length at bottom for ash-pits in station yards	50	0
(49)	Standard average depth for ash-pits in station yards	3	6
(50)	Standard depth for examining pits for carriages and waggons . . .	3	0
Engine Running Sheds—			
	Minimum width for running sheds inside in the clear:—		
(51)	For two lines of rail . . .	45	0
(52)	For one line of rail . . .	28	0
(53)	Minimum distance centre to centre of tracks in running sheds . . .	17	0

	Ft.	In.
Running shed doorways :—		
(54) Minimum width	15	0
(55) Minimum height, if flat at top	14	6
(56) Minimum height to crown of arch, if with semicircular arch	16	0
(57) Standard average depth for wash-out pits in running sheds	3	0
(58) Standard average depth for repairing pits in running sheds	3	0
TURNTABLES—		
(59) Minimum diameter for engine turntables	36	0
(60) Minimum diameter for carriage or waggon turntables	14	0
TRAVERSERS—		
(51) Minimum length for carriage or waggon traversers	14	0
WEIGH-BRIDGES—		
(62) Minimum length for weigh-bridges for ordinary stock	14	0
	Tons.	
(63) Minimum weighing power for weigh-bridges for ordinary stock	12	

VII. LOCOMOTIVE ENGINES

MAXIMUM MOVING DIMENSIONS—

(64) The maximum moving dimensions laid down for carriages and waggons apply also to locomotive engines. (*See also Diagram No.* 1.)

	Tons.
WEIGHT ON A PAIR OF WHEELS—	
(65) Maximum under any circumstances	8
(66) Maximum per foot of diameter	2.67
WEIGHT PER FOOT RUN OF WHEEL BASE—	
(67) Maximum for either engine or tender separately, in the case of tender engines	2.00
(68) Maximum for tank engines	2.67

WEIGHT PER FOOT RUN OVER BUFFERS—	TONS.
(69) Maximum for engine and tender together, in the case of tender engines . .	1.125
(70) Maximum for tank engines . .	1.333
TOTAL GROSS WEIGHT—	
(71) Maximum for engine and tender together, in the case of tender engines . .	46
(72) Maximum for tank engines . .	32

N.B.—The weights given above are the maximum permissible under any circumstances, with engine in working order and full load of fuel and water.

In exceptional cases, engines of weights in excess of the specification given above may be used under the special sanction of the Government of India. Such special sanction must be obtained *before* the engines are ordered, and the application for sanction must be accompanied by a diagram of the proposed engine giving full particulars, and by a certificate by the Government inspector that the bridges on the section over which the engines are intended to work are of sufficient strength.

VIII. CARRIAGES AND WAGGONS

MAXIMUM MOVING DIMENSIONS. (*See also Diagram No.* 1.)—

	Ft.	In.
Maximum width :—		
(73) From rail level to a height of 2 ft. 9 in. above rail level . . .	8	2
(74) From a height of 2 ft. 9 in. above rail level to a height of 10 feet above rail level	8	6

N.B.—These heights are to be taken with the vehicle unloaded and buffer centres at the maximum height of 1 ft. 11 in. from rail level. For further details see Diagram No. 1.

	Ft.	In.
Maximum height from rail level :—		
(75) For unloaded vehicle at centre . .	11	0
(76) For unloaded vehicle at sides . ..	10	0
Loading gauge for goods :—		
(77) Maximum width . . .	8	8
(78) Maximum height from rail level at centre	11	1
(79) Maximum height from rail level at sides .	10	1

	Tons.	
Maximum gross Weight—		
(80) On any pair of wheels . . .	6	
(81) Per foot run over buffers . . .	·8	

N.B.—The weights given above are the maximum permissible under any circumstances, with the vehicle fully loaded. The weight on a pair of wheels includes the weight of the wheels, axles, axle-boxes, and springs.

	Ft.	In.
Wheel Base—		
(82) Maximum rigid wheel base for passenger vehicles	12	0
(83) Maximum rigid wheel base for goods vehicles	10	0
Buffers and Couplings—		
(84) Standard distance apart from centres of buffers	—	
(85) Maximum height above rail level for centres of buffers for unloaded vehicles . .	1	11
(86) Minimum height above rail level for centres of buffers for fully loaded vehicles .	1	9
Height for Floors—		
(87) Maximum height above rail level for floor of any vehicle unloaded (with 2 ft. 4 in. wheels)	3	0
(88) Minimum height above rail level for floor of passenger vehicle fully loaded (with 2 ft. 0 in. wheels)	2	$5\frac{1}{2}$
(89) Minimum height above rail level for floor of goods vehicle fully loaded (with 2 ft. 0 in. wheels)	2	5
Wheels and Axles—		
(90) Standard wheel gauge, or distance apart for all wheel flanges . . .	3	$0\frac{5}{8}$
(91) Standard diameter on the tread for new wheels	2	4
(92) Maximum projection for flange of worn tyre below rail level	0	$1\frac{1}{4}$
(93) Minimum thickness on tread for tyres for passenger stock when worn . .	1	0

	Ft.	In.
(94) Minimum thickness on tread for tyres for goods stock when worn . . .	0	$0\frac{7}{8}$
Roof Lamps—		
(95) Standard diameter inside in the clear for rings of carriage roof lamps . .	0	$8\frac{1}{4}$
(96) Standard diameter for carriage roof lamps at level of ring	0	8

PROPOSED STANDARD DIMENSIONS TO BE OBSERVED ON RAILWAYS IN INDIA

2 feet 6 inches Gauge

Note.—The maximum, minimum, and fixed dimensions and loads given in this schedule may not be infringed under any circumstances without the special sanction of the Government of India. Where it is proposed to execute any work or to procure bridge girders, station machinery, rolling stock, or other railway material which will infringe these dimensions or loads, the sanction of the Government of India is to be obtained before such work is commenced or order given.

I. FORMATION

		Ft.	In.
Single Line—			
Minimum width of formation—			
(1) In embankment . . .		12	0
(2) In cutting (*excluding side drains*)	in earth	12	0
	in rock	11	0
Double Line—			
Minimum width of formation—			
(3) In embankment . . .		23	0
(4) In cutting (*excluding side drains*) .		23	0
(5) Standard distance centre to centre of tracks (out of stations). . . .		12	0

CURVES—

Maximum angle of curvature—

(6)	In ordinary country . . .	12° 0′ (rad. = 477½ feet.)

N.B.—The angle of curvature is taken as the angle at the centre subtended by an arc of one hundred feet in length. Thus the radius for a one degree curve is 5729.578 feet.

The maximum angle of curvature should *only be worked to in special cases* where the adoption of an easier curve would be impracticable or involve considerable extra expense. Under very exceptional circumstances, where it may appear necessary that this rule should be relaxed, the matter should be referred to the Government of India for orders.

The maximum angles of curvature given above do not apply to curves in station yards.

II. BALLAST AND PERMANENT WAY

BALLAST—

		Ft.	In.
(1)	Minimum width of ballast at rail level .	6	0
(2)	Minimum depth of ballast below sleepers .	0	6

N.B.—These minimum dimensions may be relaxed in the case of a line being opened to traffic before the banks have settled.

SLEEPERS—

Minimum dimensions for timber cross sleepers—

(3)	Length	5	0
(4)	Breadth	0	6
(5)	Depth	0	4
		No.	
(6)	Minimum number of cross sleepers per mile	1936	

N.B.—On bridges where the cross sleepers rest directly on longitudinal girders, the sleepers are to be spaced not more than 1 foot 6 inches apart, centre to centre.

RAILS—

		Ft.	In.
(7)	Maximum clearance of guard rail for points and crossings	0	1⅝
(8)	Minimum clearance of guard rail for points and crossings	0	1½

	Ft.	In.
(9) Minimum clearance of guard rail for curves and level crossings . . .	0	$1\frac{7}{8}$
N.B.—The *maximum* clearance for curves and level crossings will vary according to the radius of curve.		
(10) Minimum depth of space for wheel flange, from rail level	0	$1\frac{1}{4}$

III. FIXED STRUCTURES—IN STATIONS

	Ft.	In.
Platforms—		
(1) No platform walls; earth covered with cinders or gravel to be made up to rail level .	—	
Buildings—		
(2) Minimum horizontal distance of any building from centre of track at *passenger* platform	20	0
(3) Minimum horizontal distance from centre of track to any structure in the vicinity of a *passenger* platform (but not *on* a platform), within a height of 10 feet from rail level	8	0
N.B.—This rule does not apply to point levers between tracks, to water cranes, or to loading gauges.		
(4) Minimum horizontal distance from centre of track to any structure not in the vicinity of a *passenger* platform, from platform level, if any, or from 1 foot above rail level if there be no platform, to a height of 9 feet 6 inches above rail level .	7	0
N.B.—Under the last entry, coal or any material stacked by the side of any track is to be considered a structure in the sense in which the word is here used. A projecting overhanging roof is permissible in the case of a goods shed on a siding, if such roof extends over the centre of the track at a height of not less than 12 feet above rail level.		
Pillars, Lamps, etc.—		
(5) Minimum horizontal distance from centre of track to pillars, columns, lamps, or similar isolated structures on platforms .	9	0

Roofs, Over-bridges, etc.—	Ft.	In
(6) Minimum height above rail level, for 5 feet from centre of track, of tie-rods or underside of any continuous roof or covering in *passenger* stations . . .	16	6
(7) Minimum height above rail level for 5 feet from centre of track for passenger footbridges crossing the line in stations .	16	6
(8) Minimum height above rail level for telegraph wires crossing the line, or above surface of road where carried over roads within the boundary of a station . .	20	0

IV. FIXED STRUCTURES—OUT OF STATIONS

Buildings, etc.—		
(1) Minimum horizontal distance from centre of track to any structure, out of stations, from 1 foot above rail level to a height of 9 feet 6 inches above rail level. (*See Diagram No.* 2)	6	0

N.B.—Under this entry any material stacked by the side of the line is to be considered a structure in the sense in which the word is here used.

Where the line is on a curve the horizontal distance of a fixed structure from the centre of adjacent track is to be increased as follows :—

For a curve of 12 degrees (*477½ ft. rad.*) allow 8 in. extra
,, 8 ,, (*716 ft. rad.*) ,, 5¼ in. ,,
,, 4 ,, (*1432 ft. rad.*) ,, 2½ in. ,,
,, 2 ,, (*2865 ft. rad.*) ,, 1¼ in. ,,

and for other curves in proportion.

Over-bridges, etc.—		
(2) Minimum height above rail level for 5 feet from centre of track for over-bridges out of stations	12	0
(3) Minimum height above rail level for telegraph wires crossing the line, or above surface of road where carried over roads at level crossings . . .	20	0

N.B.—The minimum horizontal distance, from the

centre line of nearest track, at which a telegraph post may be erected, is the total height of the post plus seven feet. Also, where the line is in cutting, a telegraph post erected on the berm must be at a distance from the edge of the cutting of not less than the total height of the post.

TUNNELS—

V. STATION YARDS

	Ft.	In.
Spacing of Tracks—		
(1) Minimum distance of tracks centre to centre—		
Track nearest platform to next track .	14	0
All other tracks in station yards . .	12	0
Points and Crossings—		
(2) Minimum radius of curve . . .	175	0
(3) Standard crossings { 1 in 6; 1 in $8\frac{1}{2}$		
(4) Standard length for tongue rails . .	7	0
(5) Minimum horizontal distance from centre of track to point handle, indicator, or any part of point apparatus above rail level .	7	0

N.B.—A point handle may not, in any position, be within seven feet of the centre line of nearest track; a clear distance of seven feet is also to be preserved from centre of nearest track to any part of the point apparatus, fixed or movable, above rail level. An arrangement involving the placing of a point handle between tracks should be avoided as far as practicable; but where this arrangement is adopted, the point handle must work parallel with the rails, not at right angles thereto.

	Ft.	In.
Accommodation—		
(6) Minimum clear available length of through siding at any roadside station which may be used as a crossing station . .	600	0

N.B.—The "available length" of siding (whether the line be curved or straight) terminates where the distance between the centre line of the siding and the centre line of an adjacent track begins to be less than 10 feet.

The length of sidings may (with the sanction of the Government of India) be reduced to such an extent as may appear advisable. But for each such special case the sanction of Government is to be obtained to the proposals *before* work is commenced.

VI. STATION MACHINERY

		Ft.	In.
Water Tanks—			
	Minimum height for bottom of tank above rail level *at water column* :—		
(1)	For watering engines . . .	14	0
(2)	For washing out engines . .	20	0
(3)	Minimum distance from centre of track to face of tank house . . .	9	0
		C. ft.	
(4)	Minimum capacity of tank at any station .	500	0
Water Cranes—			
		Ft.	In.
(5)	Minimum distance in the clear from centre of track to nearest part of water column from 1 foot above rail level . .	6	0
(6)	Standard height above rail level for discharge orifice of water crane jib . .	10	6
(7)	Standard internal diameter for piping from tank to water crane . . .	0	4
Ash-pits, etc.—			
(8)	Minimum clear length at bottom for ash-pits in station yards	15	0
(9)	Standard average depth for ash-pits in station yards	3	0
(10)	Standard depth for examining pits for carriages and waggons . . .	3	0
Engine Running Sheds—			
	Minimum width for running sheds inside in the clear :—		
(11)	For two lines of rail . . .	30	0
(12)	For one line of rail . . .	18	0
(13)	Minimum distance centre to centre of tracks in running sheds . . .	12	0
	Running shed doorways :—		
(14)	Minimum width . . .	9	0
(15)	Minimum height, if flat at top . .	11	0
(16)	Minimum height to crown of arch, if with semicircular arch . .	13	0

	Ft.	In.
(17) Standard average depth for wash-out pits in running sheds	3	0
(18) Standard average depth for repairing pits in running sheds	3	0
TURNTABLES—		
(19) Minimum diameter for engine turntables .	15	0
(20) Minimum diameter for carriage or waggon turntables	12	0
TRAVERSERS—		
(21) Minimum length for carriage or waggon traversers	12	0
WEIGH-BRIDGES—		
(22) Minimum length for weigh-bridges for ordinary stock	12	0
(23) Minimum weighing power for weigh-bridges for ordinary stock . . .	Tons. 10	

VII. LOCOMOTIVE ENGINES

MAXIMUM MOVING DIMENSIONS—

(1) The maximum moving dimensions laid down for carriages and waggons apply also to locomotive engines

	Tons.
WEIGHT ON A PAIR OF WHEELS—	
(2) Maximum under any circumstances .	6
(3) Maximum per foot of diameter . .	2·25
WEIGHT PER FOOT RUN OF WHEEL BASE—	
(4) Maximum for either engine or tender separately, in the case of tender engines .	1·5
(5) Maximum for tank engines . . .	2
WEIGHT PER FOOT RUN OVER BUFFERS—	
(6) Maximum for engine and tender together, in the case of tender engines . .	0·875
(7) Maximum for tank engines . .	1

	Tons.
TOTAL GROSS WEIGHT—	
(8) Maximum for engine and tender together, in the case of tender engines . .	30
(9) Maximum for tank engines . . .	18

N.B.—The weights given above are the maximum permissible under any circumstances with engine in working order and full load of fuel and water.

In exceptional cases, engines of weights in excess of the specification given above may be used under the special sanction of the Government of India. Such special sanction must be obtained *before* the engines are ordered, and the application for sanction must be accompanied by a diagram of the proposed engine giving full particulars, and by a certificate by the Government Inspector that the bridges on the section over which the engines are intended to work are of sufficient strength.

VIII. CARRIAGES AND WAGGONS

	Ft.	In.
MAXIMUM MOVING DIMENSIONS—		
Maximum width :—		
(1) From rail level to a height of 2 feet 2 inches above rail level . .	7	6
(2) From a height of 2 feet 9 inches above rail level to a height of 10 feet above rail level	8	0

N.B.—These heights are to be taken with the vehicle unloaded and buffer centres at the maximum height of 1 foot 11 inches from rail level. For further details see Diagram No. 1.

	Ft.	In.
Maximum height from rail level :—		
(3) For unloaded vehicle at centre .	10	0
(4) For unloaded vehicle at sides . .	9	3
Loading gauge for goods in open tracks :—		
(5) Maximum width . . .	8	2
(6) Maximum height from rail level at centre	8	3
(7) Maximum height from rail level at sides	7	3

	Tons.
MAXIMUM GROSS WEIGHT—	
(8) On any pair of wheels . . .	4
(9. Per foot run over buffers	0·5

N.B.—The weights given above are the maximum permissible under any circumstances, with the vehicle fully loaded. The weight on a pair of wheels includes the weight of the wheels, axles, axle-boxes, and springs.

	Ft.	In.
Wheel Base—		
(10) Maximum rigid wheel base for vehicles .	9	0
Buffers and Couplings—		
(11) Central buffers	—	
(12) Maximum height above rail level for centres of buffers for unloaded vehicles . .	1	11
(13) Minimum height above rail level for centres of buffers for fully loaded vehicles .	1	9
Height for Floors—		
(14) Maximum height above rail level for floor of any vehicle unloaded . . .	2	5
(15) Minimum height above rail level for floor of any vehicle fully loaded . . .	2	3
Wheels and Axles—		
(16) Standard wheel gauge, or distance apart for all wheel flanges . . .	2	3½
(17) Standard diameter on the tread for new wheels	1	8
(18) Maximum projection for flange of worn tyre below rail level	0	1
Roof Lamps—		
(19) Standard diameter inside in the clear for rings of carriage roof lamps . . .	0	8¼
(20) Standard diameter for carriage roof lamps at level of ring	0	8

APPENDIX B

THE INDIAN RAILWAY ACT

Reprinted from the Gazette of India, dated 22nd March 1890

GOVERNMENT OF INDIA, LEGISLATIVE DEPARTMENT

The following Act of the Governor-General of India in Council received the assent of his Excellency the Governor-General on the 21st March 1890, and is hereby promulgated for general information :—

ACT NO. IX. OF 1890

THE INDIAN RAILWAYS ACT, 1890

CONTENTS

CHAPTER I

PRELIMINARY

CHAPTER II

INSPECTION OF RAILWAYS

CHAPTER III

CONSTRUCTION AND MAINTENANCE OF WORKS

SECTS.

7. Authority of railway administrations to execute all necessary works.
8. Alteration of pipes, wires, and drains.
9. Temporary entry upon land for repairing or preventing accidents.
10. Payment of compensation for damage caused by lawful exercise of powers under section 7, 8, or 9.
11. Accommodation works.
12. Power for owner, occupier, or local authority to causc additional accommodation works to be made.
13. Fences, screens, gates, and bars.
14. Over and under bridges.
15. Removal of trees dangerous to or obstructing the working of a railway.

CHAPTER IV

OPENING OF RAILWAYS

16. Right to use locomotives.
17. Notice of intended opening of a railway.
18. Sanction of the Government a condition precedent to the opening of a railway.
19. Procedure in sanctioning the opening of a railway.
20. Application of the provisions of the three last foregoing sections to material alterations of a railway.
21. Exceptional provision.
22. Power to make rules with respect to the opening of railways.
23. Power to close an opened railway.
24. Reopening of a closed railway.
25. Delegation of powers under this Chapter to Inspectors.

CHAPTER V

Railway Commissions and Traffic Facilities

Railway Commissions

SECTS.

26. Constitution of Railway Commission.
27. Restriction of jurisdiction of Railway Commission to cases specially referred.
28. Reference of cases to Railway Commission.
29. Constitution of Railway Commission in session.
30. Powers of Railway Commission.
31. Appeals from orders of Railway Commission.
32. Operation of orders of Railway Commission.
33. Assessors.
34. Power of the Governor-General in Council to make rules for the purposes of this Chapter.
35. Costs of proceedings under this Chapter.
36. Execution of order of Railway Commission and High Court.
37. Evidence of documents.
38. Submission to the Governor-General in Council of special reports by Railway Commission.
39. Dissolution of Railway Commission.
40. Finality of orders of Railway Commission subject to the foregoing provisions of this chapter.
41. Bar of jurisdiction of ordinary Courts in certain matters cognizable by Railway Commission.

Traffic Facilities

42. Duty of railway administrations to arrange for receiving and forwarding traffic without unreasonable delay and without partiality.
43. Undue preference in case of unequal rates for like traffic or services.
44. Provisions for facilities and equal treatment where ships or boats are used which are not part of a railway.
45. Terminals.
46. Power of Railway Commission to fix terminals.

CHAPTER VI

Working of Railways

General

Sects.

47. General rules.
48. Disposal of differences between railways regarding conduct of joint traffic.
49. Agreements with the Governor-General in Council for construction or lease of rolling-stock.
50. Powers of railway companies to enter into working agreements.
51. Establishment of ferries and roadways for accommodation of traffic.
52. Returns.

Carriage of Property

53. Maximum load for waggons.
54. Power for railway administrations to impose conditions for working traffic.
55. Lien for rates, terminals, and other charges.
56. Disposal of unclaimed things on a railway.
57. Power for railway administrations to require indemnity on delivery of goods in certain cases.
58. Requisitions for written accounts of description of goods.
59. Dangerous or offensive goods.
60. Exhibition to the public of authority for quoted rates.
61. Requisitions on railway administrations for details of gross charges.

Carriage of Passengers

62. Communication between passengers and railway servants in charge of trains.
63. Maximum number of passengers for each compartment.
64. Reservation of compartments for females.
65. Exhibition of time-tables and tables of fares at stations.
66. Supply of tickets on payment of fares.

CHAPTER VII

RESPONSIBILITY OF RAILWAY ADMINISTRATIONS AS CARRIERS

CHAPTER VIII

Accidents

Sects.

83. Report of railway accidents.
84. Power to make rules regarding notices of and inquiries into accidents.
85. Submission of return of accidents.
86. Provision for compulsory medical examination of persons injured in railway accidents.

CHAPTER IX

Penalties and Offences

Forfeitures by Railway Companies

87. Penalty for default in compliance with requisition under section 13.
88. Penalty for contravention of section 16, 18, 19, 20, 21, or 24.
89. Penalty for not having certain documents kept or exhibited at stations under section 47, 54, or 65.
90. Penalty for not making rules as required by section 47.
91. Penalty for failure to comply with decision under section 48.
92. Penalty for delay in submitting returns under section 52 or 85.
93. Penalty for neglect of provisions of section 53 or 63 with respect to carrying capacity of rolling-stock.
94. Penalty for failure to comply with requisition under section 62 for maintenance of means of communication between passengers and railway servants.
95. Penalty for failure to reserve compartments for females under section 64.
96. Penalty for omitting to give the notices of accidents required by section 83 and under section 84.
97. Recovery of penalties.
98. Alternative or supplementary character of remedies afforded by the foregoing provisions of this Chapter.

Offences by Railway Servants

SECTS.

99. Breach of duty imposed by section 60.
100. Drunkenness.
101. Endangering the safety of persons.
102. Compelling passengers to enter carriages already full.
103. Omission to give notice of accident.
104. Obstructing level crossings.
105. False returns.

Other Offences

106. Giving false account of goods.
107. Unlawfully bringing dangerous or offensive goods upon a railway.
108. Needlessly interfering with means of communication in a train.
109. Entering compartment reserved or already full, or resisting entry into a compartment not full.
110. Smoking.
111. Defacing public notices.
112. Fraudulently travelling or attempting to travel without a proper pass or ticket.
113. Travelling without pass or ticket, or with insufficient pass or ticket, or beyond authorised distance.
114. Transferring return half of return ticket.
115. Disposal of fines under the two last foregoing sections.
116. Altering or defacing pass or ticket.
117. Being or suffering person to travel on railway with infectious or contagious disorder.
118. Entering carriage in motion, or otherwise improperly travelling on a railway.
119. Entering carriage or other place reserved for females.
120. Drunkenness or nuisance on a railway.
121. Obstructing railway servant in his duty.
122. Trespass and refusal to desist from trespass.
123. Disobedience of omnibus drivers to directions of railway servants.
124. Opening or not properly shutting gates.

SECTS.

125. Cattle-trespass.

126. Maliciously wrecking or attempting to wreck a train.

127. Maliciously hurting or attempting to hurt persons travelling by railway.

128. Endangering safety of persons travelling by railway by wilful act or omission.

129. Endangering safety of persons travelling by railway by rash or negligent act or omission.

130. Special provision with respect to the commission by children of acts endangering safety of persons travelling by railway.

Procedure

131. Arrest for offences against certain sections.

132. Arrest of persons likely to abscond or unknown.

133. Magistrates having jurisdiction under Act.

134. Place of trial.

CHAPTER X

SUPPLEMENTAL PROVISIONS

135. Taxation of railways by local authorities.

136. Restriction on execution against railway property.

137. Railway servants to be public servants for the purposes of Chapter IX. of the Indian Penal Code.

138. Procedure for summary delivery to railway administration of property detained by a railway servant.

139. Mode of signifying communications from the Governor-General in Council.

140. Service of notices on railway administrations.

141. Service of notices by railway administrations.

142. Presumption where notice is served by post.

143. Provisions with respect to rules.

144. Delegation of powers of Governor-General in Council.

145. Representation of Managers and Agents of railways in Courts.

146. Power to extend Act to steam-tramways.

THE INDIAN RAILWAYS ACT, 1890.

An Act to consolidate, amend, and add to the Law relating to Railways in India.

WHEREAS it is expedient to consolidate, amend, and add to the law relating to railways in India: It is hereby enacted as follows:—

CHAPTER I

PRELIMINARY

1. (1) This Act may be called the Indian Railways Act, 1890.

(2) It extends to the whole of British India, inclusive of Upper Burma and (in so far as it has been or may be extended under the provisions of the Sindh-Pishin Railway Act, 1887) of British Baluchistan, and applies also to all subjects of Her Majesty within the dominions of Princes and States in India in alliance with Her Majesty, and to all Native subjects of Her Majesty without and beyond British India and those dominions; and

(3) It shall come into force on the first day of May 1890.

2. (1) On and from that day the enactments specified in the first schedule are repealed to the extent mentioned in the third column thereof.

(2) But all rules, declarations, and appointments made, sanctions and directions given, forms approved, powers conferred,

and notifications published under any of those enactments, or under any enactment repealed by any of them, shall, so far as they are consistent with this Act, be deemed to have been respectively made, given, approved, conferred, and published under this Act.

(3) Any enactment or document referring to any of those enactments, or to any enactment repealed by any of them, shall, so far as may be, be construed to refer to this Act or to the corresponding portion thereof.

3. In this Act, unless there is something repugnant in the subject or context,—

(1) "tramway" means a tramway constructed under the Indian Tramways Act, 1886, or any special Act relating to tramways:

(2) "ferry" includes a bridge of boats, pontoons, or rafts, a swing-bridge, a flying bridge, and a temporary bridge, and the approaches to, and landing-places of a ferry:

(3) "inland water" means any canal, river, lake, or navigable water in British India:

(4) "railway" means a railway, or any portion of a railway, for the public carriage of passengers, animals, or goods, and includes—

(*a*) all land within the fences or other boundary-marks indicating the limits of the land appurtenant to a railway;

(*b*) all lines of rails, sidings, or branches worked over for the purposes of, or in connection with a railway;

(*c*) all stations, offices, warehouses, wharves, workshops, manufactories, fixed plant and machinery, and other works constructed for the purposes of, or in connection with a railway; and

(*d*) all ferries, ships, boats, and rafts which are used on inland waters for the purposes of the traffic of a railway, and belong to or are hired or worked by the authority administering the railway:

(5) "railway company" includes any persons, whether incorporated or not, who are owners or lessees of a railway, or parties to an agreement for working a railway:

(6) "railway administration" or "administration," in the case

of a railway administered by the Government or a Native State, means the Manager of the railway, and includes the Government or the Native State, and, in the case of a railway administered by a railway company, means the railway company:

(7) "railway servant" means any person employed by a railway administration in connection with the service of a railway:

(8) "Inspector" means an Inspector of Railways appointed under this Act:

(9) "goods" includes inanimate things of every kind:

(10) "rolling-stock" includes locomotive engines, tenders, carriages, waggons, trucks, and trollies of all kinds:

(11) "traffic" includes rolling-stock of every description as well as passengers, animals, and goods:

(12) "through traffic" means traffic which is carried over the railways of two or more railway administrations:

(13) "rate" includes any fare, charge, or other payment for the carriage of any passenger, animal, or goods:

(14) "terminals" includes charges in respect of stations, sidings, wharves, depôts, warehouses, cranes, and other similar matters, and of any services rendered thereat:

(15) "pass" means an authority given by a railway administration, or by an officer appointed by a railway administration in this behalf, and authorising the person to whom it is given to travel as a passenger on a railway gratuitously:

(16) "ticket" includes a single ticket, a return ticket, and a season ticket:

(17) "maund" means a weight of three thousand two hundred tolas, each tola being a weight of one hundred and eighty grains Troy: and

(18) "Collector" means the chief officer in charge of the land-revenue administration of a district, and includes any officer specially appointed by the Local Government to discharge the functions of a Collector under this Act.

CHAPTER II

Inspection of Railways

4. (1) The Governor-General in Council may appoint persons,

by name or by virtue of their office, to be Inspectors of Railways.

(2) The duties of an Inspector of Railways shall be—

(*a*) to inspect railways with a view to determine whether they are fit to be opened for the public carriage of passengers, and to report thereon to the Governor-General in Council as required by this Act;

(*b*) to make such periodical or other inspections of any railway or of any rolling-stock used thereon as the Governor-General in Council may direct;

(*c*) to make inquiry under this Act into the cause of any accident on a railway;

(*d*) to perform such other duties as are imposed on him by this Act or any other enactment for the time being in force relating to railways.

5. An Inspector shall, for the purpose of any of the duties which he is required or authorised to perform under this Act, be deemed to be a public servant within the meaning of the Indian Penal Code, and, subject to the control of the Governor-General in Council, shall for that purpose have the following powers, namely:—

(*a*) to enter upon and inspect any railway or any rolling-stock used thereon;

(*b*) by an order in writing under his hand addressed to the railway administration, to require the attendance before him of any railway servant, and to require answers or returns to such inquiries as he thinks fit to make from such railway servant or from the railway administration;

(*c*) to require the production of any book or document belonging to, or in the possession or control of any railway administration (except a communication between a railway company and its legal advisers) which it appears to him to be necessary to inspect.

6. A railway administration shall afford to the Inspector all reasonable facilities for performing the duties and exercising the powers imposed and conferred upon him by this Act.

CHAPTER III

Construction and Maintenance of Works

7. (1) Subject to the provisions of this Act and, in the case of immovable property not belonging to the railway administration, to the provisions of any enactment for the time being in force for the acquisition of land for public purposes and for companies, and subject also, in the case of a railway company, to the provisions of any contract between the company and the Government, a railway administration may, for the purpose of constructing a railway, or the accommodation or other works connected therewith, and notwithstanding anything in any other enactment for the time being in force,—

(*a*) make or construct in, upon, across, under, or over any lands, or any streets, hills, valleys, roads, railways, or tramways, or any rivers, canals, brooks, streams, or other waters, or any drains, water-pipes, gas-pipes, or telegraph lines, such temporary or permanent inclined planes, arches, tunnels, culverts, embankments, aqueducts, bridges, roads, ways, passages, conduits, drains, piers, cuttings, and fences as the railway administration thinks proper;

(*b*) alter the course of any rivers, brooks, streams, or water-courses, for the purpose of constructing and maintaining tunnels, bridges, passages, or other works over or under them, and divert or alter, as well temporarily as permanently, the course of any rivers, brooks, streams, or water-courses, or any roads, streets, or ways, or raise or sink the level thereof, in order the more conveniently to carry them over or under or by the side of the railway, as the railway administration thinks proper;

(*c*) make drains or conduits into, through, or under any lands adjoining the railway for the purpose of conveying water from or to the railway;

(*d*) erect and construct such houses, warehouses, offices, and other buildings, and such yards, stations, wharves engines, machinery, apparatus, and other works and conveniences as the railway administration thinks proper;

(*e*) alter, repair, or discontinue such buildings, works, and conveniences as aforesaid, or any of them, and substitute others in their stead; and

(*f*) do all other acts necessary for making, maintaining, altering, or repairing and using the railway.

(2) The exercise of the powers conferred on a railway administration by sub-section (1) shall be subject to the control of the Governor-General in Council.

8. A railway administration may, for the purpose of exercising the powers conferred upon it by this Act, alter the position of any pipe for the supply of gas, water, or compressed air, or the position of any electric wire or of any drain not being a main drain:

(*a*) when the railway administration desires to alter the position of any such pipe, wire, or drain, it shall give reasonable notice of its intention to do so, and of the time at which it will begin to do so, to the local authority or company having control over the pipe, wire, or drain, or, when the pipe, wire, or drain is not under the control of a local authority or company, to the person under whose control the pipe, wire, or drain is;

(*b*) a local authority, company, or person receiving notice under proviso (*a*), may send a person to superintend the work, and the railway administration shall execute the work to the reasonable satisfaction of the person so sent, and shall make arrangements for continuing during the execution of the work the supply of gas, water, compressed air, or electricity, or the maintenance of the drainage, as the case may be.

9. (1) The Governor-General in Council may authorise any railway administration, in case of any slip or other accident happening or being apprehended to any cutting, embankment, or other work under the control of the railway administration, to enter upon any lands adjoining its railway for the purpose of repairing or preventing the accident, and to do all such works as may be necessary for the purpose.

(2) In case of necessity the railway administration may enter

upon the lands and do the works aforesaid without having obtained the previous sanction of the Governor-General in Council, but in such a case shall, within seventy-two hours after such entry, make a report to the Governor-General in Council, specifying the nature of the accident or apprehended accident, and of the works necessary to be done, and the power conferred on the railway administration by this sub-section shall cease and determine if the Governor-General in Council, after considering the report, considers that the exercise of the power is not necessary for the public safety.

10. (1) A railway administration shall do as little damage as possible in the exercise of the powers conferred by any of the three last foregoing sections, and compensation shall be paid for any damage caused by the exercise thereof.

(2) A suit shall not lie to recover such compensation, but in case of dispute the amount thereof shall, on application to the Collector, be determined and paid in accordance, so far as may be, with the provisions of sections 11 to 15, both inclusive, and sections 18 to 42, both inclusive, of the Land-acquisition Act, 1870, and the provisions of sections 57 and 58 of that Act shall apply to the award of compensation.

11. (1) A railway administration shall make and maintain the following works for the accommodation of the owners and occupiers of lands adjoining the railway, namely :—

(*a*) such and so many convenient crossings, bridges, arches, culverts, and passages over, under, or by the sides of, or leading to or from the railway as may, in the opinion of the Governor-General in Council, be necessary for the purpose of making good any interruptions caused by the railway to the use of the lands through which the railway is made, and

(*b*) all necessary arches, tunnels, culverts, drains, water-courses, or other passages, over or under or by the sides of the railway, of such dimensions as will, in the opinion of the Governor-General in Council, be sufficient at all times to convey water as freely from or to the lands lying near or affected by the railway as before the making of the railway, or as nearly so as may be.

(2) Subject to the other provisions of this Act, the works

specified in clauses (*a*) and (*b*) of sub-section (1) shall be made during or immediately after the laying out or formation of the railway over the lands traversed thereby, and in such manner as to cause as little damage or inconvenience as possible to persons interested in the lands or affected by the works.

(3) The foregoing provisions of this section are subject to the following provisos, namely :—

(*a*) a railway administration shall not be required to make any accommodation works in such a manner as would prevent or obstruct the working or using of the railway, or to make any accommodation works with respect to which the owners and occupiers of the lands have agreed to receive and have been paid compensation in consideration of their not requiring the works to be made ;

(*b*) save as hereinafter in this Chapter provided, a railway administration shall not, except on the requisition of the Governor-General in Council, be compelled to defray the cost of executing any further or additional accommodation works for the use of the owners or occupiers of the lands after the expiration of ten years from the date on which the railway passing through the lands was first opened for public traffic ;

(*c*) where a railway administration has provided suitable accommodation for the crossing of a road or stream, and the road or stream is afterwards diverted by the act or neglect of the person having the control thereof, the administration shall not be compelled to provide other accommodation for the crossing of the road or stream.

(4) The Governor-General in Council may appoint a time for the commencement of any work to be executed under sub-section (1), and if for fourteen days next after that time the railway administration fails to commence the work, or, having commenced it, fails to proceed diligently to execute it in a sufficient manner, the Governor-General in Council may execute it and recover from the railway administration the cost incurred by him in the execution thereof.

12. If an owner or occupier of any land affected by a railway considers the works made under the last foregoing section to be insufficient for the commodious use of the land, or if the local Government or a local authority desires to construct a public road or other work across, under, or over a railway, he or it, as the case may be, may at any time require the railway administration to make at his or its expense such further accommodation works as he or it thinks necessary, and are agreed to by the railway administration, or as, in case of difference of opinion, may be authorised by the Governor-General in Council.

13. The Governor-General in Council may require that, within a time to be specified in the requisition, or within such further time as he may appoint in this behalf,—

(*a*) boundary-marks or fences be provided or renewed by a railway administration for a railway, or any part thereof, and for roads constructed in connection therewith;

(*b*) any works in the nature of a screen near to or adjoining the side of any public road constructed before the making of a railway be provided or renewed by a railway administration, for the purpose of preventing danger to passengers on the road by reason of horses or other animals being frightened by the sight or noise of the rolling-stock moving on the railway;

(*c*) suitable gates, chains, bars, stiles, or hand-rails be erected or renewed by a railway administration at places where a railway crosses a public road on the level;

(*d*) persons be employed by a railway administration to open and shut such gates, chains, or bars.

14. (1) Where a railway administration has constructed a railway across a public road on the level, the Governor-General in Council may at any time, if it appears to him necessary for the public safety, require the railway administration, within such time as he thinks fit, to carry the road either under or over the railway by means of a bridge or arch, with convenient ascents and descents, and other convenient approaches, instead of crossing the road on the level, or to execute such other works as, in the circumstances of the case, may appear to the Governor-General in Council to be best adapted for removing or diminishing the danger arising from the level-crossing.

(2) The Governor-General in Council may require, as a condition of making a requisition under sub-section (1), that the local authority, if any, which maintains the road shall undertake to pay the whole of the cost to the railway administration of complying with the requisition, or such portion of the cost as the Governor-General in Council thinks just.

15. (1) In either of the following cases, namely:—

(*a*) where there is danger that a tree standing near a railway may fall on the railway so as to obstruct traffic,

(*b*) when a tree obstructs the view of any fixed signal,

the railway administration may, with the permission of any Magistrate, fell the tree, or deal with it in such other manner as will, in the opinion of the railway administration, avert the danger or remove the obstruction as the case may be.

(2) In case of emergency the power mentioned in sub-section (1) may be exercised by a railway administration without the permission of a Magistrate.

(3) Where a tree felled or otherwise dealt with under sub-section (1) or sub-section (2) was in existence before the railway was constructed or the signal was fixed, any Magistrate may, upon the application of the persons interested in the tree, award to those persons such compensation as he thinks reasonable.

(4) Such an award, subject, where made in a presidency-town by any Magistrate other than the Chief Presidency Magistrate, or where made elsewhere by any Magistrate other than the District Magistrate, to revision by the Chief Presidency Magistrate or the District Magistrate, as the case may be, shall be final.

(5) A Civil Court shall not entertain a suit to recover compensation for any tree felled or otherwise dealt with under this section.

CHAPTER IV

Opening of Railways

16. (1) A railway administration may, with the previous sanction of the Governor-General in Council, use upon a railway locomotive engines or other motive power, and rolling-stock to be drawn or propelled thereby.

(2) But rolling-stock shall not be moved upon a railway by steam or other motive power until such general rules for the railway as may be deemed to be necessary have been made, sanctioned, and published under this Act.

17. (1) Subject to the provisions of sub-section (2), a railway administration shall, one month at least before it intends to open any railway for the public carriage of passengers, give to the Governor-General in Council notice in writing of its intention.

(2) The Governor-General in Council may in any case, if he thinks fit, reduce the period of, or dispense with the notice mentioned in sub-section (1).

18. A railway shall not be opened for the public carriage of passengers until the Governor-General in Council, or an Inspector empowered by the Governor-General in Council in this behalf, has by order sanctioned the opening thereof for that purpose.

19. (1) The sanction of the Governor-General in Council under the last foregoing section shall not be given until an Inspector has, after inspection of the railway, reported in writing to the Governor-General in Council—

(*a*) that he has made a careful inspection of the railway and rolling-stock ;

(*b*) that the moving and fixed dimensions prescribed by the Governor-General in Council has not been infringed;

(*c*) that the weight of rails, strength of bridges, general structural character of the works, and the size of and maximum gross load upon the axles of any rolling-stock, are such as have been prescribed by the Governor-General in Council ;

(*d*) that the railway is sufficiently supplied with rolling-stock ;

(*e*) that general rules for the working of the railway when opened for the public carriage of passengers have been made, sanctioned, and published under this Act ; and

(*f*) that, in his opinion, the railway can be opened for the public carriage of passengers without danger to the public using it.

(2) If in the opinion of the Inspector the railway cannot be so opened without danger to the public using it, he shall state that opinion, together with the grounds therefor, to the Governor-General in Council, and the Governor-General in Council may thereupon order the railway administration to postpone the opening of the railway.

(3) An order under the last foregoing sub-section must set forth the requirements to be complied with as a condition precedent to the opening of the railway being sanctioned, and shall direct the postponement of the opening of the railway until those requirements have been complied with, or the Governor-General in Council is otherwise satisfied that the railway can be opened without danger to the public using it.

(4) The sanction given under this section may be either absolute, or subject to such conditions as the Governor-General in Council thinks necessary for the safety of the public.

(5) When sanction for the opening of a railway is given subject to conditions, and the railway administration fails to fulfil those conditions, the sanction shall be deemed to be void, and the railway shall not be worked or used until the conditions are fulfilled to the satisfaction of the Governor-General in Council.

20. (1) The provisions of sections 17, 18, and 19 with respect to the opening of a railway shall extend to the opening of the works mentioned in sub-section (2), when those works form part of, or are directly connected with a railway used for the public carriage of passengers, and have been constructed after the inspection which preceded the first opening of the railway.

(2) The works referred to in sub-section (1) are additional lines of railway, deviation lines, stations, junctions, and crossings on the level, and any alteration or reconstruction materially affecting the structural character of any work to which the provisions of sections 17, 18, and 19 apply or are extended by this section.

21. When an accident has occurred resulting in a temporary suspension of traffic, and either the original line and works have been rapidly restored to their original standard, or a temporary diversion has been laid for the purpose of restoring communication, the original line and works so restored, or the temporary diversion, as the case may be, may, in the absence of the Inspector, be opened for the public carriage of passengers, subject to the following conditions, namely :—

(*a*) that the railway servant in charge of the works undertaken by reason of the accident has certified in writing that the opening of the restored line and works, or of the temporary diversion, will not in his opinion be attended with danger to the public using the line and works or the diversion ; and

(*b*) that notice by telegraph of the opening of the line and works or the diversion shall be sent, as soon as may be, to the Inspector appointed for the railway.

22. The Governor-General in Council may make rules defining the cases in which, and in those cases the extent to which, the procedure prescribed in sections 17 to 20 (both inclusive) may be dispensed with.

23. (1) When, after inspecting any open railway used for the public carriage of passengers, or any rolling-stock used thereon, an Inspector is of opinion that the use of the railway or of any specified rolling-stock will be attended with danger to the public using it, he shall state that opinion, together with the grounds therefor, to the Governor-General in Council ; and the Governor-General in Council may thereupon order that the railway be closed for the public carriage of passengers, or that the use of the rolling-stock so specified be discontinued, or that the railway or rolling-stock so specified be used for the public carriage of passengers on such conditions only as the Governor-General in Council may consider necessary for the safety of the public.

(2) An order under sub-section (1) must set forth the grounds on which it is founded.

24. (1) When a railway has been closed under the last foregoing section, it shall not be reopened for the public carriage of passengers until it has been inspected, and its reopening sanctioned, in accordance with the provisions of this Act.

(2) When the Governor-General in Council has ordered under the last foregoing section that the use of any specified rolling-stock be discontinued, that rolling-stock shall not be used until an Inspector has reported that it is fit for use, and the Governor-General in Council has sanctioned its use.

(3) When the Governor-General in Council has imposed under the last foregoing section any conditions with respect to the use of any railway or rolling-stock, those conditions shall be observed until they are withdrawn by the Governor-General in Council.

25. (1) The Governor-General in Council may, by general or special order, authorise the discharge of any of his functions under this Chapter by an Inspector, and may cancel any sanction or order given by an Inspector discharging any such function, or attach thereto any condition which the Governor-General in Council might have imposed if the sanction or order had been given by himself.

(2) A condition imposed under sub-section (1) shall for all the purposes of this Act have the same effect as if it were attached to a sanction or order given by the Governor-General in Council.

CHAPTER V

Railway Commissions and Traffic Facilities

Railway Commissions

26. (1) For the purposes of this Chapter the Governor-General in Council shall, as occasion may in his opinion require, appoint a Commission, styled a Railway Commission (in this Act referred to as the Commissioners), and consisting of one Law Commissioner and two Lay Commissioners.

(2) The Commissioners shall sit at such times and in such places as the Governor-General in Council appoints.

(3) The Law Commissioner shall be such judge of the High Court having jurisdiction in reference to European British subjects under the Code of Criminal Procedure, 1882, in the place where the Commissioners are to sit as, in the case of a High Court established under the Statute 24 and 25 Victoria, chapter 104, the Chief Justice or, in the case of the Chief Court of the Punjab, the Senior Judge, or, in the case of the Court of the Recorder of Rangoon, the Chief Commissioner of Burma may, on the request of the Governor-General in Council, assign by writing under his hand.

(4) The Lay Commissioners shall be appointed by the Governor-General in Council, and one at least of them shall be of experience in railway business.

27. The Commissioners shall take cognizance of such cases only as are referred to them by the Governor-General in Council.

28. In any of the following circumstances, namely :—

(*a*) where complaint is made to the Governor-General in Council of anything done or any omission made by a railway administration in violation or contravention of any provision of this chapter;

(*b*) where any difference which is under the provisions of any agreement required or authorised to be referred to arbitration arises between railway administrations, and the railway administrations apply to the Governor-General in Council to have it referred to the Commissioners;

(*c*) where any other difference, being a difference between railway administrations, or one to which a railway administration is a party, arises, and the parties thereto apply to the Governor-General in Council to have it referred to the Commissioners;

the Governor-General in Council may, if he thinks fit, refer the case to the Commissioners for decision.

29. The three Commissioners shall attend at the hearing of any case referred to them for decision under this Chapter, and the Law Commissioner shall preside at the hearing.

30. (1) In hearing any such case the Commissioners shall have all the powers which may be exercised in the hearing of an original civil suit by a High Court.

(2) The decision shall, if the Commissioners differ in opinion, be in accordance with the opinion of the majority, and the final order in the case shall be by way of injunction and not otherwise.

(3) At the hearing the Commissioners may permit any party to appear before them either by himself or by any legal practitioner entitled to practise in any High Court.

31. (1) An appeal shall not lie from any order of the Commissioners upon any question of fact on which two of the Commissioners are agreed.

(2) Subject to the provisions of sub-section (1), an appeal shall lie from an order of the Commissioners—

(*a*) where the Law Commissioner was the Recorder or

Additional Recorder of Rangoon, to the High Court of Judicature at Fort William in Bengal, and

(*b*) in any other case, to the High Court of which the Law Commissioner was a member.

(3) Such an appeal must be presented within six months from the date of the order appealed from, and shall be heard by a bench of as many judges, not being fewer than three, as the High Court may by rule prescribe.

(4) In the hearing of the appeal the High Court shall, subject to the other provisions of this Chapter, have all the powers which it has as an Appellate Court under the Code of Civil Procedure, and may make any order which the Commissioners could have made.

32. Notwithstanding any appeal to the High Court from an order of the Commissioners, the order shall, unless the Commissioners or the majority of them see fit to suspend it, continue in operation until it is reversed or varied by that Court.

33. (1) The Commissioners, in the exercise of their jurisdiction under this Chapter, may from time to time, with the general or special sanction of the Governor-General in Council, call in one or more persons of engineering or other technical knowledge to act as assessors.

(2) There shall be paid to such persons such remuneration as the Governor-General in Council upon the recommendation of the Commissioners may direct.

34. The Governor-General in Council may make rules regulating proceedings before the Commissioners, and enabling the Commissioners to carry into effect the provisions of this Chapter, and prescribing fees to be taken in relation to proceedings before the Commissioners.

35. The costs of and incidental to any proceedings before the Commissioners or the High Court under this Chapter shall be in the discretion of the Commissioners or the High Court, as the case may be, and the payment of costs awarded by the Commissioners may be enforced by the Court of which the Law Commissioner was a judge, as if the payment had been ordered by a decree of a High Court.

36. (1) The Court of which the Law Commissioner was a judge may, if it appears on the application of any person who was a party to the proceedings before the Commissioners, or on appeal before the High Court, or of the representative of any such person, that an injunction made under this Chapter by the Commissioners or by a High Court has not been obeyed by the party enjoined, order such party to pay a sum not exceeding one thousand rupees for every day during which the injunction is disobeyed after the date of the order directing such payment.

(2) The payment of such sum may be enforced by the Court which made the order as if that Court had given a decree for the same, and the Court may direct that the whole or any part of the sum shall be paid to the person making the application under sub-section (1) or to the Government.

37. A document purporting to be signed by the Commissioners, or any of them, shall be received in evidence without proof of the signature, and shall, until the contrary is proved, be deemed to have been so signed, and to have been duly executed or issued by the Commissioners.

38. The Commissioners shall, as soon as may be after the disposal of each case referred to them, submit to the Governor-General in Council a special report on the case, and the Governor-General in Council shall cause the report to be published in such manner as he thinks fit for the information of persons interested in the subject-matter thereof.

39. Except for the purpose of the last foregoing section, a Railway Commission shall be deemed to be dissolved at the close of the last of the sittings of the Commissioners for the decision of the cases referred to them :—

Provided that, on the application of any person who was a party to the proceedings before the Commissioners, or of the representative of any such person, the Governor-General in Council may, if he thinks fit, in any case in which the order passed by the Commissioners is not open to appeal, reappoint the Commissioners for the purpose of hearing an application for a review of their decision, and of granting the same and rehearing the case if they think that the case should be reheard.

40. Subject to the foregoing provisions of this Chapter, and to any direction of Her Majesty in Council, an order of the

Commissioners shall be final, and shall not be questioned in or restrained by any Court.

41. Except as provided in this Act, no suit shall be instituted or proceedings taken for anything done or any omission made by a railway administration in violation or contravention of any provision of this Chapter, or of any order made thereunder by the Commissioners or by a High Court.

Traffic Facilities

42. (1) Every railway administration shall, according to its powers, afford all reasonable facilities for the receiving, forwarding, and delivering of traffic upon and from the several railways belonging to or worked by it and for the return of rolling-stock.

(2) A railway administration shall not make or give any undue or unreasonable preference or advantage to or in favour of any particular person or railway administration, or any particular description of traffic, in any respect whatsoever, or subject any particular person or railway administration, or any particular description of traffic, to any undue or unreasonable prejudice or disadvantage in any respect whatsoever.

(3) A railway administration having or working railways which form part of a continuous line of railway communication, or having its terminus or station within one mile of the terminus or station of another railway administration, shall afford all due and reasonable facilities for receiving and forwarding by one of such railways all the traffic arriving by the other at such terminus or station without any unreasonable delay, and without any such preference or advantage or prejudice or disadvantage as aforesaid, and so that no obstruction may be offered to the public desirous of using such railways as a continuous line of communication, and so that all reasonable accommodation may by means of such railways be at all times afforded to the public in that behalf.

(4) The facilities to be afforded under this section shall include the due and reasonable receiving, forwarding, and delivering by every railway administration, at the request of any other railway administration, of through traffic to and from the railway of any other railway administration at through rates :—

Provided as follows :—

(*a*) the railway administration requiring the traffic to be forwarded shall give written notice of the proposed through rate to each forwarding railway administration, stating both its amount and its apportionment, and the route by which the traffic is proposed to be forwarded. The proposed through rate for animals or goods may be per truck or per maund ;

(*b*) each forwarding railway administration shall, within the prescribed period after the receipt of such notice, by written notice inform the railway administration requiring the traffic to be forwarded whether it agrees to the rate, apportionment, and route, and if it has any objection, what the grounds of the objection are ;

(*c*) if at the expiration of the prescribed period no such objection has been sent by any forwarding railway administration, the rate shall come into operation at the expiration of that period ;

(*d*) if an objection to the rate, apportionment, or route has been sent within the prescribed period, the Governor-General in Council may, if he thinks fit, on the request of any of the railway administrations, refer the case to the Commissioners for their decision ;

(*e*) if the objection is to the granting of the rate or to the route, the Commissioners shall consider whether the granting of the rate is a due and reasonable facility in the interests of the public, and whether, regard being had to the circumstances, the route proposed is a reasonable route, and shall allow or refuse the rate accordingly, or fix such other rate as may seem to the Commissioners to be just and reasonable ;

(*f*) if the objection is only to the apportionment of the rate, and the case has been referred to the Commissioners, the rate shall come into operation at the expiration of the prescribed period, but the decision of the Commissioners as to its apportionment shall be retrospective : in the case of any other objection the operation of the rate shall be suspended until the Commissioners make their order in the case ;

(*g*) the Commissioners in apportioning the through rate shall take into consideration all the circumstances of the case, including any special expense incurred in respect of the construction, maintenance, or working of the route, or any part of the route, as well as any special charges which any railway administration is entitled to make in respect thereof;

(*h*) the Commissioners shall not in any case compel any railway administration to accept lower mileage rates than the mileage rates which the administration may for the time being legally be charging for like traffic carried by a like mode of transit on any other line of communication between the same points, being the points of departure and arrival of the through route ;

(*i*) subject to the foregoing provisions of this sub-section, the Commissioners shall have full power to decide that any proposed through rate is due and reasonable, notwithstanding that a less amount may be allotted to any forwarding railway administration out of the through rate than the maximum rate which the railway administration is entitled to charge, and to allow and apportion the through rate accordingly ;

(*j*) the prescribed period mentioned in this sub-section shall be one month, or such longer period as the Governor-General in Council may by general or special order prescribe.

43. (1) Whenever it is shown that a railway administration charges one trader or class of traders, or the traders in any local area, lower rates for the same or similar animals or goods, or lower rates for the same or similar services, than it charges to other traders or classes of traders, or to the traders in another local area, the burden of proving that such lower charge does not amount to an undue preference shall lie on the railway administration.

(2) In deciding whether a lower charge does or does not amount to an undue preference, the Commissioners may, so far

as they think reasonable, in addition to any other considerations affecting the case, take into consideration whether such lower charge is necessary for the purpose of securing, in the interests of the public, the traffic in respect of which it is made.

44. Where a railway administration is a party to an agreement for procuring the traffic of the railway to be carried on any inland water by any ferry, ship, boat, or raft which does not belong to or is not hired or worked by the railway administration, the provisions of the two last foregoing sections applicable to a railway shall extend to the ferry, ship, boat, or raft in so far as it is used for the purposes of the traffic of the railway.

45. A railway administration may charge reasonable terminals.

46. (1) The Governor-General in Council may, if he thinks fit, refer to the Commissioners for decision any question or dispute which may arise with respect to the terminals charged by a railway administration, and the Commissioners may thereupon decide what is a reasonable sum to be paid to the railway administration in respect of terminals.

(2) In deciding the question or dispute the Commissioners shall have regard only to the expenditure reasonably necessary to provide the accommodation in respect of which the terminals are charged, irrespective of the outlay which may have been actually incurred by the railway administration in providing that accommodation.

CHAPTER VI

Working of Railways

General

47. (1) Every railway company and, in the case of a railway administered by the Government, an officer to be appointed by the Governor-General in Council in this behalf, shall make general rules consistent with this Act for the following purposes, namely :—

(*a*) for regulating the mode in which and the speed at which rolling-stock used on the railway is to be moved or propelled ;

(*b*) for providing for the accommodation and convenience

of passengers and regulating the carriage of their luggage;

(*c*) for declaring what shall be deemed to be, for the purposes of this Act, dangerous or offensive goods, and for regulating the carriage of such goods;

(*d*) for regulating the conditions on which the railway administration will carry passengers suffering from infectious or contagious disorders, and providing for the disinfection of carriages which have been used by such passengers;

(*e*) for regulating the conduct of the railway servants;

(*f*) for regulating the terms and conditions on which the railway administration will warehouse or retain goods at any station on behalf of the consignee or owner; and,

(*g*) generally, for regulating the travelling upon, and the use, working, and management of the railway.

(2) The rules may provide that any person committing a breach of any of them shall be punished with fine which may extend to any sum not exceeding fifty rupees, and that, in the case of a rule made under clause (*e*) of sub-section (1), the railway servant shall forfeit a sum not exceeding one month's pay, which sum may be deducted by the railway administration from his pay.

(3) A rule made under this section shall not take effect until it has received the sanction of the Governor-General in Council, and been published in the *Gazette* of India.

Provided that, where the rule is in the terms of a rule which has already been published at length in the *Gazette* of India, a notification in that *Gazette* referring to the rule already published and announcing the adoption thereof shall be deemed a publication of a rule in the *Gazette* of India within the meaning of this sub-section.

(4) The Governor-General in Council may cancel any rule made under this section, and the authority required by sub-section (1) to make rules thereunder may at any time, with the previous sanction of the Governor-General in Council, rescind or vary any such rule.

(5) Every rule purporting to have been made for any railway under section 8 of the Indian Railway Act, 1879, and appearing from the *Gazette* of India to be intended to apply to the railway

at the commencement of this Act, shall, notwithstanding any irregularity in the making or publication of the rule, be deemed to have been made and to have taken effect under this section.

(6) Every railway administration shall keep at each station on its railway a copy of the general rules for the time being in force under this section on the railway, and shall allow any person to inspect it free of charge at all reasonable times.

48. Where two or more railway administrations, whose railways have a common terminus or a portion of the same line of rails in common, or form separate portions of one continued line of railway communication, are not able to agree upon arrangements for conducting at such common terminus, or at the point of junction between them, their joint traffic with safety to the public, the Governor-General in Council, upon the application of either or any of the administrations, may decide the matters in dispute between them, so far as those matters relate to the safety of the public, and may determine whether the whole or what proportion of the expenses attending on such arrangements shall be borne by either or any of the administrations respectively.

49. Any railway company, not being a company for which the Statute 42 and 43 Victoria, chapter 41, provides, may from time to time make and carry into effect agreements with the Governor-General in Council for the construction of rolling-stock, plant, or machinery used on or in connection with railways, or for leasing or taking on lease any rolling-stock, plant, machinery, or equipments required for use on a railway, or for the maintenance of rolling-stock.

50. Any railway company, not being a company for which the Statute 42 and 43 Victoria, chapter 41, provides, may from time to time make with the Governor-General in Council, and carry into effect, or, with the sanction of the Governor-General in Council, make with any other railway administration, and carry into effect, any agreement with respect to any of the following purposes, namely :—

(*a*) the working, use, management, and maintenance of any railway;

(*b*) the supply of rolling-stock and machinery necessary for any of the purposes mentioned in clause (*a*), and of officers and servants for the conduct of the traffic of the railway;

(c) the payments to be made and the conditions to be performed with respect to such working, use, management, and maintenance;

(d) the interchange, accommodation, and conveyance of traffic being on, coming from, or intended for the respective railways of the contracting parties, and the fixing, collecting, apportionment, and appropriation of the revenues arising from that traffic;

(e) generally, the giving effect to any such provisions or stipulations with respect to any of the purposes hereinbefore in this section mentioned as the contracting parties may think fit and mutually agree on:

Provided that the agreement shall not affect any of the rates which the railway administrations parties thereto are from time to time respectively authorised to demand and receive from any person, and that every person shall, notwithstanding the agreement, be entitled to the use and benefit of the railways of any railway administrations, parties to the agreement, on the same terms and conditions, and on payment of the same rates, as he would be if the agreement had not been entered into.

51. Any railway company, not being a company for which the Statute 42 and 43 Victoria, chapter 41, provides, may from time to time exercise with the sanction of the Governor-General in Council all or any of the following powers, namely:—

(a) it may establish, for the accommodation of the traffic of its railway, any ferry equipped with machinery and plant of good quality and adequate in quantity to work the ferry;

(b) it may work for purposes other than the accommodation of the traffic of the railway any ferry established by it under this section;

(c) it may provide and maintain on any of its bridges roadways for foot-passengers, cattle, carriages, carts, or other traffic;

(d) it may construct and maintain roads for the accommodation of traffic passing to or from its railway;

(*e*) it may provide and maintain any means of transport which may be required for the reasonable convenience of passengers, animals, or goods carried or to be carried on its railway ;

(*f*) it may charge tolls on the traffic using such ferries, roadways, roads, or means of transport as it may provide under this section, according to tariffs to be arranged from time to time with the sanction of the Governor-General in Council.

52. Every railway administration shall, in forms to be prescribed by the Governor-General in Council, prepare half-yearly, or at such intervals as the Governor-General in Council may prescribe, such returns of its capital and revenue transactions and of its traffic as the Governor-General in Council may require, and shall forward a copy of such returns to the Governor-General in Council at such times as he may direct.

Carriage of Property

53. (1) Every railway administration shall determine the maximum load for every waggon or truck in its possession, and shall exhibit the words or figures representing the load so determined in a conspicuous manner on the outside of every such waggon or truck.

(2) Every person owning a waggon or truck which passes over a railway shall similarly determine and exhibit the maximum load for the waggon or truck.

(3) The gross weight of any such waggon or truck bearing on the axles when the waggon or truck is loaded to such maximum load shall not exceed such limit as may be fixed by the Governor-General in Council for the class of axle under the waggon or truck.

54. (1) Subject to the control of the Governor-General in Council, a railway administration may impose conditions, not inconsistent with this Act, or with any general rule thereunder, with respect to the receiving, forwarding, or delivering of any animals or goods.

(2) The railway administration shall keep at each station on its railway a copy of the conditions for the time being in force

under sub-section (1) at the station, and shall allow any person to inspect it free of charge at all reasonable times.

(3) A railway administration shall not be bound to carry any animal suffering from any infectious or contagious disorder.

55. (1) If a person fails to pay on demand made by or on behalf of a railway administration any rate, terminal, or other charge due from him in respect of any animals or goods, the railway administration may detain the whole or any of the animals or goods, or, if they have been removed from the railway, any other animals or goods of such person then being in or thereafter coming into its possession.

(2) When any animals or goods have been detained under sub-section (1), the railway administration may sell by public auction, in the case of perishable goods at once, and in the case of other goods or of animals, on the expiration of at least fifteen days' notice of the intended auction, published in one or more of the local newspapers, or where there are no such newspapers, in such manner as the Governor-General in Council may prescribe, sufficient of such animals or goods to produce a sum equal to the charge, and all expenses of such detention, notice, and sale, including, in the case of animals, the expenses of the feeding, watering, and tending thereof.

(3) Out of the proceeds of the sale the railway administration may retain a sum equal to the charge and the expenses aforesaid, rendering the surplus, if any, of the proceeds, and such of the animals or goods (if any) as remain unsold, to the person entitled thereto.

(4) If a person on whom a demand for any rate, terminal, or other charge due from him has been made, fails to remove from the railway within a reasonable time any animals or goods which have been detained under sub-section (1), or any animals or goods which have remained unsold after a sale under sub-section (2), the railway administration may sell the whole of them, and dispose of the proceeds of the sale as nearly as may be under the provisions of sub-section (3).

(5) Notwithstanding anything in the foregoing sub-sections, the railway administration may recover by suit any such rate, terminal, or other charge as aforesaid or balance thereof.

56. (1) When any animals or goods have come into the possession of a railway administration for carriage or otherwise, and are not claimed by the owner or other person appearing to the railway administration to be entitled thereto, the railway administration shall, if such owner or person is known, cause a notice to be served upon him requiring him to remove the animals or goods.

(2) If such owner or person is not known, or the notice cannot be served upon him, or he does not comply with the requisition in the notice, the railway administration may within a reasonable time, subject to the provisions of any other enactment for the time being in force, sell the animals or goods as nearly as may be under the provisions of the last foregoing section, rendering the surplus, if any, of the proceeds of the sale to any person entitled thereto.

57. Where any animals, goods, or sale-proceeds in the possession of a railway administration are claimed by two or more persons, or the ticket or receipt given for the animals or goods is not forthcoming, the railway administration may withhold delivery of the animals, goods, or sale-proceeds until the person entitled in its opinion to receive them has given an indemnity, to the satisfaction of the railway administration, against the claims of any other person with respect to the animals, goods, or sale-proceeds.

58. (1) The owner or person having charge of any goods which are brought upon a railway for the purpose of being carried thereon, and the consignee of any goods which have been carried on a railway, shall, on the request of any railway servant appointed in this behalf by the railway administration, deliver to such servant an account in writing signed by such owner or person, or by such consignee, as the case may be, and containing such a description of the goods as may be sufficient to determine the rate which the railway administration is entitled to charge in respect thereof.

(2) If such owner, person, or consignee refuses or neglects to give such an account, and refuses to open the parcel or package containing the goods in order that their description may be ascertained, the railway administration may (*a*) in respect of

goods which have been brought for the purpose of being carried on the railway, refuse to carry the goods unless in respect thereof a rate is paid not exceeding the highest rate which may be in force at the time on the railway for any class of goods, or (*b*) in respect of goods which have been carried on the railway, charge a rate not exceeding such highest rate.

(3) If an account delivered under sub-section (1) is materially false with respect to the description of any goods to which it purports to relate, and which have been carried on the railway, the railway administration may charge in respect of the carriage of the goods a rate not exceeding double the highest rate which may be in force at the time on the railway for any class of goods.

(4) If any difference arises between a railway servant and the owner or person having charge, or the consignee, of any goods which have been brought to be carried or have been carried on a railway, respecting the description of goods of which an account has been delivered under this section, the railway servant may detain and examine the goods.

(5) If it appears from the examination that the description of the goods is different from that stated in an account delivered under sub-section (1), the person who delivered the account, or if that person is not the owner of the goods, then that person and the owner jointly and severally, shall be liable to pay to the railway administration the cost of the detention and examination of the goods, and the railway administration shall be exonerated from all responsibility for any loss which may have been caused by the detention or examination thereof.

(6) If it appears that the description of the goods is not different from that stated in an account delivered under sub-section (1), the railway administration shall pay the cost of the detention and examination, and be responsible to the owner of the goods for any such loss as aforesaid.

59. (1) No person shall be entitled to take with him, or to require a railway administration to carry, any dangerous or offensive goods upon a railway.

(2) No person shall take any such goods with him upon a railway without giving notice of their nature to the station-master,

or other railway servant in charge of the place where he brings the goods upon the railway, or shall tender or deliver any such goods for carriage upon a railway without distinctly marking their nature on the outside of the package containing them, or otherwise giving notice in writing of their nature to the railway servant to whom he tenders or delivers them.

(3) Any railway servant may refuse to receive such goods for carriage, and, when such goods have been so received without such notice as is mentioned in sub-section (1) having to his knowledge been given, may refuse to carry them, or may stop their transit.

(4) If any railway servant has reason to believe any such goods to be contained in a package with respect to the contents whereof such notice as is mentioned in sub-section (2) has not to his knowledge been given, he may cause the package to be opened for the purpose of ascertaining its contents.

(5) Nothing in this section shall be construed to derogate from the Indian Explosives Act, 1884, or any rule under that Act, and nothing in sub-sections (1), (3), and (4) shall be construed to apply to any goods tendered or delivered for carriage by order or on behalf of the Government, or to any goods which an officer, soldier, sailor, or police-officer, or a person enrolled as a volunteer under the Indian Volunteers Act, 1869, may take with him upon a railway in the course of his employment or duty as such.

60. At every station at which a railway administration quotes a rate to any other station for the carriage of traffic other than passengers and their luggage, the railway servant appointed by the administration to quote the rate shall, at the request of any person, show to him at all reasonable times, and without payment of any fee, the rate-books or other documents in which the rate is authorised by the administration or administrations concerned.

61. (1) Where any charge is made by and paid to a railway administration in respect of the carriage of goods over its railway, the administration shall, on the application of the person by whom or on whose behalf the charge has been paid, render to the applicant an account showing how much of the charge comes under each of the following heads, namely:—

(*a*) the carriage of the goods on the railway;

(*b*) terminals;

(*c*) demurrage; and

(*d*) collection, delivery, and other expenses; but without particularising the several items of which the charge under each head consists.

(2) The application under sub-section (1) must be in writing, and be made to the railway administration within one month after the date of the payment of the charge by or on behalf of the applicant, and the account must be rendered by the administration within two months after the receipt of the application.

Carriage of Passengers

62. The Governor-General in Council may require any railway administration to provide and maintain in proper order, in any train worked by it which carries passengers, such efficient means of communication between the passengers and the railway servants in charge of the train as the Governor-General in Council has approved.

63. Every railway administration shall fix, subject to the approval of the Governor-General in Council, the maximum number of passengers which may be carried in each compartment of every description of carriage, and shall exhibit the number so fixed in a conspicuous manner inside or outside each compartment, in English or in one or more of the vernacular languages in common use in the territory traversed by the railway, or both in English and in one or more of such vernacular languages, as the Governor-General in Council, after consultation with the railway administration, may determine.

64. (1) On and after the first day of January, 1891, every railway administration shall in every train carrying passengers reserve for the exclusive use of females one compartment at least of the lowest class of carriage forming part of the train.

(2) One such compartment so reserved shall, if the train is to run for a distance exceeding fifty miles, be provided with a closet.

65. Every railway administration shall cause to be posted in a conspicuous and accessible place at every station on its railway, in English and in a vernacular language in common use in the territory where the station is situate, a copy of the time-tables for the time being in force on the railway, and lists of the fares chargeable for travelling from the station where the lists are posted to every place for which card-tickets are ordinarily issued to passengers at that station.

66. (1) Every person desirous of travelling on a railway shall, upon payment of his fare, be supplied with a ticket, specifying the class of carriage for which, and the place from and the place to which the fare has been paid, and the amount of the fare.

(2) The matters required by sub-section (1) to be specified on a ticket shall be set forth—

(*a*) if the class of carriage to be spec fied thereon is the lowest class, then in a vernacular language in common use in the territory traversed by the railway, and

(*b*) if the class of carriage to be so specified is any other than the lowest class, then in English.

67. (1) Fares shall be deemed to be accepted, and tickets to be issued, subject to the condition of there being room available in the train for which the tickets are issued.

(2) A person to whom a ticket has been issued and for whom there is not room available in the train for which the ticket was issued, shall on returning the ticket within three hours after the departure of the train be entitled to have his fare at once refunded.

(3) A person for whom there is not room available in the class of carriage for which he has purchased a ticket, and who is obliged to travel in a carriage of a lower class, shall be entitled on delivering up his ticket to a refund of the difference between the fare paid by him and the fare payable for the class of carriage in which he travelled.

68. No person shall, without the permission of a railway servant, enter any carriage on a railway for the purpose of travelling therein as a passenger unless he has with him a proper pass or ticket.

69. Every passenger by railway shall, on the requisition of any railway servant appointed by the railway administration in this behalf, present his pass or ticket to the railway servant for examination, and at or near the end of the journey for which the pass or ticket was issued, or, in the case of a season pass or ticket, at the expiration of the period for which it is current, deliver up the pass or ticket to the railway servant.

70. A return ticket or season ticket shall not be transferable, and may be used only by the person for whose journey to and from the places specified thereon it was issued.

71. (1) A railway administration may refuse to carry, except in accordance with the conditions prescribed under section 47, sub-section (1), clause (*d*), a person suffering from any infectious or contagious disorder.

(2) A person suffering from such a disorder shall not enter or travel upon a railway without the special permission of the station-master or other railway servant in charge of the place where he enters upon the railway.

(3) A railway servant giving such permission as is mentioned in sub-section (2) must arrange for the separation of the person suffering from the disorder from other persons being or travelling upon the railway.

CHAPTER VII

Responsibility of Railway Administrations as Carriers

72. (1) The responsibility of a railway administration for the loss, destruction, or deterioration of animals or goods delivered to the administration to be carried by railway shall, subject to the other provisions of this Act, be that of a bailee under sections 151, 152, and 161 of the Indian Contract Act, 1872.

(2) An agreement purporting to limit that responsibility shall, in so far as it purports to effect such limitation, be void unless it—

(*a*) is in writing signed by or on behalf of the person sending or delivering to the railway administration the animals or goods, and

(*b*) is otherwise in a form approved by the Governor-General in Council.

(3) Nothing in the common law of England or in the Carriers Act, 1865, regarding the responsibility of common carriers with respect to the carriage of animals or goods, shall affect the responsibility as in this section defined of a railway administration.

73. (1) The responsibility of a railway administration under the last foregoing section for the loss, destruction, or deterioration of animals delivered to the administration to be carried on a railway shall not in any case exceed, in the case of elephants or horses, five hundred rupees a head, or in the case of camels or horned cattle, fifty rupees a head, or in the case of sheep, goats, dogs, or other animals, ten rupees a head, unless the person sending or delivering them to the administration caused them to be declared, or declared them, at the time of their delivery for carriage by railway to be respectively of higher value than five hundred, fifty, or ten rupees a head, as the case may be.

(2) Where such higher value has been declared, the railway administration may charge, in respect of the increased risk, a percentage upon the excess of the value so declared over the respective sums aforesaid.

(3) In every proceeding against a railway administration for the recovery of compensation for the loss, destruction, or deterioration of any animal, the burden of proving the value of the animal and, where the animal has been injured, the extent of the injury shall lie upon the person claiming the compensation.

74. A railway administration shall not be responsible for the loss, destruction, or deterioration of any luggage belonging to or in charge of a passenger unless a railway servant has booked and given a receipt therefor.

75. (1) When any articles mentioned in the second schedule are contained in any parcel or package delivered to a railway administration for carriage by railway, and the value of such articles in the parcel or package exceeds one hundred rupees, the railway administration shall not be responsible for the loss, destruction, or deterioration of the parcel or package unless the person sending or delivering the parcel or package to the administration caused its value and contents to be declared, or declared them at the time of the delivery of the parcel or package for carriage by railway, and if so required by the administration, paid or engaged to pay a percentage on the value so declared by way of compensation for increased risk.

(2) When any parcel or package of which the value has been declared under sub-section (1) has been lost or destroyed, or has deteriorated, the compensation recoverable in respect of such loss, destruction, or deterioration shall not exceed the value so declared, and the burden of proving the value so declared to have been the true value shall, notwithstanding anything in the declaration, lie on the person claiming the compensation.

(3) A railway administration may make it a condition of carrying a parcel declared to contain any article mentioned in the second schedule, that a railway servant authorised in this behalf has been satisfied by examination or otherwise that the parcel actually contains the article declared to be therein.

76. In any suit against a railway administration for compensation for loss, destruction, or deterioration of animals or goods delivered to a railway administration for carriage by railway, it shall not be necessary for the plaintiff to prove how the loss, destruction, or deterioration was caused.

77. A person shall not be entitled to a refund of an overcharge in respect of animals or goods carried by railway, or to compensation for the loss, destruction, or deterioration of animals or goods delivered to be so carried, unless his claim to the refund or compensation has been preferred in writing by him or on his behalf to the railway administration within six months from the date of the delivery of the animals or goods for carriage by railway.

78. Notwithstanding anything in the foregoing provisions of this Chapter, a railway administration shall not be responsible for the loss, destruction, or deterioration of any goods with respect to the description of which an account materially false has been delivered under sub-section (1) of section 58 if the loss, destruction, or deterioration is in any way brought about by the false account, nor in any case for an amount exceeding the value of the goods if such value were calculated in accordance with the description contained in the false account.

79. Where an officer, soldier, or follower, while being or travelling as such on duty upon a railway belonging to, and worked by the Government, loses his life or receives any personal injury in such circumstances that if he were not an officer, soldier, or follower being or travelling as such on duty upon the railway, compensation would be payable under Act No. XIII. of 1855 or to him, as the case may be, the form and amount of the compensation to be made in respect of the loss of his life or his injury shall, where there is any provision in this behalf in the military regulations to which he was immediately before his death, or is subject, be determined in accordance with those regulations, and not otherwise.

80. Notwithstanding anything in any agreement purporting to limit the liability of a railway administration with respect to traffic while on the railway of another administration, a suit for compensation for loss of the life of, or personal injury to, a passenger, or for loss, destruction, or deterioration of animals or goods, where the passenger was or the animals or goods were booked through over the railways of two or more railway administrations, may be brought either against the railway administration from which the passenger obtained his pass or purchased his ticket, or to which the animals or goods were delivered by the consignor thereof, as the case may be, or against the railway administration on whose railway the loss, injury, destruction, or deterioration occurred.

81. Where a railway administration under contract to carry animals or goods by any inland water procures the same to be carried in a vessel which is not a railway as defined in this Act, the responsibility of the railway administration for the loss, destruction, or deterioration of the animals or goods during their carriage in the vessel shall be the same as if the vessel were such a railway.

82. (1) When a railway administration contracts to carry passengers, animals, or goods partly by railway and partly by sea, a condition exempting the railway administration from responsibility for any loss of life, personal injury, or loss of or damage to animals or goods, which may happen during the carriage by sea from the act of God, the King's enemies, fire, accidents from machinery, boilers and steam, and all and every other dangers and accidents of the seas, rivers, and navigation of whatever nature and kind soever, shall, without being expressed, be deemed to be part of the contract, and, subject to that condition, the railway administration shall, irrespective of the nationality or ownership of the ship used for the carriage by sea, be responsible for any loss of life, personal injury, or loss of or damage to animals or goods which may happen during the carriage by sea, to the extent to which it would be responsible under the Merchant Shipping Act, 1854, and the Merchant Shipping Act Amendment Act, 1862, if the ship were registered under the former of those Acts, and the railway administration were owner of the ship, and not to any greater extent.

(2) The burden of proving that any such loss, injury, or damage as is mentioned in sub-section (1) happened during the carriage by sea shall lie on the railway administration.

CHAPTER VIII

ACCIDENTS

83. When any of the following accidents occurs in the course of working a railway, namely :—

(*a*) any accident attended with loss of human life, or with grievous hurt as defined in the Indian Penal Code, or with serious injury to property ;

(*b*) any collision between trains of which one is a train carrying passengers ;

(*c*) the derailment of any train carrying passengers, or of any part of such a train ;

(*d*) any accident of a description usually attended with loss of human life, or with such grievous hurt as aforesaid, or with serious injury to property ;

(*e*) any accident of any other description which the Governor-General in Council may notify in this behalf in the *Gazette* of India ;

the railway administration working the railway and, if the accident happens to a train belonging to any other railway administration, the other railway administration also shall, without unnecessary delay, send notice of the accident to the local Government and to the Inspector appointed for the railway; and the station-master nearest to the place at which the accident occurred or, where there is no station-master, the railway servant in charge of the section of the railway on which the accident occurred shall, without unnecessary delay, give notice of the accident to the Magistrate of the district in which the accident occurred, and to the officer in charge of the police-station within the local limits of which it occurred, or to such other Magistrate and police-officer as the Governor-General in Council appoints in this behalf.

84. The Governor-General in Council may make rules, consistent with this Act and any other enactment for the time being in force, for all or any of the following purposes, namely:—

(*a*) for prescribing the forms of the notices mentioned in the last foregoing section and the particulars of the accident which those notices are to contain;

(*b*) for prescribing the class of accidents of which notice is to be sent by telegraph immediately after the accident has occurred;

(*c*) for prescribing the duties of railway servants, police-officers, Inspectors, and Magistrates on the occurrence of an accident.

85. Every railway administration shall send to the Governor-General in Council a return of accidents occurring upon its railway, whether attended with personal injury or not, in such form and manner and at such intervals of time as the Governor-General in Council directs.

86. Whenever any person injured by an accident on a railway claims compensation on account of the injury, any Court or person having by law or consent of parties authority to determine the claim may order that the person injured be examined by some duly qualified medical practitioner named in the order, and not being a witness on either side, and may make such order with respect to the costs of the examination as it or he thinks fit.

CHAPTER IX

Penalties and Offences

Forfeitures by Railway Companies

87. If a railway company fails to comply with any requisition made under section 13, it shall forfeit to the Government the sum of two hundred rupees for the default, and a further sum of fifty rupees for every day after the first during which the default continues.

88. If a railway company moves any rolling-stock upon a railway by steam or other motive power in contravention of section 16, sub-section (2), or opens or uses any railway or work in contravention of section 18, section 19, section 20, or section 21, or re-opens any railway or uses any rolling-stock in contravention of section 24, it shall forfeit to the Government the sum of two hundred rupees for every day during which the motive power, railway, work, or rolling-stock is used in contravention of any of those sections.

89. If a railway company fails to comply with the provisions of section 47, sub-section (6), section 54, sub-section (2), or section 65, with respect to the books or other documents to be kept open to inspection or conspicuously posted at stations on its railway, it shall forfeit to the Government the sum of fifty rupees for every day during which the default continues.

90. If a railway company fails to comply with the provisions of section 47 with respect to the making of general rules, it shall forfeit to the Government the sum of fifty rupees for every day during which the default continues.

91. If a railway company refuses or neglects to comply with any decision of the Governor-General in Council under section 48, it shall forfeit to the Government the sum of two hundred rupees for every day during which the refusal or neglect continues.

92. If a railway company fails to comply with the provisions of section 52, or section 85 with respect to the submission of any return, it shall forfeit to the Government the sum of fifty rupees for every day during which the default continues after the fourteenth day from the date prescribed for the submission of the return.

93. If a railway company contravenes the provisions of section 53 or section 63, with respect to the maximum load to be carried in any waggon or truck, or the maximum number of passengers to be carried in any compartment, or the exhibition of such load on the waggon or truck, or of such number in or on the compartment, or knowingly suffers any person owning a waggon or truck passing over its railway to contravene the provisions of the former of those sections, it shall forfeit to the Government the sum of twenty rupees for every day during which either section is contravened.

94. If a railway company fails to comply with any requisition of the Governor-General in Council under section 62 for the provision and maintenance in proper order, in any train worked by it which carries passengers, of such efficient means of communication as the Governor-General in Council has approved, it shall forfeit to the Government the sum of twenty rupees for each train run in disregard of the requisition.

95. If a railway company fails to comply with the requirements of section 64 with respect to the reservation of compartments for females, or the provision of closets therein, it shall forfeit to the Government the sum of twenty rupees for every train in respect of which the default occurs.

96. If a railway company omits to give such notice of an accident as is required by section 83 and the rules for the time being in force under section 84, it shall forfeit to the Government the sum of one hundred rupees for every day during which the omission continues.

97. (1) When a railway company has, through any act or omission, forfeited any sum to the Government under the foregoing provisions of this Chapter, the sum shall be recoverable by suit in the District Court having jurisdiction in the place where the act or omission or any part thereof occurred.

(2) The suit must be instituted with the previous sanction of the Governor-General in Council, and the plaintiff therein shall be the Secretary of State for India in Council.

(3) The Governor-General in Council may remit the whole or

any part of any sum forfeited by the railway company to the Government under the foregoing provisions of this Chapter.

98. Nothing in those provisions shall be construed to preclude the Government from resorting to any other mode of proceeding instead of, or in addition to, such a suit as is mentioned in the last foregoing section, for the purpose of compelling a railway company to discharge any obligation imposed upon it by this Act.

Offences by Railway Servants

99. If a railway servant whose duty it is to comply with the provisions of section 60 negligently or wilfully omits to comply therewith, he shall be punished with fine which may extend to twenty rupees.

100. If a railway servant is in a state of intoxication while on duty, he shall be punished with fine which may extend to fifty rupees, or where the improper performance of the duty would be likely to endanger the safety of any person travelling or being upon a railway, with imprisonment for a term which may extend to one year, or with fine, or with both.

101. If a railway servant, when on duty, endangers the safety of any person—

(*a*) by disobeying any general rule made, sanctioned, published, and notified under this Act; or

(*b*) by disobeying any rule or order which is not inconsistent with any such general rule, and which such servant was bound by the terms of his employment to obey, and of which he had notice; or

(*c*) by any rash or negligent act or omission,

he shall be punished with imprisonment for a term which may extend to two years, or with fine which may extend to five hundred rupees, or with both.

102. If a railway servant compels, or attempts to compel, or causes any passenger to enter a compartment which already contains the maximum number of passengers exhibited therein or thereon under section 63, he shall be punished with fine which may extend to twenty rupees.

103. If a station-master or a railway servant in charge of a section of a railway omits to give such notice of an accident as is required by section 83, and the rules for the time being in force under section 84, he shall be punished with fine which may extend to fifty rupees.

104. If a railway servant unnecessarily—

(*a*) allows any rolling-stock to stand across a place where the railway crosses a public road on the level; or

(*b*) keeps a level-crossing closed against the public,

he shall be punished with fine which may extend to twenty rupees.

105. If any return which is required by this Act is false in any particular to the knowledge of any person who signs it, that person shall be punished with fine which may extend to five hundred rupees, or with imprisonment which may extend to one year, or with both.

Other Offences

106. If a person requested under section 28 to give an account with respect to any goods gives an account which is materially false, he, and if he is not the owner of the goods, the owner also shall be punished with fine, which may extend to ten rupees for every maund or part of a maund of the goods, and the fine shall be in addition to any rate or other charge to which the goods may be liable.

107. If in contravention of section 59 a person takes with him any dangerous or offensive goods upon a railway, or tenders or delivers any such goods for carriage upon a railway, he shall be punished with fine which may extend to five hundred rupees, and shall also be responsible for any loss, injury, or damage which may be caused by reason of such goods having been so brought upon the railway.

108. If a passenger, without reasonable and sufficient cause, makes use of, or interferes with, any means provided by a railway administration for communication between passengers and the railway servants in charge of a train, he shall be punished with fine which may extend to fifty rupees.

109. (1) If a passenger, having entered a compartment which is reserved by a railway administration for the use of another passenger, or which already contains the maximum number of passengers exhibited therein or thereon under section 63, refuses to leave it when required to do so by any railway servant, he shall be punished with fine which may extend to twenty rupees.

(2) If a passenger resists the lawful entry of another passenger into a compartment not reserved by the railway administration for the use of the passenger resisting, or not already containing the maximum number of passengers exhibited therein or thereon under section 63, he shall be punished with fine which may extend to twenty rupees.

110. (1) If a person, without the consent of his fellow-passengers, if any, in the same compartment, smokes in any compartment except a compartment specially provided for the purpose, he shall be punished with fine which may extend to twenty rupees.

(2) If any person persists in so smoking after being warned by any railway servant to desist, he may, in addition to incurring the liability mentioned in sub-section (1), be removed by any railway servant from the carriage in which he is travelling.

111. If a person, without authority in this behalf, pulls down or wilfully injures any board or document set up or posted by order of a railway administration on a railway, or any rolling-stock, or obliterates or alters any of the letters or figures upon any such board or document, he shall be punished with fine which may extend to fifty rupees.

112. If a person, with intent to defraud a railway administration,—

(*a*) enters in contravention of section 68 any carriage on a railway; or

(*b*) uses or attempts to use a single pass or single ticket which has already been used on a previous journey, or, in the case of a return-ticket, a half thereof which has already been so used;

he shall be punished with fine which may extend to one hundred rupees in addition to the amount of the single fare for any distance which he may have travelled.

113. (1) If a passenger travels in a train without having a proper pass or a proper ticket with him, or, being in or having alighted from a train, fails or refuses to present for examination or to deliver up his pass or ticket immediately on requisition being made therefor under section 69, he shall be liable to pay, on the demand of any railway servant appointed by the railway administration in this behalf, the excess charge hereinafter in this section mentioned, in addition to the ordinary single fare for the distance which he has travelled, or, where there is any doubt as to the station from which he started, the ordinary single fare from the station from which the train originally started, or if the tickets of passengers travelling in the train have been examined since the original starting of the train, the ordinary single fare from the place where the tickets were examined, or in case of their having been examined more than once, were last examined.

(2) If a passenger travels or attempts to travel in or on a carriage, or by a train, of a higher class than that for which he has obtained a pass or purchased a ticket, or travels in or on a carriage beyond the place authorised by his pass or ticket, he shall be liable to pay, on the demand of any railway servant appointed by the railway administration in this behalf, the excess charge hereinafter in this section mentioned, in addition to any difference between any fare paid by him and the fare payable in respect of such journey as he has made.

(3) The excess charge referred to in sub-section (1) and sub-section (2) shall,—

(*a*) where the passenger has, immediately after incurring the charge, and before being detected by a railway servant, notified to the railway servant on duty with the train the fact of the charge having been incurred, be one rupee, two annas or eight annas; and

(*b*) in any other case, be six rupees, one rupee, or three rupees,

according as the passenger is travelling, or has travelled, or has attempted to travel in a carriage of the highest class, or in a carriage of the lowest class, or in a carriage of any other class or kind:

Provided that such excess charge shall in no case exceed,—

(*a*) where the liability to pay it arises under sub-section (1), the amount of the ordinary single fare which the passenger incurring the charge is liable to pay under that sub-section; or

(*b*) where such liability arises under sub-section (2), the amount of the difference between the fare paid by the passenger incurring the charge, and the fare payable in respect of such journey as he has made.

(4) If a passenger liable to pay the excess charge and fare mentioned in sub-section (1), or the excess charge and any difference of fare mentioned in sub-section (2), fails or refuses to pay the same on demand being made therefor, under one or other of those sub-sections, as the case may be, the sum payable by him shall, on application made to any Magistrate by any railway servant appointed by the railway administration in this behalf, be recovered by the Magistrate from the passenger as if it were a fine imposed on the passenger by the Magistrate, and shall, as it is recovered, be paid to the railway administration.

114. If a person sells, or attempts to sell, or parts or attempts to part with the possession of the return half of a return ticket in order to enable any other person to travel therewith, or purchases such half of a return ticket, he shall be punished with fine which may extend to fifty rupees, and, if the purchaser of such half of a return ticket travels or attempts to travel therewith, he shall be punished with an additional fine, which may extend to the amount of the single fare for the return journey authorised by the ticket.

115. That portion of any fine imposed under section 112, or the last foregoing section, which represents the single fare therein mentioned shall, as the fine is recovered, be paid to the railway administration before any portion of the fine is credited to the Government.

116. If a passenger wilfully alters or defaces his pass or ticket so as to render the date, number, or any material portion thereof illegible, he shall be punished with fine which may extend to fifty rupees.

117. (1) If a person suffering from an infectious or contagious disorder enters or travels upon a railway in contravention of section 71, sub-section (2), he and any person having charge of him upon the railway when he so entered or travelled thereon, shall be punished with fine which may extend to twenty rupees, in addition to the forfeiture of any fare which either of them may have paid, and of any pass or ticket which either of them may have obtained or purchased, and may be removed from the railway by any railway servant.

(2) If any such railway servant as is referred to in section 71, sub-section (2), knowing that a person is suffering from any infectious or contagious disorder, wilfully permits the person to travel upon a railway without arranging for his separation from other passengers, he shall be punished with fine which may extend to one hundred rupees.

118. (1) If a passenger enters or leaves, or attempts to enter or leave, any carriage while the train is in motion, or elsewhere than at the side of the carriage adjoining the platform or other place appointed by the railway administration for passengers to enter or leave the carriage, or opens the side-door of any carriage while the train is in motion, he shall be punished with fine which may extend to twenty rupees.

(2) If a passenger, after being warned by a railway servant to desist, persists in travelling on the roof, steps, or footboard of any carriage, or on an engine, or in any other part of a train not intended for the use of passengers, he shall be punished with fine which may extend to fifty rupees, and may be removed from the railway by any railway servant.

119. If a male person, knowing a carriage, compartment, room, or other place to be reserved by a railway administration for the exclusive use of females, enters the place without lawful excuse, or having entered it, remains therein after having been desired by any railway servant to leave it, he shall be punished with fine which may extend to one hundred rupees, in addition to the forfeiture of any fare which he may have paid, and of any pass or ticket which he may have obtained or purchased, and may be removed from the railway by any railway servant.

120. If a person in any railway carriage or upon any part of a railway—

(*a*) is in a state of intoxication; or

(*b*) commits any nuisance or act of indecency, or uses obscene or abusive language; or (*c*) wilfully and without lawful excuse interferes with the comfort of any passenger, or extinguishes any lamp,

he shall be punished with fine which may extend to fifty rupees, in addition to the forfeiture of any fare which he may have paid, and of any pass or ticket which he may have obtained or purchased, and may be removed from the railway by any railway servant.

121. If a person wilfully obstructs or impedes any railway servant in the discharge of his duty, he shall be punished with fine which may extend to one hundred rupees.

122. (1) If a person unlawfully enters upon a railway, he shall be punished with fine which may extend to twenty rupees.

(2) If a person so entering refuses to leave the railway on being requested to do so by any railway servant, or by any other person on behalf of the railway administration, he shall be punished with fine which may extend to fifty rupees, and may be removed from the railway by such servant or other person.

123. If a driver or conductor of a tramcar, omnibus, carriage, or other vehicle while upon the premises of a railway disobeys the reasonable directions of any railway servant or police-officer, he shall be punished with fine which may extend to twenty rupees.

124. In either of the following cases, namely :—

(*a*) if a person, knowing or having reason to believe that an engine or train is approaching along a railway, opens any gate set up on either side of the railway across a road, or passes or attempts to pass, or drives or takes, or attempts to drive or take, any animal, vehicle, or other thing across the railway,

(*b*) if, in the absence of a gate-keeper, a person omits to shut and fasten such a gate as aforesaid as soon as he and any animal, vehicle, or other thing under his charge have passed through the gate,

the person shall be punished with fine which may extend to fifty rupees.

125. (1) The owner or person in charge of any cattle straying on a railway provided with fences suitable for the exclusion of cattle shall be punished with fine which may extend to five rupees for each head of cattle, in addition to any amount which may have been recovered or may be recoverable under the Cattle-trespass Act, 1871.

(2) If any cattle are wilfully driven, or knowingly permitted to be, on any railway otherwise than for the purpose of lawfully crossing the railway, or for any other lawful purpose, the person in charge of the cattle, or, at the option of the railway administration, the owner of the cattle, shall be punished with fine which may extend to ten rupees for each head of cattle, in addition to any amount which may have been recovered or may be recoverable under the Cattle-trespass Act, 1871.

(3) Any fine imposed under this section may, if the Court so directs, be recovered in manner provided by section 25 of the Cattle-trespass Act, 1871.

(4) The expression "public road" in sections 11 and 26 of the Cattle-trespass Act, 1871, shall be deemed to include a railway, and any railway servant may exercise the powers conferred on officers of police by the former of those sections.

(5) The word "cattle" has the same meaning in this section as in the Cattle-trespass Act, 1871.

126. If a person unlawfully—

(*a*) puts or throws upon or across any railway any wood, stone, or other matter or thing, or

(*b*) takes up, removes, loosens, or displaces any rail, sleeper, or other matter or thing belonging to any railway, or

(*c*) turns, moves, unlocks, or diverts any points or other machinery belonging to any railway, or

(*d*) makes or shows, or hides or removes, any signal or light upon or near to any railway, or

(*e*) does or causes to be done, or attempts to do any other act or thing in relation to any railway,

with intent, or with knowledge that he is likely to endanger the safety of any person travelling or being upon the railway, he shall be punished with transportation for life, or with imprisonment for a term which may extend to ten years.

127. If a person unlawfully throws or causes to fall or strike at, against, into, or upon any rolling-stock forming part of a train any wood, stone, or other matter or thing with intent, or with knowledge that he is likely to endanger the safety of any person being in or upon such rolling-stock, or in or upon any other rolling-stock forming part of the same train, he shall be punished with transportation for life, or with imprisonment for a term which may extend to ten years.

128. If a person, by any unlawful act or by any wilful omission or neglect, endangers or causes to be endangered the safety of any person travelling or being upon any railway, or obstructs or causes to be obstructed, or attempts to obstruct any rolling-stock upon any railway, he shall be punished with imprisonment for a term which may extend to two years.

129. If a person rashly or negligently does any act, or omits to do what he is legally bound to do, and the act or omission is likely to endanger the safety of any person travelling or being upon a railway, he shall be punished with imprisonment for a term which may extend to one year, or with fine, or with both.

130. (1) If a minor under the age of twelve years is with respect to any railway guilty of any of the acts or omissions mentioned or referred to in any of the four last foregoing sections, he shall be deemed, notwithstanding anything in section 82 or section 83 of the Indian Penal Code, to have committed an offence, and the Court convicting him may, if it thinks fit, direct that the minor, if a male, shall be punished with whipping, or may require the father or guardian of the minor to execute, within such time as the Court may fix, a bond binding himself, in such penalty as the Court directs, to prevent the minor from being again guilty of any of those acts or omissions.

(2) The amount of the bond, if forfeited, shall be recoverable by the Court as if it were a fine imposed by itself.

(3) If a father or guardian fails to execute a bond under sub-section (1) within the time fixed by the Court, he shall be punished with fine which may extend to fifty rupees.

Procedure.

131. (1) If a person commits any offence mentioned in sections 100, 101, 119, 120, 121, 126, 127, 128, or 129, or in section 130, sub-section (1), he may be arrested without warrant or other written authority by any railway servant or police-officer, or by any other person whom such servant or officer may call to his aid.

(2) A person so arrested shall, with the least possible delay, be taken before a Magistrate having authority to try him or commit him for trial.

132. (1) If a person commits any offence under this Act other than an offence mentioned in the last foregoing section, or fails or refuses to pay any excess charge or other sum demanded under section 113, and there is reason to believe that he will abscond, or his name and address are unknown, and he refuses on demand to give his name or address, or there is reason to believe that the name and address given by him is incorrect, any railway servant or police-officer, or any other person whom such railway servant or police-officer may call to his aid, may, without warrant or other written authority, arrest him.

(2) The person arrested shall be released on his giving bail, or, if his true name and address are ascertained, on his executing a bond without sureties for his appearance before a Magistrate when required.

(3) If the person cannot give bail, and his true name and address are not ascertained, he shall with the least possible delay be taken before the nearest Magistrate having jurisdiction.

(4) The provisions of Chapters XXXIX. and XLII. of the Code of Criminal Procedure, 1882, shall, so far as may be, apply to bail given and bonds executed under this section.

133. No Magistrate other than a Presidency Magistrate, or than a Magistrate whose powers are not less than those of a Magistrate of the second class, shall try any offence under this Act.

134. (1) Any person committing any offence against this Act, or any rule thereunder, shall be triable for such offence in any place in which he may be, or which the local Government may notify in this behalf, as well as in any other place in which he might be tried under any law for the time being in force.

(2) Every notification under sub-section (1) shall be published in the local official *Gazette*, and a copy thereof shall be exhibited for the information of the public in some conspicuous place at each of such railway stations as the local Government may direct.

CHAPTER X

SUPPLEMENTAL PROVISIONS

135. Notwithstanding anything to the contrary in any enactment, or in any agreement or award based on any enactment, the following rules shall regulate the levy of taxes in respect of railways and from railway administrations in aid of the funds of local authorities, namely :—

(1) A railway administration shall not be liable to pay any tax in aid of the funds of any local authority unless the Governor-General in Council has, by notification in the official *Gazette*, declared the railway administration to be liable to pay the tax.

(2) While a notification of the Governor-General in Council under clause (1) of this section is in force, the railway administration shall be liable to pay to the local authority either the tax mentioned in the notification or, in lieu thereof, such sum, if any, as an officer appointed in this behalf by the Governor-General in Council may, having regard to all the circumstances of the case, from time to time determine to be fair and reasonable.

(3) The Governor-General in Council may at any time revoke or vary a notification under clause (1) of this section.

(4) Nothing in this section is to be construed as debarring any railway administration from entering into a contract with any local authority for the supply of water or light, or for the scavenging of railway premises, or for any other service which the local authority may be rendering or be prepared to render within any part of the local area under its control.

(5) "Local authority" in this section means a local authority as defined in the General Clauses Act, 1887, and includes any authority legally entitled to or entrusted with the control or management of any fund for the maintenance of watchmen or for the conservancy of a river.

136. (1) None of the rolling-stock, machinery, plant, tools, fittings, materials, or effects used or provided by a railway administration for the purpose of the traffic on its railway, or of its stations or workshops, shall be liable to be taken in execution of any decree or order of any Court without the previous sanction of the Governor-General in Council.

(2) Nothing in sub-section (1) is to be construed as affecting the authority of any Court to attach the earnings of a railway in execution of a decree or order.

137. (1) Every railway servant shall be deemed to be a public servant for the purposes of Chapter IX. of the Indian Penal Code.

(2) In the definition of "legal remuneration" in section 161 of that Code, the word "Government" shall, for the purposes of sub-section (1), be deemed to include any employer of a railway servant as such.

(3) A railway servant shall not—

(*a*) Purchase or bid for, either in person or by agent, in his own name or in that of another, or jointly or in shares with others, any property put up to auction under section 55 or section 56, or,

(*b*) In contravention of any direction of the railway administration in this behalf, engage in trade.

(4) Notwithstanding anything in section 21 of the Indian Penal Code, a railway servant shall not be deemed to be a public servant for any of the purposes of that Code except those mentioned in sub-section (1).

138. If a railway servant is discharged or suspended from his office, or dies, absconds, or absents himself, and he or his wife or widow, or any of his family or representatives, refuses or neglects, after notice in writing for that purpose, to deliver up to the railway administration, or to a person appointed by the railway administration in this behalf, any station, dwelling-house, office, or other building, with its appurtenances, or any books, papers, or other matters belonging to the railway administration, and in the possession or custody of such railway servant at the occurrence of any such event as aforesaid, any magistrate of the first class may, on application made by or on behalf of the railway administration, order any police-officer, with proper assistance, to enter upon the building and remove any person found therein, and take possession thereof, or to take possession of the books, papers, or other matters, and to deliver the same to the railway administration or a person appointed by the railway administration in that behalf.

139. Any notice, determination, direction, requisition, appointment, expression of opinion, approval, or sanction to be given or signified on the part of the Governor-General in Council, for any of the purposes of, or in relation to this Act, or any of the powers or provisions therein contained, shall be sufficient and binding if in writing signed by a Secretary, Deputy-Secretary, Under-Secretary, or Assistant-Secretary to the Government of India, or by any other officer or servant authorised to act on behalf of the Governor-General in Council in respect of the matters to which the same may relate, and the Governor-General in Council shall not in any case be bound in respect of any of the matters aforesaid unless by some writing signed in manner aforesaid.

140. Any notice or other document required or authorised by this Act to be served on a railway administration may be served, in the case of a railway administered by the Government or a Native State, on the manager and, in the case of a railway administered by a railway company, on the agent in India of the railway company—

(*a*) by delivering the notice or other document to the manager or agent, or

(*b*) by leaving it at his office, or

(*c*) by forwarding it by post in a prepaid letter addressed to the manager or agent at his office, and registered under Part III. of the Indian Post-Office Act, 1866.

141. Any notice or other document required or authorised by this Act to be served on any person by a railway administration may be served—

(*a*) by delivering it to the person, or

(*b*) by leaving it at the usual or last known place of abode of the person, or

(*c*) by forwarding it by post in a prepaid letter addressed to the person at his usual or last known place of abode, and registered under Part III. of the Indian Post-Office Act, 1866.

142. Where a notice or other document is served by post, it shall be deemed to have been served at the time when the letter containing it would be delivered in the ordinary course of post, and in proving such service it shall be sufficient to prove that the letter containing the notice or other document was properly addressed and registered.

143. (1) A rule under section 22, section 34, or section 84, or the cancellation, rescission, or variation of a rule under any of those sections, or under section 47, sub-section (4), shall not take effect until it has been published in the *Gazette* of India.

(2) Where any rule made under this Act, or the cancellation, rescission, or variation of any such rule, is required by this Act to be published in the *Gazette* of India, it shall, besides being so published, be further notified to persons affected thereby in such manner as the Governor-General in Council, by general or special order, directs.

(3) The Governor-General in Council may cancel or vary any rule made by him under this Act.

144. (1) The Governor-General in Council may, by notification in the *Gazette* of India, invest, absolutely or subject to conditions, any local Government with any of the powers or functions of the Governor-General in Council under this Act with respect to any railway, and may, by that or a like notification, declare what local Government shall, for the purposes of the exercise of powers or functions so conferred, be deemed to be the local Government in respect of the railway.

(2) The provisions of section 139 with respect to proceedings of the Governor-General in Council shall, so far as they can be made applicable, apply to proceedings of a local Government exercising the powers or discharging the functions of the Governor-General in Council in pursuance of a notification under sub-section (1).

145. (1) The manager of a railway administered by the Government or a Native State, and the agent in India of a railway administered by a railway company, may, by instrument in writing, authorise any railway servant or other person to act for or represent him in any proceeding before any civil, criminal, or other court.

(2) A person authorised by a manager or agent to conduct prosecutions on behalf of a railway administration shall,

notwithstanding anything in section 495 of the Code of Criminal Procedure, 1882, be entitled to conduct such prosecutions without the permission of the Magistrate.

146. The Governor-General in Council may, by notification in the *Gazette* of India, extend this Act or any portion thereof to any tramway worked by steam or other mechanical power.

147. The Governor-General in Council may, by a like notification, exempt any railway from any of the provisions of this Act.

148. (1) For the purposes of section 3, clauses (5) (6) and (7), and sections 4 to 19 (both inclusive), 47 to 52 (both inclusive), 59, 79, 83 to 92 (both inclusive), 96, 97, 98, 100, 101, 103, 104, 107, 111, 122, 124 to 132 (both inclusive), 134 to 138 (both inclusive), 140, 141, 144, 145 and 147, the word "railway," whether it occurs alone or as a prefix to another word, has reference to a railway or portion of a railway under construction, and to a railway or portion of a railway not used for the public carriage of passengers, animals, or goods as well as to a railway falling within the definition of that word in section 3, clause (4).

(2) For the purposes of sections 5, 21, 83, 100, 101, 103, 104, 121, 122, 125 and 137, sub-sections (1), (2) and (4), and section 138, the expression "railway servant" includes a person employed upon a railway in connection with the service thereof by a person fulfilling a contract with the railway administration.

149. In sections 194 and 195 of the Indian Penal Code, for the words "by this Code or the law of England" the words "by the law of British India or England" shall be substituted.

150. For that portion of the preamble to the Sindh-Pishin Railway Act, 1887, which begins with the words "so far as it applies," and ends with the words "in its entirety," the words "should apply in its entirety to that part of the Sindh-Pishin section of the North-Western Railway which lies beyond the Province of Sindh" shall be substituted.

THE FIRST SCHEDULE

Enactments Repealed

(*See Section* 2)

Number and year	Title	Extent of repeal
	Acts of the Governor-General in Council	
III. of 1865	Carriers Act, 1865	Section 7 (so far as it relates to railways) and section 10
IV. of 1879	Indian Railway Act, 1879	The whole
IV. of 1883	Indian Railway Act, 1883	The whole
XI. of 1886	Indian Tramways Act, 1886	Section 49
XX. of 1886	Upper Burma Laws Act, 1886	So much as relates to Acts IV. of 1879 and IV. of 1883.

THE FIRST SCHEDULE

Enactments Repealed

(*See Section* 2)

Act of the Lieutenant-Governor of Bengal in Council

II. of 1882	Bengal Embankment Act, 1882	Section 16 and in section 17 the proviso to the first paragraph of that section, the words "or under the section last preceding" and the words "or railroad" wherever they occur.

THE SECOND SCHEDULE

ARTICLES TO BE DECLARED AND INSURED

(*See Section* 75)

(*a*) gold and silver, coined or uncoined, manufactured or unmanufactured;

(*b*) plated articles;

(*c*) cloths and tissue and lace of which gold or silver forms part, not being the uniform or part of the uniform of an officer, soldier, sailor, police-officer, or person enrolled as a volunteer under the Indian Volunteers Act, 1869, or of any public officer, British or Foreign, entitled to wear uniform;

(*d*) pearls, precious stones, jewellery, and trinkets;

(*e*) watches, clocks, and timepieces of any description;

(*f*) Government securities;

(*g*) Government stamps;

(*h*) bills of exchange, hundis, promissory notes, bank-notes, and orders or other securities for payment of money;

(*i*) maps, writings, and title-deeds

(*j*) paintings, engravings, lithographs, photographs, carvings, sculpture, and other works of art;

(*k*) art pottery and all articles made of glass, china, or marble;

(*l*) silks in a manufactured or unmanufactured state, and whether wrought up or not wrought up with other materials;

(*m*) shawls;

(*n*) lace and furs;

(*o*) opium;

(*p*) ivory, ebony, coral, and sandalwood;

(*q*) musk, sandalwood-oil, and other essential oils used in the preparation of *itr* or other perfume;

(*r*) musical and scientific instruments;

(*s*) any article of special value which the Governor-General in Council may, by notification in the *Gazette* of India, add to this schedule.

S. HARVEY JAMES,
Secy. to the Govt. of India.

APPENDIX C

LIST OF INDIAN RAILWAYS SHOWING LENGTHS AND OTHER STATISTICAL FIGURES, 1892

Railway.	Mean Mileage Worked.	Average Earnings per Mile per Week in 1892-93.	Average Cost per Mile. Rs. Single Track.	Working Expenses per cent of Gross Earnings.	Net Earnings per cent on the Capital Outlay on Open Line.
	Miles.	Rs.	Rs.	Rs.	Rs.
STATE LINES WORKED BY COMPANIES.					
Standard gauge—					
East Indian	1,634	580	143377	28.73	9.62
Bengal-Nágpur	862	140	96351	50.55	3.19
Indian Midland	752	129	109376	61.63	2.09
Bezváda extension (*a*)	112	80	54.906	...	...
Metre gauge—					
Rajputana-Malwa (*b*)	1,699	258	66014	41.01	10.13
South Indian	1,043	139	60887	62.89	3.64
Southern Mahratta (*c*)	1,156	87	80482	68.69	1.47
Bengal and North-Western (*d*)	756	137	58982	41.12	5.85
Rahilkund and Kumaon (Lucknow-Bareilly section)	199	66	34.268	59.72	3.51
Total	8,213	243			
STATE LINES WORKED BY THE STATE.					
Standard gauge—					
North-Western (State) (*e*)	2,509	201	132883	64.25	2.22
Oudh and Rahilkund (State)	692	235	113550	41.28	5.43
Eastern Bengal (State) (including metre and 2′ 6″ gauges)	777	292	139288[1]	44.32	6.62
Bengal Central (*f*)	125	120	68,712	59.33	3.11

Metre gauge—					
Burma (State)	728	194	72279	52.31	5.39
Special gauges—					
Jorhát (State provincial)	25	46	24.616	82.16	1.56
Cherra-Companyganj (State provincial)	8	47	41.233	95.33	0.24
Total	4,864	217			
LINES WORKED BY GUARANTEED COMPANIES.					
Standard gauge—					
Great Indian Peninsula (*g*)	1,490	513	136817	50.28	7.29
Bombay, Baroda, and Central India	461	605	148966	42.92	8.44
Madras	840	226	115749	55.40	3.58
Total	2,791	442			
TOTAL (Guaranteed and State)	15,868	271			
ASSISTED COMPANIES.					
Standard gauge—					
Delhi-Umballa-Kalka	161	132	83.672	48.00	3.69
Tarkessur	22	252	69.164	47.28	8.94
Metre gauge—					
Rahilkund and Kumaon (Company's section)	67	118	35.078	54.17	9.66
Dibru-Sadiya	78	123	79.023	68.10	2.40
Total	328	135			

(*a*) Includes the Bezváda-Godaveri section of the East Coast (State) Railway.
(*b*) Includes the Godhra-Rutlam Railway.
(*c*) Includes the Guntakal-Mysore frontier section from 1st April 1893.
(*d*) Includes the Tirhoot State Railway. Although for convenience classed amongst the State railways, the company's section of this line is the property of the Bengal and North-Western Railway Company.
(*e*) Includes the Jammu and Kashmir and the Hyderabad-Umarkot Railways.
[1] Broad gauge figures only.
(*f*) Although for convenience classed amongst the State railways, this line is the property of the Bengal Central Railway Company.
(*g*) Includes the Wardha Coal, Dhond-Manmád, Khámgaon, and Amráoti Railways.

LIST OF INDIAN RAILWAYS—*Continued.*

RAILWAY.	Mean Mileage Worked.	Average Earnings per Mile per Week in 1892-93.	Average Cost per Mile. Rs. Single Track.	Working Expenses per cent of Gross Earnings.	Net Earnings per cent on the Capital Outlay on Open Line.
	Miles.	Rs.	Rs.	Rs.	Rs.
LINES OWNED BY NATIVE STATES AND WORKED BY OTHER AGENCIES.					
Standard gauge—					
The Nizam's Guaranteed State	333	151	103668	52.35	3.35
The Gaekwar's Petlád	13	96	46453	43.25	4.89
Rájpura-Bhátinda	108	92	53.997	55.00	3.82
Metre gauge—					
Southern Mahratta (Mysore section) (*h*)	331	94	42.615	67.92	2.96
The Gaekwar's Mehsána	93	59	28.548	40.92	5.15
Kolhápur	29	67	75.349	67.72	1.23
Special gauge—					
The Gaekwar's Dabhoi	72	68	23.950	55.37	5.77
Total	979	107			
LINES OWNED AND WORKED BY NATIVE STATES.					
Metre gauge—					
Bhávnagar-Gondal-Junágarh-Porbandar	334	102	45.872	72.25	2.54
Jodhpur section	46	...	18.710	44.14	11.01
Jodhpur-Bickaneer section	364	60	21.317	67.47	2.63
Special gauge—					
Morvi	94	65	21.227	57.83	6.19
Total	838	80			
GRAND TOTAL	18,013	251			

(*h*) Includes the Nanjangúd extension and the Yesvantpur-Dodballepur section.

INDEX

THE END